From
Versailles
to
Mers el-Kébir

From Versailles to Mers el-Kébir

*The Promise of Anglo-French Naval Cooperation
1919–40*

George E. Melton

Naval Institute Press
Annapolis, Maryland

Naval Institute Press
291 Wood Road
Annapolis, MD 21402

ISBN: 978-1-61251-879-4 (hardcover)
ISBN: 978-1-61251-880-0 (eBook)

Library of Congress Cataloging-in-Publication Data is available.

Maps created by Charles Grear.

∞Print editions meet the requirements of ANSI/NISO z39.48-1992
(Permanence of Paper).
Printed in the United States of America.

23 22 21 20 19 18 17 16 15   9 8 7 6 5 4 3 2 1
First printing

To the memory of Lieutenant Commander Jack Robert Melton,
USNR, Southwest Pacific, 1943–45

CONTENTS

PREFACE

Toward the end of 1939 two fast battlecruisers made rendezvous north of Scotland and slipped unnoticed toward Iceland in search of enemy raiders. Their mission meshed neatly with a combined Anglo-French naval operation aimed at tracking down the German pocket battleship *Admiral Graf Spee*, prowling Atlantic waters south of the equator. The *Dunkerque*, a new French ship commanded by Vice-Admiral Marcel Gensoul was escorted by the light cruisers *Montcalm* and *Georges Leygues* and the destroyers *Volta* and *Mogador*. The HMS *Hood*, a handsome but older ship with capabilities similar to the *Dunkerque*, was in like manner supported by a spread of cruisers and destroyers. When the two squadrons merged, the combined force came under the orders of the highest officer on the scene, Admiral Gensoul, rather than his British opposite. The *Hood* therefore served under the orders of a French admiral for a full week until the operation ended uneventfully in early December, a few days before the *Graf Spee* was trapped off the coast of Uruguay and scuttled by her crew.

The combined operation of the *Dunkerque* and the *Hood*, unimportant and long since forgotten, stands nevertheless as an example of cordial Anglo-French naval cooperation at sea during the early months of World War II. That a British battlecruiser would come under the orders of a French admiral attests to the mutual confidence that the two naval commands shared early in the wartime alliance. At the same time, the French and British crews developed a special affection for each other's ship, as British seamen fondly referred to the *Dunkerque* as "the friend of the *Hood*."

The forging of an Anglo-French naval alliance just prior to World War II is but the happiest chapter in a disturbing history of British and French naval relations between 1919 and the collapse of the alliance in the summer of 1940. This study revisits an Anglo-French naval courtship still etched in European memories but largely forgotten among Americans. It is a study of the role of British and French naval power in early World War II and in the tangled diplomacy of the troubled prewar years when statesmen in London and Paris struggled with foreign threats at the far limits of their naval and military capabilities.

The study does not pretend to be a history of either the Royal Navy or the French fleet between the wars. It is instead a study of naval relations, of connections between naval power and diplomacy, and of connections between naval and military power. The romance between the *Hood* and the *Dunkerque* is but a brief incident in a larger pattern of diplomacy that found French and British statesmen struggling with the burdens of a swiftly changing global power balance. But the promises inherent in Anglo-French naval cooperation were not equally appreciated on both sides of the channel, as perspectives from London and Paris on the role of naval power were not identical.

Historians will remember that all of the great naval powers except Germany fought on the same side during World War I, forming what amounted to a British naval alliance with France, the United States, Italy, and Japan. The alliances with Japan and France had been concluded prior to 1914, so that London and Paris had few concerns about the security of their overseas empires during the Great War. But after the war all of these alliances collapsed, supplanted by collective arms control agreements binding the five leading naval powers to security systems that matched poorly new power relationships emerging in the 1930s.

By the mid-1930s the Royal Navy and the French fleet had become over-extended in terms of their global defense commitments, owing mainly to the collapse of the world war alliances and to an ominous shift in the balance of world naval power. The French fleet had never been large enough to protect French colonies in Asia, and the Royal Navy, badly neglected since the Great War, drifted toward obsolescence and inefficiency. At the same time, Italy and Japan moved toward an alliance with Germany, whose Kriegsmarine had by 1935 grown strong enough to threaten British and French commercial interests in the Atlantic. Although the Kriegsmarine was too small to challenge the Royal Navy in a fleet action, neither the Royal Navy nor the French Marine Nationale were strong enough to wage a naval war simultaneously against Germany, Italy, and Japan, states emerging after 1936 as the Axis powers.

The obvious first step in addressing this imbalance was the forging of an Anglo-French naval alliance so that their combined assets might be distributed or combined in a manner to maximize their power. Key to that distribution was the Mediterranean Sea. In 1939, and indeed during the latter part of the decade of the 1930s, it was only in the Mediterranean that London and Paris might expect to support diplomacy with the threat of overwhelming coercive power. Afterward, when war broke out in the summer of 1939, entente naval strategy still centered upon the Mediterranean, where London and Paris could easily combine their assets against Italy, and where geography denied the Axis powers the advantage of combining their naval assets to defend Italy. In this context, relations between the Royal Navy and the French fleet assumed an importance greater than that of Anglo-French military relations, as the limited British military contribution to the defense of the continent was less relevant than the larger contribution of the French navy to British defense needs around the globe.

This study therefore focuses on relations between the two navies and on their forging an alliance to address the operational and strategic problems thrust upon them by the shifting balance of global naval power. British and French diplomatic initiatives on the continent are treated comparatively as they related to the Mediterranean, where the strategy of combined naval power accorded London and Paris a spread of useful options. Finally, the study concludes with the collapse of the alliance in a violent clash of arms entirely out of step with happier days when the *Hood* and the *Dunkerque* together had ruled Atlantic waters at the expense of the Kriegsmarine.

ACKNOWLEDGMENTS

This study is heavily indebted to St. Andrews University for its generosity in awarding the author several grants to visit archives in Paris, London, and Washington, D.C. In this connection, special thanks are due to deans Lawrence Schulz, Robert Hopkins, and William Loftus. Professor David Herr, chair of the department of history, warmly encouraged the project. Dean Loftus, with his superb language skills, rescued the author more than once from awkward French translations. And Mary Harvin McDonald, university librarian, was always able to obtain for the author even the most obscure articles and sources from off-campus collections.

The author is also indebted to a number of friends in this country and in France. Professor Carl Hamilton Pegg of the University of North Carolina at Chapel Hill introduced him to the tangled diplomacy of the World War II era. Mr. John Taylor kept the author informed of new collections arriving at the U.S. National Archives and Records Administration. In Paris, Captain Claude Huan steered the author toward the richest files housed in the French Naval Archives at Vincennes. Madame Francine Hezez was always generous in keeping the author informed of developments in the French navy, as was Louis de la Monneraye, paymaster of the French navy, who welcomed the author to a long interview and corresponded with him afterward. Louis Hourcade shared with the author his many insights into French naval culture, as did Captain Henri Ballande, who entertained the author and his wife more than once at the French Naval Officers Club in Toulon.

Larry Addington, professor emeritus at the Citadel, The Military College of South Carolina, read the entire manuscript, contributing importantly to the clarity and accuracy of the text. Adam Nettina of the U.S. Naval Institute Press was always helpful as the author prepared the manuscript for publication. His help is much appreciated, as is that of Emily Bakely and Patti Bower. The book is indebted to all of the above, but any errors of fact or interpretation are entirely those of the author.

Finally, the author is indebted to his wife, Anne Hopkins Melton, for her efficient management of the numerous details attendant to the author's frequent travel to archives in the United States and in Europe.

Chapter 1

Toward a Global Imbalance

I n the interest of placing Anglo-French naval connections in a meaningful context, this study considers at the outset the shifting patterns of global naval relations between the world wars, for British and French naval power was but one part of a larger scene. These shifting patterns were a function of several naval arms control agreements, of the varied economic challenges facing the powers as they rebuilt their fleets, of swiftly changing naval technology, and of new diplomatic alignments. As a consequence of these changes, the global naval balance at the beginning of World War II was much different from what it had been in 1914, when a friendly distribution of naval power afforded the British and French overseas empires a measure of security. This chapter aims therefore at framing the larger picture unfolding between 1919 and 1939 so that Anglo-French naval relations during two troubled decades can be examined in the context of changing power relationships in the international arena.

The first postwar naval agreement, the naval and Asian clauses of the 1919 Treaty of Versailles, limited the size and composition of the German navy and accorded Japan an island empire in the central Pacific. Subsequent conferences held at Washington, Geneva, and London aimed at heading off naval construction races and attempted to establish security relationships among the leading naval powers—Great Britain, the United States, Japan, France, and Italy—who had fought as allies during the Great War. Naval arms control between the wars would therefore unfold along two parallel tracks, a narrow track governing the German navy and a broader one governing power relationships among the war's victorious powers.

German and Japanese Naval Power

When World War I finally ground to a halt in November 1918, London and Paris both saw the value of exploiting the Allied military victory to the end of dismantling the German navy. Paris was concerned mainly with limiting German military power, but London worried more about German naval power. David Lloyd George, head of the British delegation, and British naval experts at the 1919 Paris Peace Conference therefore intended to gain control of the Reichsmarine and to prevent German naval rearmament. Signed on June 28, 1919, the Treaty of Versailles, with its seventeen naval clauses, was an imperfect instrument that ended the threat of German naval power in the 1920s but gave unintended birth to a new generation of German warships early in the next decade.

The armistice of November 11, 1918, had required the interning of a portion of the German fleet in an Allied port, which turned out to be Scapa Flow, in northern Scotland.[1] But at the expiration of the armistice on June 28, 1919, German officers scuttled ten battleships, five battlecruisers, and five cruisers interned there.[2] Of the remaining fleet units, nine battleships and numerous lighter craft were delivered to the victorious powers, converted to merchant ships, or scrapped in accordance with various terms of the treaty. In addition, article 191 of the Versailles treaty forbade Germany to possess any submarines. Reduced to a small surface force, the Reichsmarine would never again be large enough to challenge the Royal Navy in a Jutland-type fleet action.

The treaty was flawed, however, in its concern to condemn the German navy to obsolescence. The Reichsmarine would inherit thirty-six ships, of which the largest were six battleships launched between 1904 and 1908, each mounting four 11-inch guns. These ships, obsolescent even at their launching, were outclassed by the British *Dreadnought* types mounting up to ten 12-inch guns. The treaty, therefore, denied the Reichsmarine any modern capital ships. But article 190 permitted Germany to replace its battleships at a tonnage discount after they had attained an age of twenty years, so a 14,000-ton battleship could be replaced in the late 1920s with a ship of no more than 10,000 tons, presumably too light to mount 11-inch guns.[3] The treaty no doubt intended to phase out the German battleship fleet and reduce the future Reichsmarine to ships no heavier than cruisers. These treaty provisions, however, set the stage for German naval architects to design light battleships in the early 1930s, at the very moment when other arms control agreements made it illegal for the Royal Navy to match them.

By the end of the Great War, Japan had emerged as the dominant naval power in Asia. Japanese naval construction had proceeded briskly during the war, which Japan had entered promptly in 1914. When the United States finally entered in 1917, Japan had already occupied the Marshall, Caroline, and Marianas island groups, former German colonies in the central Pacific. The Versailles treaty recognized Japanese control of these islands as mandated territories under the League of Nations. Although the treaty forbade their fortification, that restriction would not long endure, so that Japanese control of these islands threatened the security of the Philippines and of British and French colonies south of the equator. The rise of Japanese naval power therefore threatened the imperial interests of all the victorious Western powers, except Italy, and influenced the direction of their naval construction programs between the wars.

Background of the Washington Naval Conference

Shifting security relationships among the five leading naval powers in the wake of World War I bore upon Anglo-French naval relations in a manner to isolate France and undermine the security of her sprawling colonial empire. During the war French naval power had declined relative to that of Great Britain. While British naval construction had proceeded briskly with the launching of ten battleships between 1914 and 1918, French construction ground nearly to a halt. No French battleships were launched during the war, and by 1921 the Marine Nationale had been reduced to eighteen cruisers, assorted lighter craft, and ten battleships, the newest being the *Bretagne*, *Provence*, and *Lorraine*, all launched in 1913.[4] The French fleet was therefore small and obsolescent, incapable of protecting France's colonial empire, which stretched as far as Indochina and New Caledonia.

In contrast, the British fleet of 1919 consisted of 61 battleships, 9 battle-cruisers, and 30 cruisers. In addition, there were in commission 90 light cruisers, 23 flotilla leaders, 443 destroyers, and 147 submarines.[5] The Royal Navy was, moreover, considerably more modern than the French fleet. There were also additional new ships under construction, so Great Britain entered the postwar era with the world's most powerful navy. In terms of useful warships in all classes, it was larger than the American and Japanese navies combined.[6] Moreover, British colonial possessions in Asia had been secured diplomatically by the 1902 Anglo-Japanese Treaty, which had been renewed in 1912.

Although the Japanese alliance had served British security needs well enough since 1902, it soon became a focus of tension between London and Washington, where American naval officers regarded it as a threat. Should the United States become involved in a war with Japan, the American navy risked the threat of a two-front war—one in the Pacific and another in the Atlantic—at the expense of Canada, who had no interest in an Anglo-American war. But the Japanese treaty remained popular at the Admiralty, for it protected by diplomacy Singapore, Hong Kong, and other Asian and Pacific possessions at the far limits of British naval capabilities.

With the German menace now abated, there remained no reasons for London to continue with the French alliance, which had lent tacit security to France's Asian empire. The breakdown of the Anglo-French entente therefore undermined the security of France's Asian empire, which lay well beyond the orbit of French naval capabilities. Indochina and French colonies in the Pacific, such as New Caledonia, were now indefensible against Japan or, indeed, any of the Washington Naval Treaty powers, except Italy. Isolated without any naval allies, France could afford no more than a symbolic naval presence in her Asian colonies.

After the war, one current of public opinion in the United States demanded naval disarmament in the interest of lowering taxes and reducing international tensions. To many Americans, it made no sense to continue with the construction of battleships that had remained largely on the sidelines during the Great War. But other powerful interests, supported by a simmering Anglophobia, insisted upon completing the ambitious 1916 and 1918 naval construction programs to build an American navy "second to none," which meant building battleships to the level of the Royal Navy. By 1920 the three leading naval powers—Great Britain, the United States, and Japan—were in the process of completing their wartime naval construction programs. They had already entered into a race with each other to build battleships.

At the same time, changing technology had led the smaller naval powers—France and Italy—to redefine their security needs. During World War I, undersea technologies had surged ahead of naval aviation to produce efficient and inexpensive weapons systems well suited to the needs of the smaller powers, which could ill afford battleships. Consequently, as the major naval powers entered into a race to construct *Dreadnought*s for operations on the high seas, France and Italy raced against each other to construct submarines and light surface ships suitable for service in the Mediterranean.

The Washington Naval Conference

The Washington Naval Conference, which opened on November 12, 1921, addressed a spread of security needs but failed to dissolve a pattern of tensions already emerging between London and Washington, between Paris and Rome, and between the Admiralty and the French naval command at the Rue Royale in Paris. With German naval power momentarily restrained by the Versailles treaty, the political leadership of Great Britain, the United States, and Japan came together to head off battleship construction races among themselves and to address by diplomacy their security needs in the Far East. France and

Italy were not expected to play leading roles. The United States, with its huge industrial power, enjoyed an important coercive advantage. Should the remaining powers drag their feet on fleet reductions, Washington could unleash its massive industrial might to outdistance the other powers in naval construction. But Washington preferred instead to negotiate fleet reductions within the framework of regional security agreements to restrain Japanese power in Asia, a policy that matched American interests at the expense of the Admiralty's special relationship with the Imperial Japanese Navy.

The French delegation to Washington, headed by parliamentarian Albert Sarraut, included Admiral Jean de Bon, chief of the French naval staff. The French delegation assumed that the deliberations would proceed on the basis of imperial security needs rather than that of existing fleet tonnage. Sarraut and de Bon expected the conference to permit France to rebuild its fleet to a level matching its commitment to defend the French Empire, the world's second largest.[7]

But Secretary of State Charles Evans Hughes' dramatic statement opening the conference called for substantial tonnage reductions and acceptance of the current tonnage levels as the standard for the future strength of each navy. In addition, capital ship tonnage would become the measure of naval strength with proportional limitations on aircraft carriers, cruisers, destroyers, and submarines.[8] De Bon expected that the proposals would narrow the gap between France and the larger naval powers.[9] He was mistaken, however, for the decline of French naval power during the war had placed France at a disadvantage relative to the other powers. France had nothing to gain from the current strength standard, which promised only to perpetuate French naval inferiority.

Afterward, when the American, British, and Japanese delegations excluded the French and Italian delegations from the deliberations of the Under-Commission for Naval Limitations, French concerns began to mount. Just moments before the undercommission reassembled on December 15, Hughes informed Sarraut that French capital ship strength would be limited to no more than 175,000 tons. And in the official session that followed, Hughes announced that British, American, and Japanese strength would be governed by a ratio of 5-5-3, respectively, which translated into 525,000 tons for Great Britain and the United States and 315,000 tons for Japan. Sarraut also learned that Italy would receive parity with the French navy at a ratio of 1.67 each.[10] Justifiably outraged, Sarraut protested that French imperial defense needs far exceeded those of Italy, whose empire was regional rather than global. More than any other item, the decision for Franco-Italian tonnage equality thrust France into an antagonistic posture for the remainder of the conference and, indeed, for more than a decade afterward.

The Five-Power Treaty, with its tonnage ratios, affected the Royal Navy and the Marine Nationale in different ways. For the Royal Navy, it meant conceding legal equality with the United States in capital ships and in total fleet tonnage should the ratios be extended downward to include lighter ships. It also meant scrapping numerous battleships, many of them out of date but some of them unfinished or planned, including four super-*Hood*s. Despite a ten-year construction holiday for capital ships, Britain was permitted to precede with construction of the 35,000-ton *Nelson* and *Rodney*. And while Washington committed itself not to fortify its bases in the Philippines, London was permitted to go ahead with the fortification of Singapore.

As for France, the Rue Royale and public opinion objected stoutly to the imposition of capital ship equality with Italy. But this restriction was largely symbolic, for France lacked in 1922 the financial capacity to compete with the larger naval powers in the construction of *Dreadnought*s. French interests demanded instead the construction of lighter ships. The treaty, however, contained in part II, section III, a clause permitting France and Italy to replace obsolete battleship tonnage in 1927 and 1929. Significantly, this obscure provision liberated both France and Italy to resume capital ship construction prior to the other powers, in the early 1930s, when new construction in Germany threatened both France and Britain and when new French capital ship construction would figure importantly in the European power balance. This provision would permit a revision of French construction priorities after 1930, while the three leading naval powers remained under a construction holiday until the end of 1936. In retrospect, it seems clear that the Five-Power Treaty served the long-term interests of the French navy in a way not fully appreciated in 1922.

Secretary Hughes would have preferred to apply the tonnage ratios to auxiliary warships, most importantly cruisers, destroyers, and submarines. But Sarraut and de Bon stoutly refused to consider any downward extension of the ratios. So Hughes appealed directly to Premier Aristide Briand, who agreed to the 175,000-ton limitation on French capital ships, but on condition that the ratios not include cruisers and other light warships.[11] French opposition to the downward extension of the ratios made it unnecessary for the British delegation to take that stand. Because of the French objections, the Washington Naval Treaty exempted lighter ships from the ratios, with the result that the Royal Navy was free to maintain in service the world's largest cruiser and destroyer fleets—30 cruisers, 90 light cruisers, and 443 destroyers in 1918.[12] At the same time, France was now legally entitled to rebuild her fleet with the construction of a variety of innovative and affordable light ship designs and, if finances should permit, to outdistance Italy's Regia Marina in the construction of all designs except battleships and aircraft carriers.

The Washington Naval Treaty therefore imposed no quantitative limits on the construction of cruisers. It imposed instead qualitative limits intended to make a clear distinction between auxiliary ships and capital ships governed by the ratios. The Washington-class cruisers, or Treaty Cruisers, as they came to be called, were new ship designs of no more than 10,000 tons mounting up to 8-inch guns, in contrast to battleships, which were heavier vessels mounting guns of more than eight inches.[13] The failure to impose a quantitative cap on cruiser tonnage set in motion a race between Britain and Japan in the construction of Treaty Cruisers, and between France and Italy in the construction all classes of auxiliary ships, including Treaty Cruisers. Since France could not compete with Japan in the construction of Treaty Cruisers, the Marine Nationale would compete instead with Italy's Regia Marina to construct a mixed fleet of heavy and light cruisers supplemented by submarines and other light vessels that often did not fit neatly into standard design classifications.

While British and French interests largely coincided on the need for light surface vessels for imperial defense, their interests clashed on the question of submarines. British naval officers viewed the submarine as an illegal intruder that threatened the central tactical role of their most cherished weapon, the battleship. For this and a host of other reasons, including wartime memories of U-boat attacks, the Admiralty insisted that submarines be abolished or subjected to quantitative limitations. In contrast, the Rue Royale regarded the submarine as a legitimate weapon suitable for the defense of distant colonies or for operations against a coastal blockade. But the French submarine was mainly intended for service in the Mediterranean, where the Italian undersea fleet had surged ahead of its French counterpart during the Great War. In Paris the submarine was viewed as an ideal weapon for a smaller naval power, one of an assortment of inexpensive ships funded in a tight budget that accorded the navy only about 20 percent of total defense expenditures.[14]

Although the British delegation at Washington offered to scrap its entire submarine fleet, Sarraut stubbornly insisted upon building the French undersea fleet to 90,000 tons. These negotiations dragged British and French naval relations to a low ebb. The British delegation, led by former Prime Minister Arthur Balfour, felt threatened at the French intention to expand its submarine fleet. "Who is this expansion directed against," Balfour insisted, "if it is not against England?"[15] The French delegation refused to compromise on the submarine issue. Consequently, the treaty imposed no limitations on undersea craft, with the result that France continued to build submarines that the Admiralty perceived as a threat to the Royal Navy.

An important American objective at the Washington Naval Conference was to stabilize international relations in the Far East, which meant imposing diplomatic restraints upon Japan. Geography accorded Japan important naval and military advantages in the far Pacific, where Japanese imperial ambitions had by no means subsided. Washington therefore proposed multiateral treaties to prop up the status quo in Asia, where American and European defense commitments lay at the far limits of their naval capabilities. The most important of these was the Four-Power Treaty, which abrogated the Anglo-Japanese Alliance. The treaty committed the United States, Britain, France, and Japan to respect each other's possessions in the Far East. Significantly, it lent less security to British interests than had the Japanese alliance, but it matched French interests as it brought Indochina under the umbrella of a collective security agreement.

In sum, the Washington treaties served reasonably well the interests of the three leading powers by heading off wasteful battleship construction during a peaceful decade when changing technology had not yet determined the future patterns of naval warfare. On the other hand, in failing to head off construction races between France and Italy and between Great Britain and Japan in the construction of auxiliary ships, the treaties set off a decade-long obsession to construct expensive Treaty Cruisers. At the same time, the Four-Power Treaty poisoned relations between Washington and London, where the Admiralty had assigned considerable security value to the Anglo-Japanese Treaty.[16] The Admiralty, lamenting the abrogation of the treaty and blaming the Americans for it, also smarted under the Five-Power Treaty, whose definition of cruisers coincided better with American than with British needs at a moment when Japan began to emerge as a potential enemy.

From Washington to Geneva: New Construction Races

The postwar naval races between France and Italy and between Great Britain and Japan were anticipated by the failure of the Washington treaty to restrain aggressive Japanese and Italian construction of auxiliary vessels under way since 1919. Italian construction of 15 destroyers between 1919 and 1923 threatened France, whose navy had decayed noticeably after 1914. The Japanese construction of more than 60 warships between 1919 and 1922 emerged as a serious threat to British Asian interests after the abrogation of the Anglo-Japanese Treaty in 1922 turned the Japanese ally into a potential enemy. The Royal Navy emerged from the Great War with the world's largest fleet of auxiliary ships, which included 30 cruisers, 90 light cruisers, 23 flotilla leaders, and 443 destroyers.[17] But many of the British ships were older or worn out from wartime service, due to be retired or scrapped faster than they could be replaced.

With modern warships under construction in Japan and Italy, and in France after 1922, the key to future naval balance lay with a new generation of ships yet to be built, rather than with the backlog of older World War ships. But in 1919 the British government, inspired by Secretary of State for War and Air Winston Churchill, adopted the controversial Ten-Year Rule, which assumed no major war for a decade. Renewed several times, it justified governmental restraints on shipbuilding.[18] Consequently, not one cruiser or destroyer was authorized between 1919 and the end of 1923.[19] The Ten-Year Rule promoted obsolescence and contributed to a shortage of modern ships needed for imperial defense at a moment when other naval powers were already beginning to rebuild their fleets.

The growing obsolescence of auxiliary ship tonnage in the Royal Navy therefore coincided with sharp increases in new tonnage on the part of Italy, France, and especially Japan. Of the European powers, Italy seized the initiative between 1919 and 1922 to authorize 14 destroyers in the range of 600 to 800 tons (to supplement a fleet of 84 World War–era destroyers) and in the mid-1920s two heavy cruisers of the *Trento* class.[20] Responding, the French launched in 1922 an ambitious naval construction program so that by the end of 1927 France had launched or authorized 7 new cruisers, 36 destroyers, and 41 submarines.

The creator of the modern French navy was Minister of Marine Georges Leygues.[21] Under his inspiration, France's newest ships consisted of an assortment of destroyers, submarines, and cruisers, including 2 cruisers of the 10,000-ton *Duquesne* class and 3 of the 7,249-ton *Duguay-Trouin* class, a lighter cruiser design that the British Admiralty would in time demand in larger numbers. France also moved in 1922 to construct 6 super destroyers, contre-torpilleurs, of the *Jaguar* class, slightly in excess of 2,100 tons. The 6 contre-torpilleurs and 6 larger versions of the same type, the 2,400-ton *Guépard* class laid down in 1926 and 1927, plus 26 1,500-ton standard destroyers of the *Simoun* and *L'Adroit* classes were designed to outmatch the more numerous but lighter Italian destroyers built during or shortly after the war.[22]

Great Britain followed between 1924 and 1927 with 13 cruisers, 11 destroyers, and 12 submarines. The total number of cruisers, destroyers, and submarines built or authorized by the three European powers during the years 1919–1927 were 84 by France, 56 by Italy, and 37 by Great Britain. Although Britain authorized during those years more cruisers than Italy and France combined, the Royal Navy neglected the construction of destroyers, launching only 11. The Admiralty had already begun to assign a higher value to cruisers than to destroyers. The slowdown in destroyer construction reflected Admiralty assumption that the Treaty of Versailles had ended the German U-boat threat, that the development of new submarine detection technology called Asdic had reduced the need for large destroyer fleets, and that the defense of Asia against Japan demanded a stronger presence of cruisers than of destroyers.

Japan surged ahead between 1919 and 1927 with the construction of 143 ships in these categories, including 21 cruisers, 66 destroyers, and 56 submarines. During those same years, the United States lagged behind, authorizing only 8 cruisers, 12 destroyers, and 3 submarines, a total of 23 ships.[23] These figures taken together suggest that after 1918, construction of auxiliary warships proceeded briskly but in uneven proportions among the five naval powers. While Japan, Italy, and France built a total of 112 submarines during that period, Britain built only 11 destroyers. But with Japan laying down 13 cruisers between 1919 and 1923, years when Great Britain built none, and with Tokyo authorizing 8 Treaty Cruisers in 1922, the Admiralty had little choice but to respond with 17 ships of similar type rather than with destroyers.[24] Not surprisingly, the swift acceleration of Japanese and British cruiser construction set off alarms in Washington.

In the wake of the Washington conference, Japan and the United States surged ahead of the European powers in the emerging new field of naval aviation. France got off to a good start with the completion of the 22,000-ton carrier *Béarn* in 1927, at about the same time the United States commissioned the 37,000-ton *Lexington* and *Saratoga* and Japan the *Akagi* and *Kaga*. Constructed on the hulk of an unfinished battleship, the slow-moving *Béarn* conformed to the qualitative requirements of the Washington treaty, but the Rue Royale moved slowly to develop aviation technology and doctrine. The narrow Mediterranean, where French naval interests focused most sharply, was less friendly to carrier operations than was the vast Pacific. But France moved ahead of Italy, who built not even one aircraft carrier between the wars.

During World War I, Great Britain had pioneered in the development of naval aviation. With the seaplane carrier *Ark Royal* and two true carriers, the 19,000-ton *Furious* and the 14,450-ton *Argus*, the Royal Navy built the first carrier fleet. Although these ships were intended to play reconnaissance roles in service to the battle fleet, the *Furious* operated independently in 1918 to mount history's first carrier attack against a shore target. The Admiralty added the 21,630-ton *Eagle* in 1920, the 10,850-ton *Hermes* in 1924, and in 1925 the *Furious* was renovated. But all of these ships were technically inferior to the *Lexington* and *Saratoga*, each operating sixty-three aircraft as opposed to twenty for the *Hermes* and thirty-six for the *Furious*.[25]

British naval aviation was also burdened by organizational problems. In 1917 the Royal Naval Air Service was placed under the command of the Royal Flying Corps, later the Royal Air Force, whose priorities were slanted toward strategic bombing at the expense of the special needs of naval aviation. This awkward arrangement circumvented the Admiralty and placed the training of naval aviation personnel under the command of an air service with little interest in carrier-based operations. At about the same time that American naval aviation liberated itself from the Army Air Corps to form an independent naval air arm, British naval aviation entered into two decades of servitude that condemned naval aircraft to technical backwardness and imposed a heavy drag on training and doctrinal development.[26]

While naval aviation remained in its infancy, the Admiralty focused attention after 1924 on the construction of cruisers, whose qualitative standards defined by the Washington treaty poorly served British imperial defense needs. Among the first generation of the Treaty Cruisers were the thirteen British *County* class and the two American *Pensacola*-class ships, built to the treaty standard of 10,000 tons and 8-inch guns. They were slightly slower but better protected than their French and Italian opposites, the *Duquesne* and *Trento* classes. The finest of the new Treaty Cruisers were the Japanese *Myoko* class of four ships, each displacing more than 13,000 tons, exceeding the treaty standard.[27] Between 1919 and 1927 Japan authorized or constructed twenty-two cruisers, more than Great Britain and the United States combined.[28] Aggressive Japanese naval construction coincided with the idealistic crusade for peace and disarmament in the mid-1920s, but the Admiralty was quick to see that Tokyo was out of step with that mood.

Meanwhile, naval and military disarmament negotiations began anew in the spring of 1926 when the Preparatory Commission for World Disarmament opened in Geneva under the auspices of the League of Nations. In these negotiations the French delegation proposed limits on total national tonnage distributed among four ship classes—battleships, aircraft carriers, surface ships below 10,000 tons, and submarines—with each navy free to shift tonnage from one class to another.[29] The French proposal to define a new category of surface ships as those under 10,000 tons reflected the French construction program already in progress, one that assumed the right of the Rue Royale to build light ships in quantity and quality conforming to French defense needs and budget limitations. It also protected the French right to shift large tonnage into the construction of submarines, ships suitable for service in the Mediterranean or out of colonial harbors.

Not surprisingly, the British delegation opposed the French proposal on the grounds that it placed too few restrictions on ship classes below 10,000 tons. The British proposed instead a rigid structure of nine ship classes with tonnage limitations on each class.[30] The formula reflected the British intent to deny France the option of shifting tonnage to submarines. There was little chance that the French delegation would accept the British proposal, not because of any plan to unleash submarines against Britain but because it cramped the French need to shift tonnage from one class to another and demanded that French ships conform to British design categories. Despite their failure, the deliberations in the Preparatory Commission set the scene for the Admiralty to move closer to the French position, which was friendly to emerging British demands for light cruisers.

Tensions at Geneva

In the meantime, American president Calvin Coolidge had issued in February 1927 a call for a new naval conference with the announced intention of curbing government spending by extending downward the Washington treaty ratios to the construction of auxiliary ships.[31] France, having no reason to enter into negotiations that risked imposing limits on light ships, declined the invitation but sent an observer, as did Italy. The Geneva Conference, sometimes called the Coolidge Conference, which opened in late June, addressed the construction interests of the United States, Great Britain, and Japan, but its outcome led to a surprising turn in Anglo-French naval relations.

The conference opened with little prior communication, so the British and American delegations clashed on technical details that might have been addressed in advance. The British delegation proposed a long agenda that included a cap on the construction of 10,000-ton Treaty Cruisers and the introduction of a new class of light cruisers displacing up to 7,500 tons and mounting 6-inch guns. This formula would enable the British to build heavy cruisers to serve the needs of the battle fleet, match the Japanese program, and build numerous less-expensive cruisers suitable for patrolling distant shipping lanes from bases in close proximity. Specifically, London wished to construct seventy cruisers (twenty-five heavy and forty-five light cruisers) for a total of 562,000 tons.[32] The British proposal reflected the Admiralty's need to rebuild the Royal Navy in a pattern to address its remote defense commitments within the limits of a budget growing increasingly tight. Even though funds to build seventy cruisers might not be immediately available, the Admiralty wished to ensure legality for construction up to the limits of British industrial capacity.

In contrast, the American delegation insisted upon Washington-type cruisers, heavy ships of greater endurance suitable for long-range Pacific operations. The U.S. Navy had fewer needs for light cruisers. The American delegation opposed British demands for increased naval construction, insisting at the same time upon the right of parity with Great Britain in the construction of all classes of ships. The United States had already laid down two of eight heavy cruisers authorized by Congress in 1924, and contracts for the remaining six had been let on condition that they could be canceled upon the conclusion of a disarmament agreement.[33] Alarmed at the construction races among the other naval powers and wanting to reduce his defense budget, Coolidge had summoned the conference at a moment when a disarmament agreement would have made it possible for him to cancel construction contracts for the remaining six cruisers.

There is no need to recount here the prolonged and heated exchanges attendant to the American delegation's rejection of several British proposals, all reflecting the urgent British need for increased construction to defend its distant Asian communications against Japan.[34] The Geneva Conference finally broke down because the American demand for naval disarmament clashed with British demands for increased construction. Afterward Coolidge made no move to withdraw the contracts for construction of the remaining cruisers under the 1924 program, so by the end of 1929 there were eight American cruisers under construction.[35]

The Anglo-French Naval Agreement

Although the Geneva Conference damaged Anglo-American naval relations, it set the scene for the Admiralty and the Rue Royale to revisit a spread of problems common to British and French construction needs. The Admiralty, isolated in the wake of the Geneva Conference, had good reasons to court the Rue Royale, for a naval agreement might enable London and Paris to present a common front against the United States when the powers met again as scheduled in 1930. Prompted by the Admiralty, Foreign Secretary Austen Chamberlain initiated discussions with his French counterpart, Aristide Briand. Chamberlain hinted at the reduction of ship categories from nine to five with the right of transferring tonnage among categories, which the French had long favored. The result was the Anglo-French Naval Agreement of July 4, 1928, a compromise agreement negotiated secretly in Paris and Geneva, where French and British naval officers represented their respective staffs at the League of Nations. The agreement, which resolved key differences that had burdened the negotiations in the Preparatory Commission, coincided with broader negotiations to conclude the Kellogg-Briand Pact, which aimed at repudiating war as an instrument of national policy.

The Anglo-French Naval Agreement proposed quantitative limitations on 10,000-ton cruisers. All five of the powers would be accorded parity in heavy cruisers and long-range submarines, with a tonnage ceiling to be determined for these classes, to the end of phasing out construction of Treaty Cruisers and of appeasing British fears of excessive French tonnage in submarines. The agreement would lend legality to increased construction of light cruisers.

Left unrestricted were 600-ton submarines, which the Admiralty accepted as coastal defense weapons posing no threat to overseas trade. London and Paris expected the agreement to serve as the basis for an arms control agreement among the five Washington treaty powers.[36] The question was whether it could be advanced as a constructive proposal or whether it would instead be viewed as a power play intended to advance the British cruiser agenda that the Americans had already rejected at Geneva.

The news of the agreement, which leaked to the press before its terms had finally been determined, unleashed a storm of controversy that requires here no more than a brief summary.[37] The French press, for the most part supportive of closer Anglo-French relations, applauded the agreement, suggesting moreover that it finally liberated France from the humiliating Washington treaty.[38] British opinion was more divided. Official voices supported the agreement, insisting that it was a constructive proposal to set an agenda for future naval disarmament. Other British opinion opposed it, usually on the grounds that the agreement was a narrow Anglo-French alliance standing in the way of a more useful alignment with Washington or that it undermined the mood of peace attendant to the Kellogg-Briand negotiations.

Sharp objections to the agreement were articulated in public addresses and press releases of senior British statesmen. Former foreign secretary Earl Grey denounced the agreement as a new entente between Great Britain and France, a step backward at the expense of Anglo-American relations, a disastrous foreign policy mistake that would provoke the United States to build additional heavy cruisers.[39] Former Prime Minister David Lloyd George described the agreement as the "most sinister event since the war." He warned that "to antagonize America is sheer madness."[40] And at a dinner honoring the American ambassador, former First Lord of the Admiralty Viscount Lee of Fareham insisted that there were no reasons for any disputes between Great Britain and the United States, that naval experts ought not to guide policy, and that statesmen could easily settle any issue outstanding between the two countries.[41]

Coolidge thought along the same lines. Receiving the British ambassador, Sir Esme Howard, on November 7, the president assigned the blame for failed disarmament discussions to naval technicians whose endless haggling over guns and tons, he said, wrongly assumed the possibility of war. He insisted with Howard upon the need of broad-minded statesmen who would assume from the beginning that there would be no war between the United States and Great Britain.[42] Coolidge left open the door for future discussions with Great Britain. Nevertheless, he moved forward with the 1929 naval bill to authorize construction of fifteen additional heavy cruisers.

Despite its popularity in France, the Anglo-French Naval Agreement failed to find approval in London. But the fact that the agreement had been negotiated in the first place suggests that the British and French naval staffs had edged closer to each other in defining their future construction needs, that British and French naval interests were more similar than different, and that their technical differences might be resolved by staff negotiations. Although the agreement was premature and abortive, it nevertheless anticipated the Anglo-French naval alliance to be concluded a decade later. On the other hand, the failure of the agreement indicated that British political relations with Washington were paramount—at the expense of relations with France, at least for the moment—when the world was speaking peace and when no one but the Admiralty worried much about the massive build-up of Japanese naval power.

Background of the London Naval Conference

With disarmament in the air, naval authorities everywhere could easily see the advantage in rushing forward their construction programs prior to the 1930 London Naval Conference. Washington moved aggressively toward completion of twenty-three heavy cruisers, eight under the 1924 program and fifteen under the 1929 program.[43] In France, four 10,000-ton cruisers, one light cruiser, seventeen destroyers, and thirty-six submarines, all laid down after 1924, were either completed or under construction by 1930. A program of similar distribution, including twenty-two submarines, was under way in Italian shipyards.[44] At the end of 1929 Japan had under construction or had recently commissioned four heavy cruisers, six destroyers, and six submarines. Funds for eight additional destroyers, six submarines, and an aircraft carrier had been appropriated. Japanese cruisers under construction exceeded by as much as 30 percent the 10,000-ton limit required under the Washington treaty.[45]

In contrast to the brisk building programs under way among the other powers, British construction lagged. While members of the government argued endlessly over what kind of cruisers should be built, the Treasury imposed a strict retrenchment that left the Royal Navy badly undernourished. In 1929, after the June elections had unseated the Conservatives, the Labor government of Ramsay MacDonald slashed the 1928 program, suspending construction not yet begun and canceling plans for two 10,000-ton cruisers. MacDonald promptly contacted American president Herbert Hoover, and the two statesmen summoned a naval disarmament conference to meet in 1930, with the view of imposing limits on the construction of auxiliary ships.[46]

In February 1929 construction had begun in Germany for the first of three cruisers intended to replace battleships that had become overaged after twenty years, as provided by the Treaty of Versailles. But German naval architects seized a technical advantage with the construction of a new type of ship out of step with the Washington treaty definition of cruisers. Known as Panzerschiffe or pocket battleships, each of these ships could mount six 11-inch battleship guns on an announced 10,000-ton cruiser platform. They in fact displaced 11,700 tons. With a top speed of twenty-six knots, these ships could outgun any cruiser capable of overtaking them.[47] They were designed as commerce raiders, to prowl distant seas and to prey upon merchant ships. The presence of even one of these ships in vast Atlantic waters would require a British or French commitment many times their number to chase them down.

Significantly, MacDonald prepared to enter Great Britain into a new arms control conference summoned to lock into place cruiser designs ill-suited to match the new and heavier German battlecruisers. In sum, the five Washington treaty powers moved toward new naval limitations at the moment when a sixth naval power, governed by a different treaty, had begun to liberate itself from its restrictions. Ironically, it would be the French rather than the British who would address the new German threat with suitable construction.

The London Naval Conference

In February 1930, after London and Washington had drawn closer together on the cruiser question, delegations of the five Washington treaty powers assembled in London. Not everyone shared the Anglo-American agenda of extending downward the Five-Power Treaty ratios to included auxiliary vessels. France, already locked in a race with Italy to construct cruisers, destroyers, and submarines, refused to accept parity with Italy or to sign the articles limiting tonnage in these categories. It was finally arranged for France and Italy to resume discussions afterward at Geneva, with Great Britain acting as intermediary.

For the other three powers, the ratios were extended downward and adjusted in detail to govern construction of auxiliary ships. Imposing a tonnage cap on heavy cruisers and lending legitimacy to a new class of light cruisers mounting 6.1-inch guns, the London treaty shifted for a time the emphasis in Great Britain toward construction of light cruisers. It accorded the British 192,000 tons of the light design with the option of shifting to cruiser tonnage up to 10 percent of that allotted to destroyers. This was less than the Admiralty had desired, but it meant that the Royal Navy could now build light cruiser types the Americans had opposed at Geneva in 1927. Japan, whose navy had always opposed the 5-5-3 ratios for capital ships, accepted a complex arrangement that fell just short of the overall 10-10-7 ratio that the Japanese delegation had requested.[48]

In France the trend also moved toward light cruisers, whose lower construction costs liberated scarce funds for the construction of heavier ships. The

London Naval Treaty extended until 1936 the holiday for the construction of capital ships, but France and Italy were permitted to undertake overdue battleship construction authorized by the Washington treaty. For France, this led in the 1930s to the *Dunkerque* and *Strasbourg*, 26,000-ton battlecruisers designed to outclass the German Panzerschiffe. Italy was not far behind, laying down in 1934 the battleships *Vittorio Veneto* and *Littorio*.[49] In sum, the London Naval Treaty authorized France to outmatch the Panzerschiffe and Italy to build two modern battleships that threatened France more than Germany. Great Britain remained locked into the construction holiday for capital ships during years when Germany proceeded with the construction of three Panzerschiffe, Italy with two battleships, and France with two battlecruisers. Britain would commission not even one battleship or battlecruiser during the 1930s. In authorizing France to construct two battlecruisers, the London Naval Treaty set the stage for the Marine Nationale to become an attractive ally of the Royal Navy toward the end of the decade.

Crisis in British Naval Power

The construction limitations imposed by the London Naval Treaty was but one part of a larger scene that ushered the Royal Navy into a new crisis during the early 1930s. The treaty restrictions made it difficult for the Royal Navy to regain lost ground when the global balance soon shifted in favor of the emerging Axis powers. The treaty authorized for Britain fifty modern cruisers, as opposed to the seventy that the Admiralty had demanded at the Geneva Conference. It left the Royal Navy with only 120 destroyers, nearly half of which would be obsolete by 1936.[50] Between 1930 and 1935 the government authorized annually nine new destroyers, the equivalent of one flotilla per year.[51] But this construction served only to replace ships becoming obsolete. With both Japan and Nazi Germany emerging as potential enemies in the early 1930s, British construction until 1936 produced too few cruisers to address the Asian problem and too few destroyers to deal with any future German U-boat menace. Moreover, the London Naval Treaty locked the Royal Navy into the traditional ship categories at the expense of inventive ways to match the German Panzerschiffe.

At the same time, financial austerity imposed by the Great Depression deprived the navy of resources essential to fulfilling the global mission that history and geography had imposed upon it. During those years the national government, under Ramsay MacDonald and Stanley Baldwin, starved the navy of supply, personnel, and equipment important to morale and operational efficiency. And British naval aviation continued to languish under the unhappy marriage to the Royal Air Force. The naval air service, which might have been developed in the 1930s as a useful defense against German surface raiders and submarines, struggled without doctrinal focus and with its too few aircraft becoming obsolescent.

Symptomatic of the starving of the Royal Navy was the September 1931 Invergordon mutiny, in which pay reductions prompted lower deck personnel on the *Hood*, *Nelson*, and other heavy ships to ignore orders from their officers.[52] Although the problem was quickly corrected, the threat of widespread indiscipline shook the navy to its core. The reduction in pay was but one part of a larger pattern of neglect that burdened the Royal Navy during the Great Depression. Numerous other problems ranged all the way from spoiled gunpowder to the failure to fortify Singapore, whose security was vital to any British defense of its Pacific possessions against Japan.

The nadir of British naval power occurred in June 1935 with the Anglo-German Naval Agreement. A bilateral agreement concluded at the expense of France and of the Versailles treaty, the agreement permitted the Reich to build up to 35 percent of the British navy, up to 45 percent in submarines, and at Berlin's discretion up to parity in submarines. That led to an announced German program to build by 1942 six battleships, 44,000 tons of aircraft carriers, eighteen cruisers, 37,500 tons of destroyers, and 17,500 tons of U-boats.[53] In 1935 the Royal Navy was locked into the terms of the London Naval Treaty, until the end of 1936, so that the German agreement increased by eighteen months the head start the Reich had seized in battleship construction.

For reasons related as much to the neglect of the fleet as to construction restraints, the Royal Navy was too weak to risk a clash with Italy during the 1935 Abyssinian crisis. The fact of British naval decline was well understood in Paris, where French intelligence services reported in 1935 that "for the first time in perhaps 230 years, Great Britain is unable by herself to supervise her maritime traffic, at least not between Gibraltar and Suez."[54]

The Renaissance of French Naval Power

During the half dozen years following the 1930 London Naval Conference, as the Marine Nationale struggled to keep ahead of the Regia Marina and to address the challenge imposed by the new German Panzerschiffe, French naval construction shifted its focus from Treaty Cruisers to battlecruisers and light cruisers. Franco-Italian naval disarmament negotiations, which began in late 1930 at Geneva and continued into 1931, made no progress as the French refused to accept parity with Italy or to reduce French submarine construction, which British intermediary Sir Robert Craigie had insisted upon. The French delegation, headed by René Massigli, French delegate to the League of Nations, and naval expert Rear-Admiral Jean François Darlan, offered several compromise proposals, all of which were rejected either by the British or the

Italians. Darlan observed that Craigie and the British naval experts were biased toward the Italians, whose smaller but growing submarine fleet was somehow less threatening than the French. Darlan suspected that the British motive at Geneva was to negotiate a reduction in French submarine construction.

On the other hand, Massigli and Darlan understood that France and Britain shared similar defense commitments, which the abortive 1928 naval staff agreement had implied. Each nation held distant colonial possessions, and neither had sufficient naval resources to defend them. The obvious first step in addressing the problem was a naval alliance under which the two powers might combine their assets against a common enemy. But London backed away from a French agreement, with the result that the Geneva negotiations bore upon the balance of French and Italian naval power. They finally broke down in 1931 when Massigli and Darlan refused to cancel construction intended to address the dual threat of mounting Italian and German naval power.[55]

With its vast colonial empire stretching from Africa to the Caribbean to Indochina, and in the Pacific as far as New Caledonia, France could hardly accept tonnage parity with Italy, whose defense commitments stretched mainly to nearby Libya. In the absence of an alliance with Great Britain, France would have to build heavy ships to outclass the three German commerce raiders that threatened France rather than Italy and also light ships to protect the distant trade routes and preserve the French margin over the Regia Marina in the Mediterranean. France therefore went ahead with construction that included the *Dunkerque*, authorized in 1932 and commissioned in 1937, and the *Strasbourg*, authorized in 1934 and commissioned in 1938, after the cruiser construction program had been phased out with the final authorization of four light cruisers in 1933. The two *Dunkerques*—battlecruisers of 26,000 tons mounting 13-inch guns at twenty-nine knots—were designed to outgun and outdistance the *Deutschland*, launched in May 1931, and two sister ships, *Graf Spee* and *Admiral Scheer*, launched in 1933 and 1934. The construction of the *Dunkerque* and the *Strasbourg* attest to the astute leadership of the French command, whose stubborn defense of French construction rights at London and Geneva enabled the Rue Royale to proceed with the construction of ship designs that the Washington and London treaties had denied the Royal Navy.[56]

By 1933, when the last class of cruisers was authorized, France had built an impressive variety of auxiliary ships designed primarily to outclass the Regia Marina. The most impressive of these were seven 10,000-ton cruisers beginning with the *Duquesne* class in the mid-1920s and ending with the *Suffren* class that included the *Colbert*, *Foch*, *Dupleix*, and *Algèrie*, all of which were in service by the early 1930s. And twelve light cruisers, including six 7,600-ton ships of the *La Galissonnière* class built between 1931 and 1935, would patrol Mediterranean and more distant waters. All of the French cruisers, fast at the expense of armor protection, were consistent with the French need to address the Italian challenge in the Mediterranean.

Paris had always protected the French right to adopt innovative designs, which resulted in the construction of thirty-two contre-torpilleurs, of which the most modern, the 2,800-ton *Mogador* class, carried 5.4-inch guns and 21.6-inch torpedo tubes, to outmatch Italian destroyers or any destroyer afloat prior to World War II. In addition, French shipyards produced by 1939 thirty-eight light and standard destroyers that included twenty-six ships of the 1,300-ton *Bourrasque* and *L'Adroit* classes. The French also pushed forward with the construction of submarines so that there were seventy-seven in service by 1939.[57]

Nevertheless, the French fleet of the 1930s, like the Royal Navy, was stretched too thin to fulfill its global defense commitments. In the wake of the 1935 Anglo-German Naval Agreement, the Reich proceeded with the construction of the battlecruisers *Scharnhorst* and *Gneisenau*, to match the *Dunkerque* and *Strasbourg*, and later with the battleships *Bismarck* and *Tirpitz*. Italy, moreover, proceeded with two 35,000-ton battleships, the *Vittorio Veneto* and *Littorio*, while Japan surged ahead with construction that included the massive 65,000-ton *Yamato*. In 1936 Berlin took the first steps to negotiate with Rome and Tokyo the Axis alliance, which shifted the global naval balance decisively against Britain and France.

French naval construction could not match that of the three Axis powers, and British naval rearmament did not get under way in earnest until 1937, after the 1936 London Naval Treaty had ended the construction holiday for capital ships. British construction of heavy ships lagged behind the French, owing mainly to London's prolonged commitment to arms control agreements, so the Admiralty could not expect to commission the first of the *George V* class battleships until 1940. At the same time, the Marine Nationale enjoyed no decisive margin over the Regia Marina. French naval officers had long understood that the best hope for Britain and France lay in the conclusion of an alliance that would enable them to combine their naval assets in the Mediterranean to the end of establishing a clear margin over Italy. But forging that alliance would not be easy because statesmen clung to appeasement as a safer option than power in addressing the emerging threat of fascist aggression in the Mediterranean.

Chapter 2

Fascist Aggression in the Mediterranean

Fascist aggression in the Mediterranean was but one part of a larger challenge that threatened British and French security needs in the mid-1930s. Crisis in Ethiopia, German designs on the Rhineland, Japanese aggression in Asia, and the forging of an alliance among the three Axis powers threatened London and Paris alike, but in different ways, based on geography. The only area where massively superior power might have been employed to support French and British diplomacy against any of the aggressor states was the Mediterranean. But that option was more daring than the diplomacy of appeasement. Accordingly, French and British statesmen were tempted to address Mediterranean problems from a posture of weakness rather than of strength.

Geographic Differences

France and Great Britain had much in common in terms of overseas defense needs, but their military commitments on the European continent were sharply different. With 60 million Germans just beyond her northern frontier, France had good reason to fear a resurgence of German military power. Accordingly, Paris defended the Treaty of Versailles; negotiated a network of defensive alliances with eastern European states, including Poland and Czechoslovakia; and began construction of the Maginot Line to blunt any attack across the Franco-German frontier between Switzerland and Belgium. Memories of two German invasions since 1870 remained fresh in the minds of the French, and they were not inclined to think that Germany would act much differently in the future.

In contrast, geography accorded Great Britain a measure of security that promised London the option of keeping France at arm's length. British statesmen, remembering the unspeakable horrors of World War I, assumed that the United Kingdom would have no reason to enter again into a continental war or to maintain a large army in the event of one. French military commitments to eastern Europe heightened London's fears that close relations with France would drag Great Britain into precisely the kind of war that the English were determined to avoid. Except for the naval disarmament agreements, London therefore pursued in the 1920s a foreign policy of aloofness, refusing to undertake any military commitments beyond the 1925 Locarno treaty that guaranteed the Rhineland frontiers of Germany, France, and Belgium against unprovoked military aggression.

British isolationism was nourished on the domestic scene by a mood of pacifism and Francophobia that assumed France to be the main threat to peace. Many English believed that France stood for militarism, that Paris exploited the Treaty of Versailles to punish Germany, and that French fears of another German war were exaggerated. With channel waters to protect them against any German invasion, it was easy for the English to think along these lines. Many of the assumptions that had governed Anglo-French relations in the 1920s lingered to perpetuate in London a mindset geared toward avoiding intimate relations with France. London remained obsessed with working strictly within the framework of the League of Nations in the pursuit of collective security, a safer alternative than bilateral relations with France.

Nevertheless the flexing of Italian naval muscles in the Mediterranean would in time force London to consider whether closer relations with France might after all be useful. The French navy stood as the logical British ally in the Mediterranean. But any Anglo-French naval alliance to protect the Mediterranean risked drawing Great Britain closer to France on the continent and closer to an unwanted war against Germany or Italy. British Mediterranean policy in the mid-1930s was therefore marked by an awkward ambivalence. On the one hand, there was the dominant temptation to try to keep Italian dictator Benito Mussolini in line by diplomatic means, which meant concluding with him a Mediterranean settlement. On the other hand, there persisted an underlying current of opinion that any negotiations to restrain Mussolini would have to be backed up by the threat of naval power. In 1935, when Italian aggression thrust Europe into the Abyssinian crisis, the threat of combined Anglo-French naval power in the Mediterranean remained a viable option. It was, indeed, the strongest card that London and Paris had to play. Ironically, it was a French rather than an English statesman who first refused to play that high card.

The Enigma of Stresa

During the 1920s London had always thought it important to maintain cordial relations with Italy, and in 1931, at the Geneva naval disarmament negotiations, British statesmen had lined up with Italy to isolate France. Afterward the European scene grew considerably more complex and threatening to all three powers. In 1933 Chancellor Adolf Hitler abruptly withdrew Germany from the World Disarmament Conference and from the League of Nations, and in 1934 Austrian Nazis staged an abortive coup d'état in Vienna that collapsed only when Mussolini threatened armed intervention to protect Austria from impending German aggression. In March of 1935 Berlin announced plans for compulsory military conscription with the creation of an army of thirty-six divisions, in defiance of the military restrictions of the Versailles treaty.

Alarmed, Mussolini invited London and Paris to send delegates to Stresa, Italy, for discussion of collective measures to oppose German rearmament.[1] Although the Stresa Front of April 14, 1935, came to nothing, a bilateral Anglo-Italian declaration attached to the accord announced a spirit of cooperation upon which London would attempt to build better relations with Italy, who appeared capable of unleashing military power against the Reich. London's temptation to flirt with Mussolini in 1934 reflected the fact that Great Britain, a naval power, had no good way to restrain Germany, no way to back up British diplomacy on the continent with the threat of military power. On the other hand, London's temptation to turn Mussolini against Hitler clashed with the option of employing the threat of naval power to confront a pattern of fascist aggression spreading throughout the Mediterranean in the mid-1930s.

The Stresa accords marked only the beginning of Europe's reaction to German rearmament. In early May of 1935 French premier Pierre Laval concluded with Moscow the Franco-Soviet Treaty of Mutual Assistance. But that accord, which seemed to amplify the chances of war on the continent, reinforced British determination to keep France at arm's length. In June, moreover, the Anglo-German Naval Agreement gave sanction to German naval rearmament that France could not easily match, keeping Anglo-French relations at low ebb. In the meantime, Mussolini had stirred up a crisis in Abyssinia that threatened to poison Anglo-Italian relations and cause London to consider the value of cooperation with France in the Mediterranean, where it was possible to confront Mussolini with the threat of combined Anglo-French naval power.

Crisis in the Mediterranean

When Mussolini's armies invaded Abyssinia on October 3, 1935, the League of Nations promptly declared Italy the aggressor and voted to impose economic sanctions, to go into effect on November 18. Although Mussolini's aggression in Abyssinia posed no serious threat to British imperial interests, it threatened to weaken the influence of the League, whose friendly arena had long provided London a substitute for any binding commitments to France. And although public opinion in the United Kingdom demanded sanctions against Italy, statesmen in both London and Paris understood that imposing them risked driving Mussolini into the arms of Hitler.

Since Britain had taken the lead at Geneva to impose sanctions, the Admiralty naturally worried about possible Italian reprisals. Italian naval power, though not overwhelming in 1935, was nevertheless sufficiently strong in submarines to threaten the Royal Navy. Responding, the Admiralty increased its naval presence in the region, sending to Gibraltar two squadrons centered on the *Hood* and *Renown*. But London preferred not to employ force against Italy, mainly out of concern to find instead a diplomatic settlement.[2] Nevertheless, should the crisis somehow lead to war, the Royal Navy would require French assistance in the Mediterranean. Naval operations against Italy would require British use of French bases. British warships, for example, might need to put into Toulon, France, or Bizerte, Tunisia, for fuel, repairs, or other services available only ashore. This assistance would require Anglo-French naval cooperation that might easily escalate into combined operations against Italy. Accordingly, in the interest of finding allies against Italy, London concluded in the autumn of that year defense agreements with several of the Mediterranean states, most importantly France. At the same time, negotiations to find a peaceful settlement continued at diplomatic levels.

As early as September, when the question of economic sanctions was being discussed at Geneva, British undersecretary of foreign affairs Anthony Eden pressed Paris to give London assurances of French naval support in the event that sanctions provoked an Italian attack against British possessions in the Mediterranean.[3] Responding to this initiative, the French and British naval staffs under Rear-Admiral Jean Decoux and Admiral Sir Ernle Chatfield, First Sea Lord, worked in London in October to draft a proposal that included making French naval bases available to the Royal Navy in the event of unprovoked Italian aggression against either power.[4] These negotiations suggest that the Admiralty and the Rue Royale were in step with each other should there be a need to confront Mussolini with the threat of combined naval power. But even as these negotiations proceeded, Laval dragged his feet on the question of Anglo-French naval cooperation.

Laval, whose January 1935 Franco-Italian Agreement had given Mussolini what amounted to a green light in Abyssinia, was miffed at the British naval buildup in the Mediterranean, which clashed with his policy of appeasing

Mussolini. He stated publicly his willingness to support the Royal Navy in any role to help enforce decisions of the League of Nations. At the same time he insisted that withdrawal of British ships from the Mediterranean would ease tensions and increase the chances of a negotiated settlement and that a strong French pledge of support to the Royal Navy would close the door on any diplomatic settlement.[5] With considerable support in the French press, Laval aimed at a diplomatic settlement to satisfy Mussolini's ambitions in Abyssinia in exchange for Italian support, should the Reich threaten French interests in Europe. Many French could not understand why London would object so stoutly to Mussolini's Abyssinian ambitions, which posed no threat to Europe, and simultaneously ignore Hitler's mounting arms buildup opposite the Rhineland.[6]

Eden insisted that Britain and France stand together against Italian aggression, and he threatened to withdraw British military commitments under the Locarno pact should Paris fail to give London full support in the Mediterranean. Eden's linking the Locarno pact to the Ethiopian crisis struck a hard blow at French security expectations, for Paris had long regarded Locarno as an unqualified British guarantee of France's Rhineland frontier. Now London was holding that guarantee hostage to French naval support in the Mediterranean. Finally, on October 18, after Anglo-French relations had been strained to the limit, Laval passed on to Eden a note containing assurances of French support in the event of an Italian attack resulting from British participation in any collective effort undertaken by the League of Nations.[7]

The Anglo-French naval agreement concluded on November 2 went further than Laval's assurances had intended. According to American naval attaché reports from Paris, the agreement authorized ships of the Royal Navy to use French Mediterranean ports, including Toulon and Bizerte, for purposes of docking, refueling, and repair. France, moreover, would call up naval reserves, and French ships would be moved to strategic points in the Mediterranean. Any British warships moved out of the Mediterranean would be replaced by French ships to monitor the Italian fleet and report ship movements to the British Admiralty. In a second phase, to begin at the outset of any hostilities, the French and British naval general staffs would quickly come together to draft plans for combined operations against the common enemy.[8] The agreement suggests that Anglo-French naval staff relations resonated clearer than Anglo-French political relations and that the French political and naval leadership were out of step with each other.

Not surprisingly, Laval backed away from the Anglo-French naval agreement, moving instead to appease Rome. He made no effort to call up French reserves, to move French warships to strategic positions in the Mediterranean, or to prepare any French harbor to receive British warships. At the same time, he assured Italy that "France has gone as far as it cares to for the time being in pledging naval cooperation with Britain in the Mediterranean."[9] He continued to complain, moreover, about the British naval buildup at Gibraltar, such that London began to question whether France could be trusted to lend the Royal Navy much support. Laval had never given London a pledge of unqualified naval support. The policy he clearly rejected was that of enlisting the threat of combined Anglo-French naval power in the service of diplomacy.

Although London had never abandoned the thought of negotiating a diplomatic settlement with Mussolini, British statesmen in 1935 were more inclined than French statesmen to employ naval power to support their diplomacy, as their sending two battlecruisers to Gibraltar attests. They were therefore displeased with Laval's ambivalent attitude, which discounted the value of Anglo-French naval cooperation as an alternative to appeasement. Laval's ambivalence caused London to question the reliability of France as a potential ally.

In December, when Laval and British foreign secretary Samuel Hoare finally settled upon a plan that rewarded Italy with a generous slice of Ethiopia, both men fell from power, with Eden succeeding Hoare as foreign secretary. Laval's policy of appeasement failed to drive a wedge between Mussolini and Hitler, and his refusal to support the Royal Navy in the Mediterranean made it easier for London, in 1936, to hedge on its Rhineland commitments under the Locarno treaty. In 1935 the threat of combined Anglo-French naval power in the Mediterranean was the strongest card that Paris and London held, but it was the Frenchman Laval who refused to play it.

An Upturn in Anglo-French Naval Relations

With Laval now out of the way, the Rue Royale took the initiative in early 1936 to repair its relations with the Admiralty, to underscore the intention of the French naval staff to honor its commitments under the November agreement. On January 3 the director of naval intelligence in London received the French naval attaché, who delivered a message for Admiral Chatfield from the chief of the French naval staff, Admiral Georges Durand-Viel, reporting a spread of measures the French navy had undertaken to fulfill its obligations, including efforts to prepare Toulon and other ports to receive British warships. According to the British account of the interview, Durand-Viel "hoped during his visit to the South to be able to inspect the many preparations that France had been making in the last two months, secretly, to be more ready to support us in the event of hostilities. He told me these preparations had been made entirely by the Naval Staff, without even the knowledge of their Minister of

Marine, and were, therefore, very secret." The record of the interview concludes with the observation that the French officer "had evidently come to give me the impression that the French Naval Staff were trying to do their utmost to help and to be more ready."[10] In closing, the French attaché offered the services of Admiral Georges Robert, who would be available should the Admiralty need additional information.

Chatfield could easily see that the Rue Royale, mistrustful of its own political leadership, nevertheless wished to fulfill its commitments under the November agreement and to renew Anglo-French discussions at the staff level. He was puzzled, however, at the French obsession with secrecy, that the French naval staff would conceal the agreement from its own minister of marine. He could see that the French naval staff was out of step with the French government and that the Rue Royale might not be able to fulfill its commitments under the agreement.[11] But what the French communication had implied, and what Chatfield clearly did not miss, was that the Rue Royale wished to stay in step with the Admiralty and cooperate with the British naval staff on questions vital to their common defense interests.

Discussions were renewed on January 15, when Chatfield received Admiral Robert at the Admiralty. There they agreed informally upon the outlines of plans that would govern Anglo-French naval cooperation in the Mediterranean in the event of war with Italy. Robert made it clear that French Mediterranean ports now stood ready to receive and service British warships and that French officers were prepared to discuss technical details concerning entry into the ports. The two admirals agreed to a tentative division of the Mediterranean into British and French zones of responsibility. Liaison officers would be exchanged so that each navy would have representation at the Admiralty, at the Rue Royale, and with the major naval commands in the Mediterranean. Early in the war British warships would help escort French troop convoys from Africa to France, and French destroyers would help patrol waters near Gibraltar against Italian submarines. Afterward France would station submarines in the eastern Mediterranean to attack Italian communications with Libya, and French warships would cooperate with the Royal Navy to bombard ports along the Italian coast. The two navies would, however, operate most often in their assigned zones, rather in close proximity to each other.[12] This informal and confidential agreement, though short of a formal Anglo-French naval alliance, reflected the fact that the two naval staffs were at that moment more in step with each other than were their governments.

The naval staffs met again on April 15 and 16 in London under the Locarno treaty, this time in response to Hitler's reoccupation of the Rhineland in early March. These meetings, which involved military and air staffs as well as the naval staffs, also included representatives from Belgium. The meetings between the British and French naval staffs now assumed different dimensions, for the potential enemy had become Germany rather than Italy. The Reich's three new battlecruisers, *Deutschland*, *Admiral Scheer*, and *Graf Spee*, had already been launched. On the other hand, their French counterparts, *Dunkerque* and *Strasbourg*, remained under construction, and Great Britain had not yet begun to rebuild its battleship fleet, so that the Kriegsmarine emerged as an enemy more formidable than the Italian navy. And the Reich was poised to wage an entirely different kind of naval war, one of commerce raiding in the vast Atlantic, where combined British and French naval power would be stretched thin against the three swift Panzerschiffe.

With Great Britain and France only marginally prepared to wage a naval war against the German commerce raiders, the April staff discussions were limited in scope so as not to appear provocative to Germany. They were geared mainly toward the exchange of information rather than to operations. Whereas the 1935 staff meetings had focused on making French Mediterranean ports available to the Royal Navy, those in 1936 aimed at making British home ports available to French ships, with the obvious view of moving French assets northward for service in British home waters.

The British naval staff was especially interested in making their home ports accessible to French contre-torpilleurs and destroyers. Given the British shortage of destroyers, the Admiralty could easily see the advantages of the French ships operating under their own command for coastal patrol to liberate British destroyers for service with the battle fleet. The April staff discussions established a system of communications, which turned out to be mainly an exchange of information intended to match French naval needs with fuel, docking, and other facilities available in British home ports.[13] As it turned out, these discussions had no immediate outcome, for Paris and London managed to avoid war by appeasing German ambitions in the Rhineland. Nevertheless, the discussions again reflected a community of interest between the two navies that would become more useful with the completion of the two French battlecruisers.

The events from the autumn of 1935 to the spring of 1936 defined for the moment the perimeters limiting Anglo-French naval cooperation. For the first time since the World War, London had solicited French naval assistance in both the Mediterranean and the Atlantic. That marked the beginning of a shift in British naval policy toward France without, however, ruling out a policy of appeasing Italy. London's overtures to the French navy during the Ethiopian crisis reflected a naval balance in the Mediterranean where combined Anglo-French power against Italy remained a useful option. But the Rhineland crisis, which exposed British weakness in the Atlantic and underscored London's reluctance to enforce the Locarno treaty, suggested that an Anglo-French naval alliance against the Reich remained, in London, a poorer option than the diplomacy of appeasement.

The Rhineland crisis underscored the overextension of the Royal Navy in terms of its global defense commitments, which could have easily tempted London to neutralize Italy by diplomacy, rather than by naval power, at the expense of a naval entente with France. Paris might therefore have worried that London might someday abandon France altogether, or might accord France but half of an alliance, a naval entente against Italy to protect British Mediterranean communications, and a policy of isolationism toward the continent, leaving France to stand alone against mounting German military power on its northern frontier.[14]

What is clear, however, is that French political leadership under Laval had pursued a policy of appeasement that forfeited a viable opportunity to employ the threat of combined Anglo-French naval power to back up British and French diplomacy toward Italy, and both French and British political leadership had opted in the Rhineland crisis to appease the Reich at a moment when Anglo-French naval power in the Atlantic was too thin to support a more muscular policy. With the *Dunkerque* and *Strasbourg* still unfinished, France had little at the moment to offer Britain in terms of a naval entente against Germany.

On the other hand, the British and French naval staffs had cooperated with each other reasonably well after the fall of Laval, and they had grown to understand better their differences and common interests. The French naval staff, assigning special significance to the Admiralty's soliciting French naval support in 1935, assumed prematurely that British naval sentiments had shifted against Italy and in the direction of an informal entente with France.[15] Nevertheless, both admiralties could appreciate the possibility of Anglo-French naval cooperation in the Mediterranean, where their combined assets could be more easily deployed against Italy than they could in the Atlantic against Germany.

Nevertheless, there always lurked in the background a French concern that London might be tempted to forfeit the advantages of Anglo-French naval cooperation in the interest of negotiating directly with Rome to find solutions to Mediterranean problems. Their suspicions were on target, for there had already emerged in the Admiralty a concern that closer relations with the Marine Nationale would risk dragging Britain into a Mediterranean war when Rome might be neutralized instead by diplomacy.

The Spanish Civil War from a Naval Perspective

When the Spanish Civil War broke out in July 1936, French political leadership had already shifted its focus from Rome to London. Following the fall of Laval, the Popular Front government of Léon Blum with the Anglophile Yvon Delbos at the Quai d'Orsay had committed itself to a restoration of the Anglo-French entente of the Great War years. Moreover, the rising star of the French navy, Admiral Jean François Darlan, had been summoned from a sea command to serve the Popular Front, first as chief of the military cabinet of the Ministry of Marine and later as commander in chief of the navy. Darlan, son of an important Radical-Socialist family, was well suited to serve the left-leaning Popular Front government built around a coalition of the Socialist and Radical Socialist parties, and he already understood that Anglo-French naval cooperation might help to draw France and Britain closer together. His appointment, moreover, implied that the Rue Royale and the French government would close ranks and cooperate better than they had under Laval.

The Spanish Civil War quickly assumed international dimensions. The insurgent Nationalist regime of General Francisco Franco would receive material support from Fascist Italy (and later from Nazi Germany), while the Spanish Republicans would receive support from the Soviet Union. Most of the outside support arrived by sea, so any power or combination that controlled Spanish waters might influence the outcome of the war if they were willing to use their naval power to that end. The question was whether London and Paris would enlist their naval power to support a common diplomatic policy toward the war or would they instead forfeit their local advantage and let the dictators exploit the Spanish scene? The question was complicated by the fact that the flexing of Anglo-French naval muscle in Spanish waters risked provoking the Reich at a moment when neither the Admiralty nor the Rue Royal had sufficient naval might to protect their Atlantic trade routes against the three German pocket battleships.

At the outbreak of the Spanish conflict, Darlan realized that Paris and London acting together could control the waters around Spain. He understood that France and Britain enjoyed a strategic advantage in that they could easily concentrate their combined naval power in the Mediterranean against Italy. In contrast, Germany and Italy, separated at sea by geography, could not so easily combine their naval assets. Darlan therefore believed that combined or coordinated Anglo-French naval power could influence the outcome of the Spanish conflict to the advantage of both France and Britain. A man of the moderate Left, he worried that nonintervention would risk the establishment of an extreme right-leaning state in Spain and that Italy and Germany might lodge themselves in the Balearic and Canary Islands to threaten both French and British naval communications.

While Darlan's strategic ideas made sense in terms of the local scene, his political perspective and that of Blum fit poorly into the ideological milieu that the Spanish Civil War had created in France and Britain. Blum and Darlan naturally favored the Spanish Republican government, which stood to the left of the French Popular Front. But Franco's Nationalist movement enjoyed considerable support in France, especially among Roman Catholics. And in Britain, conservatives overwhelmingly found Franco more acceptable than the leftist Republican government in Spain. So when Blum proposed intervention to assist the Spanish Republicans, he encountered stiff opposition both at home and abroad. Blum therefore backed away from intervention. In mid-July both Paris and London moved toward a policy of nonintervention despite the fact that their fleets could control Spanish waters.

The Darlan-Chatfield Interview

At the end of July, when two Italian aircraft landed short of fuel in French North Africa, Blum had evidence in hand that Mussolini was already sending aid to the Franco faction. He therefore considered whether it might after all be possible to send aid to the republic. Accordingly, he sent Admiral Darlan to London to confer with Admiral Chatfield, who might use his influence with the British Cabinet. Darlan's mission aimed at exploring with Chatfield whether France and Great Britain might employ their naval power to the end of influencing to their mutual advantage the outcome of the civil war in Spain. But the scene had changed since London had approached France for naval support against Italy in 1935, when British public opinion demanded sanctions against Mussolini. In the case of Spain, conservative opinion in Britain ran deep in support of Franco so that there was no public mandate for intervention in the Spanish war.

When he received Darlan on August 5, Chatfield was of course well aware of Franco's popularity among British conservatives, and he understood better than Darlan the weakness of the Royal Navy at the moment. Nevertheless, he listened patiently as the French admiral made his case for Anglo-French naval intervention in the Spanish conflict to protect both British and French interests. Darlan reported information he had received of Italian and German designs on the Balearic and Canary Islands, warning that the dictators would be tempted to take these islands by force. Darlan insisted that nonintervention in Spain would probably lead to the triumph of the Nationalists and to closer relations among the three dictators, which he thought would be dangerous to British and French interests. On the other hand, he added, Anglo-French intervention could head off both the Fascists and Communists and lead to the establishment of a friendly and broadly based democratic government in Spain.

Chatfield, with fresh memories of French staff officers concealing information from their own government, suggested that the Quai d'Orsay communicate French concerns directly to the Foreign Office in a formal note. Darlan agreed, but he returned quickly to his agenda, inquiring whether it might be useful to station French or British warships in the Balearics, then under the control of the Spanish government. Chatfield rejected that option, suggesting that it would afford the Italians a pretext for intervention there. But he suggested that French and British warships might be sent to the islands in brief visits for the purposes of observation. Standing his ground, Darlan then proposed that the two navies cooperate to protect British and French citizens stranded in the war zone. Chatfield replied evasively, insisting that Paris and London had already accepted nonintervention as the proper policy. When Darlan suggested that London and Paris cooperate to mediate the Spanish conflict in the interest of installing a democratic government friendly to both Great Britain and France, Chatfield rejected the proposal on the grounds that it risked dragging the two countries into a situation beyond their control, which meant the risk of provoking a naval war against the Reich.[16]

The interview ended cordially enough, but Darlan could see that Chatfield viewed the Spanish situation from another perspective. The failure of the Darlan-Chatfield interview exposed the wide gap separating French and British intentions concerning the use of naval power in Spanish waters. Whereas the Rue Royale stood ready to flex naval muscles to address local French interests in the Mediterranean, the Admiralty could identify no interest there sufficient to risk complications in the broader international arena, especially with Germany. The interview signaled to Paris that London would persist with a policy of nonintervention and that France had little choice but to follow in the same pattern.

Problems of Nonintervention

In August 1936, Europe's main powers—France, Britain, Germany, Italy, and the Soviet Union—entered into a nonintervention agreement. In September a nonintervention committee, created to enforce the agreement, held its first meeting in London, where it would remain for the duration of the Spanish conflict. Germany and Italy, however, continued to deliver supplies and volunteers to assist the Nationalists, and the Soviets sent aid to the Republicans. The Non-Intervention Agreement therefore restrained mainly France and Britain, who stood by while the other powers exploited the agreement to assist one side or the other and to justify mounting Italian and German naval power in Spanish waters.

On August 3, two days before Darlan met with Chatfield, the battlecruiser *Deutschland* put into Ceuta in Spanish Morocco, where German naval officers lunched with General Franco. Within a few days Nationalists forces seized Majorca, in the Balearics, with its seaport at Palma, soon to become an important base for German and Italian warships. Early in September London protested to Rome at the arrival of Italian aircraft at Majorca.[17] It seems clear that Germany and Italy were beginning to exploit the Spanish conflict in the manner that Darlan had anticipated in his interview with Chatfield.

In Paris French naval officers at the Rue Royale kept close watch on Spanish developments, predicting that Franco would impose a naval blockade of the Spanish coast and that serious violations of international naval law would soon follow. They expected Berlin and Rome to extend diplomatic recognition to Franco and perhaps supply him with submarines to enforce the naval blockade. Observing that German and Italian surface ships had already arrived in Spanish waters, the French naval staff worried that the Germans and Italians would entrench themselves in Spanish Morocco and the Balearics, both of which stood astride vital French maritime routes. Italian entrenchment at Majorca was especially worrisome, for naval and air forces stationed there might easily threaten French communications with North and West Africa and between French naval squadrons based on Mediterranean and Atlantic shores. The French command also noted that the German and Italian presence in Spanish waters threatened British interests in much the same way. Thoroughly alarmed, the French naval staff in early November prodded the government to act in concert with London to protest the Italian naval buildup in the western Mediterranean, and it suggested a need for Anglo-French naval staff consultations.[18]

Nothing, however, came of that proposal. Just as the Rue Royale had predicted, Franco imposed a blockade of the Spanish coast, on November 17, and he threatened to attack foreign ships in Republican harbors and at sea. On the following day, Berlin and Rome in concert extended diplomatic recognition to the Franco regime. The blockade made Spanish waters all the more dangerous, and Mussolini would soon be tempted to unleash his submarines, just as the Rue Royale had predicted. Up until this time the Spanish crisis had not been threatening enough to provoke London into action. But the stage was being set for the crisis to assume dimensions that might after all justify the flexing of Anglo-French naval muscles in the Mediterranean.

Shifting Balance of World Naval Power

In the meantime, trends already afoot in international relations began to mature in a way that would thrust the two Western democracies into a naval crisis of global dimensions. At the beginning of the Spanish Civil War, the French naval staff focused its attention on the changing balance of naval power in the Mediterranean. As the Spanish war continued into the autumn of 1936, it became clear that the Admiralty and the Rue Royale stood in the presence of a more formidable problem, one that promised to shift the global naval balance decisively against the Western democracies. This new balance, which had been anticipated earlier by subtly shifting diplomatic currents, would impose substantially heavier burdens on the French and British navies, making it more important than ever for them to cooperate with each other. The Admiralty was of course long aware of these trends and understood that British sea power had become overextended. By contrast, the Rue Royale understood earlier than the Admiralty the imperative of forging an Anglo-French naval entente to address the massive problems to be imposed by what soon would become the Axis alliance.

Studies prepared in early 1934 under the authority of Admiral Darlan anticipated an ominous shift in the balance of world naval power. Reading these studies, French naval authorities at the Rue Royale realized that Germany was already liberating herself from the naval restrictions of the Versailles treaty and that the Reich's new battlecruisers were capable of prowling the vast oceans to raid distant French and also British commerce. They could see that Germany was drawing closer to Italy as well as Japan, who seemed poised to launch new aggressions in Asia. With the British and French navies badly overextended in the face of emerging new combinations, Darlan and the French naval staff concluded that the security of both Great Britain and France depended more than ever upon the forging of an Anglo-French naval alliance.[19]

Later in 1934, when Japan denounced the 1922 Washington Naval Treaty, and in 1935, when Japan and Italy both withdrew from the scheduled London Naval Conference, French fears of a new combination against them seemed justified. The 1936 Second London Naval Treaty, signed by Britain, France, and the United States, liberated Paris to proceed with new capital ship construction and London to launch a comprehensive program to entirely rebuild the Royal Navy. The 1936 treaty assumed a community of interest among the three democratic powers, but it amounted to considerably less than an alliance. The Rue Royale could see that the United States would likely remain neutral at the outset of any European war, and British intentions regarding any European or Asian conflict remained uncertain. With Germany, Italy, and Japan no longer restricted by any collective naval agreement, Paris could do little more than proceed with the construction of the battleships *Richelieu* and *Jean Bart* and hope that France would not have to face Japan or more than one European enemy in any future war.

In 1936 the world naval balance did indeed begin to shift, much in the way that the Rue Royale had anticipated. The Rome-Berlin Axis, concluded in

October of that year between Hitler and Mussolini, marked but the first step in the shifting balance. A month later, in November, Berlin and Tokyo concluded the Anti-Comintern Pact, which Italy would join in 1937. The Axis alliance, though fragile in the beginning, nevertheless thrust London and Paris into a new era of crisis, underscoring the fact that the French and British navies were stretched too thin to address all of their defense commitments.

But the weakest link in the Axis chain was Italy, whose fleet and empire lay exposed to the threat of combined Anglo-French naval power in the Mediterranean. There was little that London and Paris could do to restrain German ambitions in eastern Europe or Japanese ambitions in Asia, for in each case geography prevented their moving enough military assets into the area to lend substance to their diplomacy. They were, however, capable of assembling on short notice massive naval assets in the Mediterranean to support any diplomatic initiative to restrain Mussolini. Should Paris and London stand together, there would be no reason to appease him.

A "Gentleman's Agreement"

London and Paris, however, remained out of step on precisely that point. During the autumn of 1936 Mussolini took the initiative to open discussions with London, but not with Paris. Foreign Secretary Eden, worried about a spread of Mediterranean problems that included the continuing Italian naval buildup in the Balearics, was willing to listen to Mussolini's proposals. Il Duce, as Mussolini was known, was no doubt motivated to gain British recognition of the Italian conquest of Ethiopia and drive a wedge between Paris and London. In the course of preliminary conversations with Count Dino Grandi, Italian ambassador to London, Eden made it clear that London would not recognize the Italian conquest of Ethiopia, but with the Cabinet insisting upon some kind of agreement with Italy, he caved to Mussolini's demand that France be excluded from the negotiations.[20] When French ambassador Charles Corbin gently protested that Mussolini's motives might be precisely to exclude France from any Mediterranean agreement, Eden answered that the French fears appeared to be exaggerated. Paris accepted the affront with good grace.[21] Nevertheless, London's decision to go ahead with bilateral negotiations with Italy ruined for the moment any chance of confronting Mussolini with a united Anglo-French diplomatic front in the Mediterranean.

The Anglo-Italian Declaration of January 2, 1937, known as the Gentleman's Agreement, contained a transit clause that recognized the vital interests of both nations to enter, exit, and pass through the Mediterranean. The transit clause was an obvious benefit to Italy, whose weaker navy was unable to deny the Royal Navy access to either end of the Mediterranean. It ceded to Italy the right of exit that British naval power otherwise could easily deny. The declaration also contained a disclaimer clause whereby each government denied any desire to change the territorial status quo in the Mediterranean, which Eden and Mussolini both understood to mean that Italian naval and military forces would evacuate the Balearics and all Spanish territory at the conclusion of the Spanish Civil War. Moreover, the declaration contained an agreement whereby each government undertook "to discourage any activities liable to impair the good relations which it is the object of the present declaration to consolidate."[22] Rome could interpret that clause as a British commitment to keep France at arm's length, but London understood it as an Italian commitment to make no increases in its naval or military forces already involved in the Spanish conflict.

The hypocrisy of the Gentleman's Agreement became evident two days later, on January 4, when additional Italian volunteers arrived in Spain, a clear a violation of the spirit of the Anglo-Italian Declaration just concluded.[23] Meanwhile, Paris had stood on the sidelines as London negotiated with Mussolini as an equal on important Mediterranean naval matters. In concluding the worthless Gentleman's Agreement with Italy, Eden had frittered away an opportunity to stand firm with Paris to deny Mussolini the prestige of dealing directly with London at French expense.

Disappointed at the Italian buildup in Spain, which continued into 1937, Eden began to question the value of any future negotiations with Mussolini, but he did not rule them out altogether.[24] Others in London, less alarmed at Italian intervention in Spain, still hoped for a general settlement with Mussolini. Sir Robert Vansittart, permanent undersecretary of the Foreign Office, and several key members of the Cabinet leaned toward extending de jure recognition of Italy's Abyssinian empire as a means of settling with Mussolini and heading off his moving closer to Hitler.[25] But Eden, now believing Mussolini to be entirely unreliable, stood firm against extending recognition. While London debated its Italian policy, the Italian buildup in Spain continued. British statesmen, with fresh memories of Laval's refusal to lend naval support during the 1935 Ethiopian crisis and fearful of being dragged into a naval conflict with the Reich, gave little thought to building a solid Anglo-French naval front in the Mediterranean as an alternative to further negotiations with the dictator.

The Nonintervention Patrol

London moved in 1937 toward collective naval agreements in the expectation of curbing outside intervention in Spain. With Eden taking a leading role, the Non-Intervention Committee still sitting in London agreed in early March on a system of naval patrols to enforce the 1936 Non-Intervention Agreement. The Royal Navy and the French navy were assigned patrol zones along the northern, western, and southern coasts of Spain, where deliveries were known to arrive from Germany and Italy. In turn, the German and Italian navies were assigned zones along the east coast, where Soviet shipments to the Republicans usually arrived. In addition, Italy was assigned Minorca. The French navy would patrol Spanish Morocco, Ibiza, and Majorca.[26] The Soviet Union had no zone, to the disadvantage of the Spanish Republicans. Moreover, Italian and German warships were able to enforce or ignore the Non-Intervention Agreement in their zones, according to the wishes of their governments, and simultaneously claim that their ships were posted in the region as a service to the international community. Significantly, the patrol scheme lent legitimacy to the presence of German warships in Mediterranean waters, where Britain and France enjoyed a decisive naval advantage over Italy.

Neville Chamberlain, who succeeded Stanley Baldwin as head of a Conservative government in May of 1937, had always gotten along well enough with Eden, but he was too ambitious to confer upon his foreign secretary a monopoly on Italian relations. The new Prime Minister was already disposed to negotiate personally with Mussolini and to breathe new life into the failed Gentleman's Agreement of the previous January.[27] The stage was set for Chamberlain to launch the policy of appeasement, for which he would be long remembered. In late July, without bothering to notify Eden, Chamberlain corresponded directly with Mussolini, proposing new conversations. In a friendly reply Mussolini expressed agreement and indicated his wish to meet personally with the Prime Minister.[28]

In August, however, the dictator unleashed at sea a pattern of violence that undermined Chamberlain's private diplomacy and played directly into the hands of Eden. That episode of fascist aggression soon drew the British and French navies into an informal alliance that would supplant the naval patrol and enable Britain and France to seize control of the Mediterranean in the autumn of 1937.

Chapter 3

Tensions in Spanish Waters

Mussolini's decision to unleash his submarines against Mediterranean shipping came in the midst of a long string of mysterious naval and aerial incidents in Spanish waters. Despite the imposition of the international naval patrol, or perhaps because of it, deliveries of armaments and reinforcements continued to arrive in Spain during the spring and summer of 1937. There was also a large volume of legal trade in such items as petroleum and foodstuffs. With warships of four naval powers already in Spanish waters, and with merchant ships of many nationalities carrying both legal and illegal cargo, the potential for violence was nearly limitless. There were frequent clashes between Spanish warships, between Spanish warships and Spanish merchant ships, and between Spanish aircraft and ships of all kinds and nationalities. In the confusion, it was not always easy for Spanish warships or aircraft to know the nationality of ships they attacked, and sometimes they deliberately attacked warships assigned to the international naval patrol. Moreover, foreign warships lent artillery support to Nationalist military operations along the Spanish Mediterranean coast. All of those incidents were a normal part of a civil war, in contrast to the calculated and deliberate policy of piracy that Mussolini would impose on the Mediterranean during the summer of 1937.

Violence in Spanish Waters

The French naval archives contain reports of nearly fifty attacks on neutral shipping in 1937. They included bombings and strafing by aircraft, shelling by surface craft, the planting of mines in crowded shipping lanes, and attacking with deck guns and torpedoes by submarines. The majority of these attacks occurred in the western basin of the Mediterranean. In most cases the identity of the aggressor was unknown.[1] By August, when Mussolini unleashed his submarines, tensions in Spanish waters had already reached dangerous proportions.

Tensions in the Mediterranean began to rise in early 1937, when ships of all four European naval powers were involved in violent incidents near the Spanish coast. On January 18 unidentified aircraft attacked the French destroyer *Maille-Breze*, on patrol off Catalonia. Although six bombs exploding near the vessel caused no damage, Admiral Jean François Darlan ordered French warships in the region to defend themselves in the event of further attacks.[2] At the same time, violence flared along the southern coast of Spain. The *New York Times* reported Nationalist air attacks on the coastal towns of Malaga and Almeria, with "mysterious foreign warships" lending offshore support with their heavy guns.[3]

In February and March, prior to the introduction of the international naval patrol, seven British ships were attacked near Spain in separate incidents, all carefully documented by French naval intelligence. These attacks caused no casualties, but on May 13 the destroyer *Hunter* suffered serious damage when it struck a mine off Almeria. The ship was towed back to Gibraltar, carrying nine wounded and eight dead.[4] These attacks, launched most likely by one or the other of the Spanish factions, foreshadowed more serious events soon to come.

By May of 1937 the international naval patrol was in place so that Italian and German warships now operated in Spanish waters along with British and French ships as a service to the Non-Intervention Committee. In this service ships of different nationalities would sometimes put into various Spanish or French Mediterranean ports to replenish supplies and give crewmen short periods of rest. Such was the case on May 26, when the British destroyer *Hardy*, the German destroyer *Albatros*, the Italian cruiser *Barletta*, and several smaller Italian warships lay anchored at Palma in Majorca, a big port under Nationalist control widely known as a staging point for Italian supply deliveries to Franco. Suddenly, nine Loyalist aircraft attacked. Bombs found their mark on the *Barletta*, killing six officers. The Non-Intervention Committee deplored the incident and recommended to the Spanish Republican government at Valencia the recognition of a safety zone for all ships of the naval patrol operating out of Palma. Valencia answered that ships of the naval patrol had no right to operate within Spanish territorial waters.[5] Italian warships had operated out of Majorca since the Nationalists seized the island early in the conflict, but now the legitimacy accorded them by the patrol agreement justified their being at Palma and obscured their covert mission to support Italian intervention in the Spanish war.

Meanwhile, on that same day, Republican aircraft again attacked the harbor at Palma, where additional Italian lives were lost. Responding two days later, Nationalist aircraft based at Majorca staged an early-morning air raid on Valencia. Forty bombs struck the city, killing more than twenty civilians. A British merchant ship, the *Pinzon*, was damaged, but there were no casualties.[6] With the air war now spreading into the Balearics, the stage was set for incidents of even greater magnitude.

From Ibiza to Wilhelmshaven

Toward the end of May the German battlecruisers *Deutschland* and *Admiral Scheer*, accompanied by four destroyers, patrolled waters off the east coast of Spain. Although Spanish waters were dangerous, Berlin had chosen to include among the ships stationed there two of its three modern battlecruisers. Captain Paul Fanger, commander of the *Deutschland*, reported later that these ships were carrying out their assignments under the international naval patrol.[7] Everyone knew that smaller ships were more suitable for the naval patrol, but neither London nor Paris wished to quarrel with Berlin as to whether the newest ships in the Kriegsmarine were in fact required or whether they were instead sent there to flex German naval muscle.

Patrol duty in Spanish waters was demanding, so all personnel remained alert, ready to man their stations should any unidentified craft approach by sea or suddenly by air. Having been summoned from meals and sleep more than once during the long voyage, ship crews looked forward to brief periods of rest when their ships would withdraw to a safe port. Since Palma had been under air attack, Captain Fanger turned the *Deutschland* toward the small harbor of Ibiza, a Nationalist stronghold a hundred miles southwest of Majorca. He arrived there late in the afternoon of Saturday, May 29. The *Deutschland* dropped anchor in the roadstead, while the destroyer *Leopard* moored at a pier in the harbor. The German tanker *Neptun* stood nearby, ready to refuel the two warships.

With the dangerous voyage now over, the *Deutschland* let down its guard. Many of the crew remained below, lounging in the mess after their evening meal. Others had come topside to enjoy band music as the sun dropped low in the west. But suddenly, toward 10:00 p.m., two Spanish Republican aircraft approached swiftly out of the sun, flying low to attack the big ship before any defense could be mounted. The alert sounded just as two 550-pound bombs found their mark, one striking a starboard gun turret to kill or wound several crewmen, some of whom were blown overboard. The other exploded in the mess below, killing perhaps twenty seamen and injuring many more.[8]

Although the attack had caused heavy loss of life, the *Deutschland* had not suffered vital damage. The ship immediately set sail for Gibraltar, arriving there the next afternoon, Sunday, May 30, where Captain Fanger delivered fifty-three wounded and about twenty dead crewmen to the British military hospital. Despite swift airlift of additional medical personnel from England, several of the wounded crewmen died at Gibraltar. The *Deutschland* quickly put out to sea on Monday morning, not awaiting the services for more than twenty dead seamen to be buried that afternoon in a nearby cemetery.

Berlin no doubt had reasons for the big ship to exit Gibraltar in haste. On Sunday afternoon the Reich's top military leaders had assembled in Berlin to discuss reprisals. According to reports reaching Paris, they agreed to stage a naval bombardment of a Spanish coastal town. Almería was chosen because it stood as a stronghold of Republican resistance to a Nationalist offensive that had stalled short of the town. Further, Germany would reinforce its fleet in Spanish waters to guard against future incidents and to take additional reprisals should Berlin fail to obtain satisfactory compensation for the *Deutschland* incident.[9]

The departure of the *Deutschland* from Gibraltar coincided almost exactly with the German bombardment of Almería. At dawn that same Monday morning, a German cruiser and four destroyers hurled three hundred shells into the city, killing thirteen men, five women, and a child and injuring fifty-five other civilians. Shore batteries returned fire before the German squadron disappeared around Cape Gata at the eastern end of Almería bay.[10]

In London that same day German ambassador Joachim von Ribbentrop announced the Reich's withdrawal from the naval patrol. Italy followed with a similar announcement. Tensions mounted as France in turn threatened to open wide the door of her Spanish frontier to increased arms delivery to the Loyalists. London, however, managed to restrain Paris. In the meantime, Berlin filed a complaint in the Non-Intervention Committee and announced plans to reinforce its naval strength in Spanish waters, a move that seemed inconsistent with German withdrawal from the patrol.[11] In sum, Berlin threatened to increase German naval power in the region in a manner that it would operate outside of the authority of the Non-Intervention Committee. But Germany and Italy returned to the patrol by the middle of June.[12]

Throughout the crisis, discussions in the Non-Intervention Committee had focused on Loyalist aggression against the *Deutschland* rather than the brutal German bombardment of Almería. Since the naval patrol agreement lent legitimacy to the presence of German warships in Spanish waters, Berlin was able to turn the *Deutschland* affair into a propaganda victory that obscured the firing of angry Nazi guns in waters important to British and French naval interests.

In the wake of the *Deutschland* incident, Berlin reinforced its naval strength in Spanish waters, but only modestly. The *Deutschland* soon arrived in Germany for repairs, leaving behind her sister ship, the *Admiral Scheer,* and four destroyers. The cruisers *Koln* and *Leipzig* were sent to join them. Four submarines departing Germany in early June would proceed only as far as Lisbon, to operate west of Gibraltar rather than in the Mediterranean. Eleven German warships would therefore remain in Spanish waters to resume patrol duty and to maintain their liberty of action in the event of another Spanish attack.[13]

Axis naval strength in Spanish waters remained less than British strength, and considerably less than British and French naval strength combined. During the summer of 1937 Italy usually kept fewer than half a dozen small surface ships in Spanish Mediterranean waters. At the same time, Britain and France kept more than thirty warships on station there, which included the Bay of Biscay, with nearly all of their heavy ships held in reserve elsewhere.[14] Should any emergency arise, Britain and France could quickly double or triple their naval assets in the Mediterranean—as, indeed, they did toward the end of the summer.

In the meantime, the epilogue of the *Deutschland* drama unfolded at Wilhelmshaven on June 17, when Hitler presided over memorial services for thirty-one German seamen killed at Ibiza. That same day he visited the *Deutschland*, undergoing repairs at Wilhelmshaven. Toward the end of the day, in a final act of closure, he dismissed Captain Fanger, who had been responsible for the lives of his crewmen when the *Deutschland* had dropped anchor three weeks earlier at Ibiza.[15]

Republican Piracy in the Mediterranean

During the second week of June Spanish Republican radio at Bilbao announced the formation of a new submarine unit with the mission of driving German and Italian warships out of Spanish waters. The Spanish threat was apparently more than a bluff, for within days the captain of the cruiser *Leipzig* reported two torpedo attacks against his ship, on June 15 and another three days later, in waters near Oran. All of the torpedoes missed their mark. Nevertheless, Ambassador Ribbentrop in London demanded a protest demonstration from the four patrol navies, which presumably meant a combined naval attack against another Loyalist town.

British foreign secretary Eden, however, doubted whether Valencia had mounted the attacks or, indeed, whether any attacks had in fact taken place. The British and French press promptly labeled the reported attacks a myth, a German invention designed to justify a naval buildup in the Mediterranean. Finally, when Ribbentrop got no satisfactory response from London, Berlin and Rome again withdrew their ships from the naval patrol. German warships remained in Spanish waters, along with a smaller number of Italian ships, but they did not return to the patrol.[16] There now followed an interval during July in which no major incidents in Spanish waters were reported.

Italian and Nationalist Violence Combined

In August violence erupted again in the Mediterranean, this time with such obvious design and of such wide proportions that Europe was swiftly dragged into a major naval crisis. The August violence was anticipated on July 29, when the Spanish Loyalist merchant ship *L'Andutz-Mendi* was attacked by a mysterious submarine off Le Grau du Roi, near Marseilles. Witnesses reported that the submarine, attacking on the surface, resembled the Italian *Archimede* class, with its distinctive tower flanked by two deck guns fore and aft. But since the Insurgent navy was known to possess three Italian-made submarines, there was no compelling reason to think that the attack had been mounted by any navy other than Franco's.[17] Nevertheless, the aggressor may indeed have been an Italian submarine. Mussolini had sent his submarines to attack neutral shipping in the Mediterranean in early 1937 only to call them back in mid-February in the wake of unsatisfactory results.[18]

In August the violence spread into the eastern basin of the Mediterranean in a pattern of attacks far beyond the capabilities of Franco's tiny navy. Early in the month Franco had received reports of Soviet plans to reinforce the Loyalists with arms deliveries, which, according to press reports, included 600 tanks, 10,000 machine guns, 20,000 rifles, 300 aircraft, and important quantities of ammunition.[19] Franco therefore wired Mussolini on August 3, requesting either the use of Italian ships or direct Italian intervention to intercept the Soviet shipments as they passed through the straits south of Sicily. He suggested that any Italian ships involved might be supplied with Spanish officers who would hoist the Nationalist flag at the moment of contact. As for ships already en route, Franco asked that Italian warships follow them and report their positions to the Spanish navy. On August 5 Mussolini expressed himself in principle to agree with the Spanish request. He promptly delivered two submarines and two destroyers to Franco, who presumably would assume responsibility for any action they would undertake.

But Mussolini would also commit privately a number of his own submarines to operate in Sicilian waters with the understanding that they would hoist the Spanish Nationalist flag should they be forced to the surface. Il Duce had reason to think that the reports of the Soviet deliveries, though perhaps exaggerated, were substantially correct, for shortly thereafter five Spanish Republican ships—*Campeador*, *L'Aldecoa*, *Ciudad de Cadiz*, *Lealtad*, and *Cabo*

San Augustin—departed the Black Sea toward the Mediterranean.[20] Their departure set the stage for Mussolini's submarines and destroyers to spring into action, not only in Sicilian waters but further afield as well.

In the meantime, the first incidents of renewed violence flared suddenly along the coast of Algeria. On Friday morning, August 6, just before 6:00 a.m., the French steamer *Djebel Amour* was attacked by an aircraft bearing Nationalist insignia. The aircraft sprayed the bridge with machine-gun fire, but there were no casualties. At about the same time aircraft with similar markings attacked the tanker *British Corporal*. No bomb found its mark, but of more than twenty dropped, fragments from several near misses struck the British ship. A machine-gun attack followed, but there was no loss of life. On Sunday, August 8, the British steamer *Noemi Julia* was attacked by air not far from the site of the *British Corporal* incident.[21]

Two hours later that same morning, just after 8:00 a.m., the Italian cargo ship *Mongioia* was attacked north of Algiers by an unidentified airplane. Three bombs were dropped, and fragments from a near miss wounded the captain, who later died of his injuries. In an ironic twist of events, an Italian ship had been attacked by aircraft bearing Nationalist insignia. Days later, when the British chargé d'affaires in Rome, Edward Ingram, gently complained about the attack on the *British Corporal*, which he hinted had been mounted by Italian aircraft based at Palma, Italian Foreign Minister Count Galeazzo Ciano already knew that the *Mongioia* had been the unintended victim of friendly fire, so he deftly sidetracked the British complaint, insisting that all of the attacks that morning had been launched by Spanish Republican aircraft rather than Italian.[22]

In the wake of the August 6 incidents, French naval intelligence officers observed that Nationalist warships and aircraft had increased their surveillance activities west of Sicily for the purpose of intercepting maritime traffic between the Black Sea and Spain. They noted the close naval surveillance of French territorial waters off Tunisia and Algeria and the increase of aerial patrols southeast from Palma. From reports of the French submarine *Iris*, on patrol off Palma, they learned that several trimotor monoplanes with Nationalist insignia were based on the island; that one of these, bearing the number 9138, had attacked the *British Corporal*; and that another, number 9133, had attacked the *Mongioia*. The French officers could not know for sure the nationality of the aircraft crews, whether they were Spanish or Italian.[23] Nevertheless, they could see that the *Mongioia* had been attacked by friendly aircraft and that all of the attacks off Algeria on August 6 had been mounted by Spanish Nationalist or Italian aircraft rather than Loyalist.

Early in the next week violence in the Mediterranean mounted sharply as Italian and Nationalist warships struck in widely scattered areas. It began late in the night on Tuesday, August 10, when the Spanish tanker *Campeador* was attacked by gunfire and torpedoes between Sicily and Tunisia, where the Italians had expected the vessel to appear. It was one of several ships that Franco had asked Mussolini to intercept in those waters. Carrying nine thousand tons of gasoline, the ship burned furiously before it finally sank early Wednesday morning. Survivors reported that the *Campeador* had been followed by the Italian destroyer *Saeta* and an unidentified destroyer. The Nationalist cruiser *Canarias*, which had patrolled Sicilian waters for several days, may also have been involved in the attack. A day later, on Thursday, the Danish steamer *Edith* was attacked and sunk near Barcelona by four Insurgent aircraft. The crew, however, was rescued.[24]

On that same day, August 12, the Loyalist destroyers *Almirante Antequera* and *Churruca* were attacked by unidentified submarines in Spanish waters near Cartagena, a hundred miles up the coast from Almería. The *Churruca* was struck by a torpedo and badly damaged. The next day the scene shifted abruptly to the Sicilian Channel, where the French cargo ship *Parame* was attacked by an unidentified submarine near Bizerte; however, the torpedo missed its mark. These incidents were the first of several attacks launched by mysterious submarines in the Mediterranean during August and early September. The fact that the two attacks took place in widely separated parts of the Mediterranean suggested to French naval intelligence that Italian submarines had become involved. British intelligence, having penetrated Italian naval codes, knew that Mussolini had unleashed his submarines on Thursday, August 12, the day of the attack on the *Churruca*.[25]

At the same time, the violence continued on the surface. On Friday, the Spanish steamer *Conde de Absolo* was torpedoed by a surface ship, reportedly an Italian destroyer, just west of Malta. Twenty-seven crewmen were lost. The next day the Panamanian tanker *George W. McKnight*, steaming from Syria to Le Havre, was attacked by surface ships near Pantelleria in the Sicilian Channel, not far from the site of the previous attack. Struck by several shells, the *McKnight* was set ablaze and abandoned before it finally sank. The crew was rescued by a British merchantman that happened upon the scene. Afterward the captain of the stricken ship insisted that the attack had been launched by two Italian destroyers.[26]

Italian Piracy in the Eastern Basin

During the next week the violence spread into the eastern basin of the Mediterranean. On Monday, August 16, a mysterious submarine lurked in Aegean waters near the mouth of the Dardanelles. It bore the number C3, that of a Spanish Nationalist submarine, but the vessel mounted two deck guns rather than a single gun the C3 was known to carry. On that same day the Spanish steamer *Ciudad de Cadiz*, loaded with trucks and gasoline, departed the Dardanelles to enter Aegean waters. Suddenly, as it steamed past the island of Tenedos, a submarine surfaced nearby, hoisted the Nationalist flag, and fired a torpedo that found its mark. The crew quickly took to the boats as the ship settled in the water and sank.

Two days later, on Wednesday, the Spanish steamer *Amuru*, loaded with Soviet wheat destined for Spain, entered those same waters only to be sunk off Tenedos late in the afternoon by a mysterious submarine. Fortunately the crew of the *Amuru* was rescued by a Turkish ship. Afterward, the captain of the *Ciudad de Cadiz* described the submarine, noting that it carried the marking C3 but bore the appearance of the Italian *Archimede* class with its distinctive tower flanked by two deck guns.[27] With these attacks so distant from Spanish waters, British and French newsmen might easily suspect that Italian submarines were on the prowl.

London Divided

In the meantime, Neville Chamberlain had set his heart on concluding a diplomatic settlement with Mussolini. On August 10, just before Il Duce unleashed his submarines, British statesmen assembled at the Foreign Office to discuss whether to extend de jure recognition to the Italian conquest of Abyssinia, regarded as an essential item prior to any negotiations with Mussolini. After prolonged discussion, it was tentatively agreed that the British delegation would be prepared to raise the question of Ethiopian recognition in the League Assembly, scheduled to meet at Geneva on September 13. Anglo-Italian conversations would follow, aimed at settling a list of problems that included the eventual withdrawal of Italian volunteers from Spain and the Balearic Islands. As a part of a general diplomatic settlement, London was willing to enter into a military agreement provided that it should extend no further than the exchange of military information.[28]

Three days later the three service chiefs of staff reported their support of a diplomatic settlement. The chiefs agreed that any Italian settlement would include a military agreement justified by the current state of British naval weakness, by the need for time to complete British military and naval rearmament, and by the need to keep Italy neutral in the event of a war with Germany or Japan. Projecting only two options, the report insisted that "our sea communications through the Mediterranean can only be made really secure either by maintaining friendship with Italy, or by establishing ourselves in such military strength in the Mediterranean as would permanently deter Italy from embarking on war against us."[29]

The chiefs therefore recommended the option of restraining Mussolini by diplomacy rather than by power. The report gave no consideration to any other option, such as that of Anglo-French naval cooperation in the Mediterranean. What the report reveals is the Admiralty's basic strategic assumption of the imperative of peace in the Mediterranean at any cost, to the end of keeping open naval communications between Gibraltar and Singapore. Significantly, that assumption would dominate the Admiralty's strategic perspective for the remainder of the decade and into the early months of World War II.

That perspective would tempt the Admiralty to solve Mediterranean problems through negotiations with Italy rather than France, whose Mediterranean ambitions risked dragging Great Britain into an Italian war not worth the price of interrupting communications with Asia. The chiefs therefore understood that an Anglo-Italian military agreement would damage British relations with France. But discounting that point, they went ahead to recommend a military agreement that appealed to weakness rather than to strength. They recommended a candid exchange of military information they knew would reveal British naval weakness, such as marginal antiaircraft defenses at Malta. They would share the most confidential information with Mussolini, whose "knowledge of our weakness might allay the suspicion . . . that we are bent on aggression against him, and might therefore result in a cessation of his counter-preparations."[30]

The chiefs therefore expected the Foreign Office to neutralize Italy by diplomacy. The Admiralty preferred pandering to Mussolini instead of considering whether combined Anglo-French naval power in the Mediterranean was sufficient to restrain him. They chose instead to appease Mussolini because it was safer than flexing Anglo-French naval muscles that might risk dragging Great Britain into a war with Italy. In contrast, Eden remained uncomfortable with the drift toward negotiations with Mussolini, whom he mistrusted and disliked personally. Eden was therefore out of step with the Admiralty and with the Prime Minister. But the swift renewal of piracy in the Mediterranean strengthened Eden at the expense of Chamberlain, still bent upon flirting with the Italian dictator.

Piracy Renewed

The chances for an Italian settlement fell sharply on August 17, when Eden informed key ministers of startling news—the Admiralty had reliable information that Italian submarines had been ordered to attack neutral and British oil tankers in the Mediterranean. When the ministers met late that Tuesday afternoon, the reports of Italian intentions were so explicit that they might easily have suspected that the Admiralty was reading confidential Italian codes. They heard that "the Admiralty had reliable information that submarine attack upon British ships approaching Spanish Government ports was contemplated, and that such attack might take place at any moment."[31]

The question was whether to unleash British warships to respond to any Italian submarine attack or instead to await approval of the Prime Minister, then on vacation. Impatient of any delay, Eden insisted with the support of the Admiralty that an attack was imminent or may already have occurred and that to leave British warships without instructions was unthinkable. The ministers had little choice but to agree. Accordingly, the Mediterranean command was immediately authorized to counterattack any aggressor submarine. The Prime Minister would be informed by telephone of the decision to strike back. The press was informed shortly thereafter, but the statement did not identify Italy as the aggressor.[32]

The next day, Admiral Sir Dudley Pound, commander in chief Mediterranean, issued guidelines to govern the British response to any surprise submarine attack. Battleships and cruisers, too valuable to risk chasing submarines, were ordered to confine themselves to rescue work. Destroyers, ideal for antisubmarine warfare, were ordered to secure the safety of the crew of any stricken ship and then to hunt and destroy any submerged submarine within five miles of the scene. Any remaining on the surface or beyond the five-mile limit should be forced to disclose their identity.[33] With that order, the Royal Navy entered into a new era of antisubmarine warfare. At about the same time, also in response to the mounting violence in the Mediterranean, the Rue Royale renewed orders in effect since April for French warships to intervene, should any French merchant ship be attacked on the high seas.[34]

Although Eden knew by the middle of August that Italian warships and aircraft had authored much of the violence in the Mediterranean, he instructed the British chargé d'affaires at Hendaye, France, on August 25 to protest with Franco the Nationalist air attacks on British shipping.[35] By that time British journalists had already come to suspect Italian involvement in the violence. On Friday the *Manchester Guardian* carried more than one article hinting at Italian involvement, one of them stating, "It is far from certain that all of this damage was done by the unaided efforts of Franco's fleet."[36]

Eden, realizing that the press was poised to pin the blame on Mussolini, instructed Ingram in Rome to express London's concern that any new incident might upset the projected Anglo-Italian conversations. When Ciano received Ingram on August 23, the Englishman hinted at Italian authorship of the violence, and he cautioned tactfully that any further incidents might lead to publicity harmful to cordial Anglo-Italian relations. And on Friday, August 27, after an Italian airplane had harassed a British ship near Malta, Ingram again cautioned Ciano, this time with greater urgency.[37] Ciano clearly understood London's concern that the projected conversations with London were now in danger, but he did nothing to rein in Italian aircraft and warships.

If Ciano took little note of the British protests, it was probably because London acting alone was unable to support its diplomacy with the threat of naval power. On Wednesday, August 25, before delivering the second protest, Eden asked the chief of naval aviation whether it might be possible to have "a few aircraft flying about from an aircraft carrier."[38] Eden had in mind a press release announcing a naval buildup in the Mediterranean to reinforce the protest that Ingram would deliver to Ciano.

He learned, however, that a naval air patrol was impractical, that British naval strength in the Mediterranean was sorely lacking, that there were not enough British naval bases in the region to support an effective patrol, and that there was not even one cruiser available to reinforce the western Mediterranean fleet. There were, however, a few ships scheduled to pass through the Mediterranean in late August and in September. Eden therefore had to settle for a tepid announcement on Friday that London would maintain its naval strength in the western basin and that other British warships would soon pass through those waters.[39] Neither Ciano nor Mussolini would be much impressed with that admission of British naval timidity.

In contrast, the news from Rome that same Friday expressed boundless confidence in Italian military power. During that week the Republican stronghold of Santander had fallen to the Spanish Nationalists, prompting Mussolini to send Franco a public message expressing his pride in the contribution of Italian volunteers to the victory. Il Duce's boastful message, which stood in sharp contrast to Eden's restrained press release of the same day, did nothing to appease the angry mood among British and French journalists. Moreover, in a bombastic speech delivered at Palermo that same Friday, Mussolini dismissed the recent Mediterranean violence as nothing more than "regrettable incidents." At the same time he railed against Bolshevism, vowing not to tolerate it in the Mediterranean.[40]

In London and Paris, the press quickly shifted its attention to Mussolini. The *Manchester Guardian*, interpreting the speech to mean that Mussolini would support Franco to the end, questioned whether there were any grounds upon which an Anglo-Italian understanding might be built. In Paris, even the right-wing press expressed reservations about Il Duce's speech. The *Echo de Paris*, quick to see the key issue, insisted that France could not allow Mussolini to threaten French Mediterranean communications under the cover of a campaign against Bolshevism.[41]

Toward the end of August public opinion in both France and Britain grew increasingly indignant of Mussolini. The press in both countries had moved ahead of Eden and especially of Chamberlain, still set upon negotiating a settlement with Il Duce. With British and French opinion moving swiftly toward common ground, the option of confronting Mussolini with a united Anglo-French front grew more promising to statesmen in Paris. Chamberlain's policy of accommodating Rome could not easily survive—at least not in the short term—another round of violence in the Mediterranean.

Nevertheless, the violence returned quickly, just as Eden had predicted, and this time with a vengeance that struck at the heart of Chamberlain's plans. The first of a series of incidents occurred on Sunday, August 29, when the British merchant ship *Carpio* was attacked by an unidentified submarine near Gibraltar, the torpedo passing just a few feet astern. Late that same afternoon, the Spanish cargo ship *Ciudad de Reus*, en route from Marseilles to Barcelona, was damaged by gunfire from an unidentified submarine off Sète in the Gulf of Lion. On Monday afternoon the Soviet steamer *Timiryazev*, having departed the British port of Cardiff two weeks earlier bound for Port Said with a load of coal, was shadowed off Algeria by an Italian destroyer, thought to be the *Turbine*. According to the Soviet captain, the Italian ship disappeared only to appear again on the horizon at dusk. Then suddenly, after dark, the *Timiryazev* was struck by two torpedoes that wrecked the engine room. As the ship foundered and sank, the crew of twenty-six men and three women was rescued by an Algerian fishing boat.[42]

The violence spread swiftly and deliberately. The British destroyer *Havock*, on patrol off Cape San Antonio on the eastern coast of Spain, sprang swiftly into action late that same Monday night when a torpedo passed just a few yards astern. Within minutes the Italian submarine *Iride* shook violently under the impact of depth charges launched by the fast destroyer. The counterattack continued as five British destroyers—*Heparin, Hardy, Hereford, Hasty*, and *Hero*—rushed to the scene. Despite use of the highly regarded Asdic detection device, the counterattack of six British destroyers failed to sink or flush the *Iride*, which was badly shaken before it finally slipped away.[43]

The French and British press, reacting sharply to the attacks, now began to use the word "piracy" to describe them. There was common agreement in London and Paris that stern measures against those responsible must be undertaken. Since Franco clearly could not have staged all of the attacks, journalists in both cities concluded that Italy was responsible for them, and that the violence could not be tolerated much longer. The *Manchester Guardian* stated bluntly that the piracy was authored mainly by Italy, long pledged to a policy of nonintervention. But nonintervention, the *Guardian* insisted, had come to mean Italian naval control of the Mediterranean in the interest of supporting Franco. In Paris, the French government was prepared to call Mussolini's bluff, either by opening the Spanish frontier to unrestricted trade or by taking naval action in the Mediterranean. There was widespread agreement in Paris that Il Duce had gone too far and that France would have to take action, preferably with British support but alone if necessary. There were reports, moreover, that the French government had already solicited London with proposals for common action.[44]

Nevertheless, the violence continued to mount in the Mediterranean. On Wednesday, September 3, the British tanker *Woodford* was torpedoed and sunk off Valencia by an unmarked submarine reported by the captain to be Italian. One crewman was killed, and six were injured. And on Thursday the Soviet steamer *Molakiev* was torpedoed in the Aegean Sea by a submarine bearing Nationalist markings.[45] Everyone could see that the piracy had spread from one end of the Mediterranean to the other.

Toward Anglo-French Naval Cooperation

In the meantime, public opinion in France pressed the government of Camille Chautemps to take action against the piracy. At the Quai d'Orsay, Foreign Minister Yvon Delbos had already decided that London's policy of pampering Mussolini would fail to restrain the dictator. In his view, the only effective solution would be the application in the Mediterranean of concerted Anglo-French naval power. The French Council of Ministers, however, was divided as some feared that stern measures against Italy might undermine French relations with Germany.[46] The debates in Paris over the direction of French policy grew increasingly bitter, but the mounting violence in the Mediterranean in August strengthened Delbos' hand. Toward the end of the month he felt strong enough to feel out the British position on the question of concerted Anglo-French action in the Mediterranean. At the same time he would test London's commitment to its policy of seeking a rapprochement with Mussolini.

On Thursday, August 26, Eden received in his office French chargé d'affaires Roger Cambon, who raised the question of the impending Anglo-Italian conversations insofar as they related to the recent violence in the Mediterranean. The Frenchman took care to remind Eden that Italian aggression in the Mediterranean would impose a heavy burden on any effort to settle with Rome. He stated that his government, much concerned about these incidents and sure that Italy had authored many of them, would welcome Anglo-French-Italian conversations prior to the meeting of the League Assembly in September at Geneva, mainly to head off trouble there. Eden replied that he shared the French concern to ease tensions at Geneva, but he was unsure about the objectives of any three-way conversations with Rome. Cambon therefore would inquire further about his government's specific intentions. They agreed that Cambon would report back early the next week.[47]

Over the weekend, however, Mussolini had delivered his intemperate message to Franco, followed by his bombastic speech at Palermo, which further strengthened Delbos' hand and made it possible for the Quai d'Orsay to present Eden with specific proposals. When Cambon returned on Monday, August 30, Eden remained preoccupied with the Abyssinian question. Cambon, however, made it clear that Italian violence in the Mediterranean precluded any French support at Geneva in regard to Abyssinia. Seizing the initiative, he handed Eden a note from Delbos containing three proposals, one for a Mediterranean pact and another for an Anglo-French protest in the Non-Intervention Committee, both of which Eden promptly rejected. But Eden could see from Cambon's earnest remarks that France was determined to take stern measures to address the crisis in the Mediterranean.[48]

Cambon's third proposal, to arrange a meeting at Geneva of the Mediterranean and possibly the Black Sea powers to discuss Mediterranean security, seemed to Eden more promising. According to the plan, the French and British delegations to the League Assembly meeting on September 10 would extend invitations to Greece, Turkey, Egypt, and Yugoslavia, but not Italy, to consider measures to address the piracy. The riparian states—the USSR, Bulgaria, and Romania—would be summoned later if necessary. Although the details were not yet clear, Eden was impressed with the proposal, which he would bring to the attention of his government. He promised to communicate again with Cambon, who answered that his government would be most grateful for an early reply.[49]

When the interview had ended, Eden could see that Paris was at the point of taking drastic action to protect French interests in the Mediterranean. He could also see that Paris had seized the initiative and that London had little choice but to work within the options that Delbos had thrust upon him. At that moment, neither Eden nor Delbos saw clearly the problems inherent in Cambon's third proposal or the vast opportunities implicit in it. Nor could they see that France and Britain had just taken the first step along the road that would lead them to confront Mussolini with combined Anglo-French naval power.

Chapter 4

The Road to Nyon

The bold French initiative to draw London and Paris into a plan of common action could not have been advanced in a timelier manner. The torpedo attack of August 29 on the *Carpio*, followed by similar attacks during each of the next four days on the *Timiryazev*, *Havock*, *Woodford*, and *Molakiev*, coincided with the delivery to Undersecretary Anthony Eden of the French proposal for a meeting of the Mediterranean powers at Geneva. The violence in the Mediterranean had reached its peak just at the moment when Eden considered his response to Paris. The torpedo attack on the *Havock* on Tuesday, September 2, followed in quick order by the sinking of the *Woodford* on Wednesday, underscored for Eden the urgent need for effective measures to restrain the aggressor. With the French proposal on his desk, he had no better alternative than to consider its possibilities. At that moment, however, it remained unclear whether the aggressor was Mussolini alone or Mussolini and Franco together.

A Search for Solutions

In the meantime, Eden and the Admiralty moved toward solutions consistent with that of armed action implicit in the French proposal. On August 31, in a meeting with Admiralty officials, Eden suggested the sinking of the Nationalist cruiser *Canarias* should another attack occur, but that option was quickly abandoned for a host of reasons, among them the concern that Franco could easily respond with an artillery attack on Gibraltar. Other forms of retaliation were also considered, such as a blockade of Nationalist coasts, raids on Insurgent seaports, and seizure of Majorca or other Nationalist territory. But all of these options were abandoned as they risked provoking Germany or Italy.[1]

Another solution, that of concentrating British destroyers in areas where pirate submarines were known to operate, seemed more promising. Should any British ship be attacked, a full flotilla of nine destroyers would search and destroy any submarines in the area. This option would have the support of public opinion, and any protest—whether by Spain, Germany, or Italy—would betray the identity of the pirates. The Admiralty believed that if a public announcement of British intentions should fail to stop the aggression, the sinking of a pirate submarine would put an end to it.[2]

The Admiralty, obviously thinking in terms of winning one major victory to send a message to the aggressor, could see that any prolonged operation would be burdened by a shortage of destroyers, by inadequate naval aviation, and by the lack of British naval bases between Gibraltar and Malta. Only later would they consider that solutions to all of these problems were implicit in the French proposal of August 30, which assumed Anglo-French naval cooperation in the Mediterranean. With its strong fleet of modern destroyers and with a string of naval and air bases on both sides of the Mediterranean, France was the key to the success of any plan to drive aggressor submarines from the sea. Should London and Paris find ways to cooperate with each other, they could assemble superior naval power in the Mediterranean. Moreover, Yvon Delbos had already taken the initiative to seek British cooperation in a crisis whose solution lay beyond the capabilities of the Royal Navy acting alone.

Events moved swiftly forward in early September. In a telephone conversation with Neville Chamberlain, on vacation in Scotland, Eden gained the Prime Minister's approval on September 1 to put the whole question of Abyssinia on hold, with the understanding that it might be raised later at Geneva should Anglo-Italian relations undergo improvement. Chamberlain raised no objections to a discussion of the French proposal at Geneva, and he gave his assent to an increase of British destroyer strength in the region, "if such a course was practicable."[3]

With Chamberlain's support of the French proposal in hand, Eden had no reason to seek further approval of it when he met informally with key members of the Cabinet at the Foreign Office late Thursday morning, September 2. He merely reported the contents of the French proposal. But he needed to know whether reinforcement of the destroyer fleet in the Mediterranean was practicable. Eden made clear his view that the Spanish Nationalists could not possibly have authored all of the violence. He pointed out that Britain had twice addressed Rome on the question of Mediterranean security, that British public opinion had grown restive at the attacks on British shipping, and that the press pointed to Italian submarines as the guilty party. He insisted that "if this state of affairs continued, it would be quite impossible for His Majesty's government to enter upon the proposed Anglo-Italian Conversations."[4]

Addressing the question of reinforcing the British destroyer fleet in the Mediterranean, Rear Admiral John Cunningham reported that there were no British ports near the areas where the attacks had taken place. British destroyers patrolling these distant waters would therefore be placed in a dangerous position. He added that it would require a very large fleet of destroyers to reduce the number of incidents occurring off the coast of Spain. But when the meeting resumed in the afternoon, Cunningham indicated that, in view of the urgent political situation, four additional destroyers might be sent to the Mediterranean. It was therefore agreed that British destroyer strength in the Mediterranean would be reinforced and that Eden would make yet another representation to Rome on the question of Mediterranean security, without directly accusing Italy of the attacks.[5]

Press reports of that same day revealed the growing impatience of public opinion in both Britain and France. The London press, indignant at the attack on the *Havock*, demanded armed action. In an article under the heading "Track Them Down," the *Daily Mail* insisted that these "grievous outrages cannot be tolerated." The *Times*, describing conditions in the Mediterranean as "fast becoming intolerable," insisted upon counterattack as the only way to discourage further outrages. In France, the entire press condemned the outbreak of "piratical submarine warfare," with the Left press insisting that Italy was the author of it.[6]

Problems with Invitations

By the end of that long Thursday afternoon, Eden had attained his immediate objective: to reinforce British destroyer strength in the Mediterranean. He therefore promptly summoned French chargé d'affaires Roger Cambon, informing him that London was ready to participate in the proposed conversations at Geneva involving the Mediterranean and possibly the Black Sea powers to address the problem of violence in the Mediterranean. In a communication with Cambon later that same day, Eden indicated his preference that the Geneva meeting might include only the Mediterranean powers. He was not adamant on that point, however, conceding that the question of invitations could be discussed afterward at Geneva.[7]

Neither Eden nor Delbos would have the luxury of awaiting the Geneva meeting to send out invitations, however, for news of the impending Mediterranean conference had already leaked to the press. On the very next day, Friday, September 3, the German chargé d'affaires in London inquired of

Eden as to whether Germany would be invited to the conference. Caught by surprise, Eden replied evasively, taking care not to shut the door to German participation.[8] On the same day Eden received a wire from the British chargé d'affaires in Rome, Edward Ingram, reporting inquiries by British journalists in Rome as to whether Italy would be invited. Ingram cautioned that Italy would probably refuse to attend a meeting in Geneva, and he questioned whether any such meeting would be possible without Italy in attendance.[9] Eden could now see that the invitations could not await the opening of the League of Nations session on September 10. Nor could the meeting be held at Geneva if invitations were to be sent to Berlin and Rome.

When Eden received Cambon that Friday afternoon, he learned that Paris was equally concerned to quickly settle the question of the invitations. Paris, Cambon reported, wished to expand the invitation list to include the Black Sea powers, which Eden realized would mean an invitation to the Soviet Union. Objecting, Eden countered that the invitations should be extended only to the Mediterranean powers, which he said were the ones most directly concerned and were best able to take action against the piracy. Eden went on to name them—Italy, Yugoslavia, Albania, Greece, Turkey, and Egypt. Though he made no comment, Cambon could see that Eden's including Italy at the exclusion of the Soviet Union might cause problems in Paris. Eden went on to inform Cambon of the proposal he had in mind for the meeting.

Key to it was a collective warning to the two Spanish parties that any submarine found submerged outside of Spanish territorial waters would be pursued and destroyed. This solution required an understanding that the remaining powers confine their submarines to specified safe areas near their coasts, because any submerged submarine in the Mediterranean would risk being attacked. Eden intended this measure to provide a graceful out for Mussolini, who could attend the conference and afterward confine his submarines in his own safe zones. The technical plan therefore meshed neatly with Eden's intention to invite Italy to send a representative. Eden suggested that the invitations might be sent out the next day, Saturday, September 4, under joint Anglo-French signature. Cambon, answering that the proposals seemed largely technical and therefore uncontroversial, would submit them to his government that Friday with the expectation of having a response on Saturday.[10]

Eden's technical proposals were uncontroversial, at least for the moment, but his proposed invitation list provoked a storm of controversy in Paris. When Cambon's report arrived there late that Friday evening, the French cabinet realized that Eden would exclude the Soviet Union and extend an invitation to Italy. Delbos, however, had never intended to include Italy. Resuming their meeting Saturday morning, the cabinet held firmly to the position of excluding

Italy and inviting the Soviet Union, who had suffered important losses at the hand of Italian submarines.[11] Paris and London therefore stood poles apart. London would invite Italy and exclude the Soviet Union, while Paris would do the opposite.

The differences between London and Paris in fact ran deeper than that of sending invitations. Despite the obvious Italian involvement in the Mediterranean piracy, Chamberlain was still determined to negotiate a settlement with Rome after the piracy problem had been solved. Eden, therefore, had to proceed under the burden of providing Mussolini a graceful exit from the trap that Paris and London were about to set for him. It was thus important that Italy be sent an invitation. But Delbos felt no need to coddle Mussolini or to send him an invitation. He expected instead to solve the piracy problem with a technical agreement built around French and British naval power. Delbos had no interest in according Mussolini a graceful exit from the corner he had painted himself into.

The deadlock over the invitations was finally broken on Saturday afternoon in the course of two long telephone conversations between Delbos and Eden. Delbos insisted that he would have to resign should London insist upon the exclusion of the Soviet Union, and that London would be responsible for the ministerial crisis in Paris. Eden therefore had little choice but to accept the Soviet Union. They agreed finally that Italy, the Soviet Union, and Germany would be invited. But Eden agreed to the Soviet invitation with reservations, warning Delbos that the Kremlin might attempt to undermine the conference.[12] They also agreed, because Italy had already withdrawn from the League, that the conference would be held at Nyon, a small town in Switzerland thirteen miles from Geneva, with the opening session scheduled for September 10. Accordingly, invitations in the name of Britain and France were prepared the next day, Sunday, September 5, for delivery to the Mediterranean powers, the Black Sea powers, and to Germany.

In the meantime, Mussolini and Ciano had come to realize that Britain and France were poised to seize control of events in the Mediterranean. On Thursday, September 2, Ciano had observed in his diary that public opinion, particularly in England, had become aroused. He wrote on Friday, "Full orchestra—France, Russia, Britain. The theme—piracy in the Mediterranean. Guilty—the Fascists."[13] He obviously feared a clash at sea with Britain and France, who could do him more harm than could the Soviet Union. Mussolini and Ciano could see that London and Paris had seized the initiative at a moment when Rome expected the League to recognize the new Italian empire in East Africa. They clearly had no interest in a meeting of the Mediterranean powers. On the other hand, they could not easily reject an invitation, for a rejection would underscore Italian responsibility for the piracy. Ciano now realized that Rome had stumbled into a dilemma.

Accordingly, on Saturday, September 4, when the submarine campaign was beginning to enjoy its greatest success and Franco pressed hard for its continuation, Ciano abruptly suspended it. In his diary, Ciano remarked that the campaign would be suspended "for the moment," which suggests that he was prepared to resume it as soon as the threat had passed.[14] It seems clear that Ciano had suspended the submarine campaign out of fear of combined Anglo-French sea power about to be unleashed against him.

At the same time, Rome began to drag its feet on the question of attending the Mediterranean conference, complaining to Ingram about the choice of Geneva as the site of the meeting, about the lack of diplomatic preparation, and about the apparent decision to proceed without Germany.[15] Eden, though, was already addressing the Italian objections. Accordingly, with the meeting to be held at Nyon rather than at Geneva, and with Germany to receive an invitation, Mussolini would have no good excuse to reject the invitation soon to arrive at Rome.

On Monday, before the invitation could be delivered to Rome, Ingram met again with Ciano, who suggested that the proposed Anglo-Italian conversations could hardly deal with any item other than recognition of the Italian empire in Ethiopia and that recognition of Abyssinia by the League would open the door for an Italian return to Geneva.[16] Rome, therefore, continued to fish for recognition of the Italian empire. London, however, had already ruled out that option, at least for the moment, and had closed ranks with Paris to convene a conference at Nyon. Mussolini, with no good excuse to back out of the conference, was trapped in a corner with no easy exit.

Since London and Paris together had summoned the Nyon conference, it was proper that the invitation should be presented jointly by the British and French diplomatic representatives in Rome. Thus on Monday evening, September 6, Ingram and French chargé d'affaires Jules Blondel handed Ciano the invitation to send a representative to the conference.[17] From this point on, all communications with Rome regarding Nyon might easily have been delivered jointly, not merely as protocol but to underscore Anglo-French solidarity. Yet, for whatever reasons, Eden failed to exploit that advantage, as he later allowed Ingram to see Ciano in the absence of Blondel.

The Soviet Bombshell

In the meantime, relations between Rome and the Kremlin had grown increasingly tense. Early in September, while the Italian submarine campaign took a heavy toll on Soviet shipping, the Soviet press unleashed a spirited protest against the piracy. On September 3, *Pravda* openly accused "Fascist bandits" of "monstrous provocations" in the Mediterranean and complained that Paris and London had failed to take collective measures to end the violence. *Isvestia* carried similar articles as well as protests by Soviet workers, soldiers, and intellectuals demanding government action to end the violence and to teach the fascist bandits a lesson.[18]

The Soviet press campaign, obviously orchestrated by the Kremlin, anticipated the strong Soviet protest that arrived in Ciano's office on Monday afternoon, September 6. Submitted as "a decisive protest," the Soviet note bluntly accused the Italian government of mounting the submarine attacks. Insisting that the Soviet government had undeniable proof of Italian aggression against Soviet merchant ships, it cited specific examples, including the sinking of the *Timiryazev* on August 30. These acts of aggression, the note continued, "are absolutely contrary not only to the principles of humanity but also to the most elementary and generally recognized standards of international law." The note pointed directly to Italian responsibility for the attacks, demanding that the aggression be stopped, that compensation be granted for the damages, and that those guilty of ordering the attacks be punished.[19]

Receiving the Soviet note early Monday afternoon prior to his appointment with Ingram and Blondel, Ciano saw in it the opportunity to evade the Nyon conference or perhaps to destroy it altogether. "We must turn it to our advantage—force toward Russia, smiles for the rest," he wrote in his diary.[20] When Ingram and Blondel arrived for their scheduled appointment Monday evening, Ciano pretended that his government had intended to accept the invitation. But the Soviet note, he insisted, would make it nearly impossible for his government to sit at the same table with the Soviets. Summarizing the Soviet communication to Ingram and Blondel, he added that the note "seemed to him to have successfully torpedoed the conference."[21] He therefore merely acknowledged receipt of the invitation pending a later reply. Much to Blondel's surprise, Ingram then inquired of Ciano "whether it would not be possible in the circumstances to make use of machinery of the Non-Intervention Committee."[22]

Ciano had hoped that an Italian rejection of the invitation would wreck the Nyon conference before it met, and now Ingram's inept comment opened the door to yet another escape route. Accordingly, Ciano and Mussolini agreed on September 8 that Italy would not accept the Nyon invitation. They would advance instead an alternate proposal: to discuss the question of Mediterranean security in the London committee rather than at Nyon. That same day, Ciano shared the proposal informally with Ingram, flattering him upon his initiating it in their prior conversation.[23] Ciano did not reject the Nyon invitation, nor did he advance the alternate proposal in any formal sense. He clearly hoped that London would accept the alternate proposal as a substitute for the Nyon conference.

The suggestion to shift the Mediterranean agenda to London reveals the inconsistency of Ciano's position as well as his duplicity. Ciano's stated objection to Nyon—to avoid sitting at the same table with the Soviets—would obviously find no satisfaction in the Non-Intervention Committee, where the Italian representative had from the beginning sat at the same table with the Soviets. Ciano's proposal makes sense only in terms of his unspoken agenda, which was to escape the Nyon conference or to wreck it. Understanding Ciano's motives, Ingram wired Eden Tuesday morning that both he and Blondel "feel that Moscow has unconsciously played into Italian hands and that the Italian Government rather welcome this way of getting out of a conference for which they clearly had no great taste."[24]

Eden could see that the invitation to Nyon had backed Ciano into a tight spot, but he refused to consider shifting the discussion to London. On that same Tuesday morning, September 7, he wired Ingram that "we do not want the question of piracy in the Mediterranean to be dealt with by the Non-Intervention Committee, since the question of security on the high seas is one which transcends any question arising out of the Spanish Civil War and it would only confuse the issue to link it up with the problem of non-intervention in Spain."[25] Eden had already informed Ingram of his hope that Rome would accept the invitation despite the Soviet note, indicating that Italian cooperation in a conference to end the piracy in the Mediterranean "would be a most useful prelude to Anglo-Italian conversations."[26]

Later that Tuesday, Eden expressed these sentiments to Italian ambassador Dino Grandi in a manner to suggest that the proposed Anglo-Italian conversations hinged upon Rome's cooperation at Nyon to stabilize the unsettled situation in the Mediterranean.[27] Eden's attitude exposes the fragility of the common Anglo-French front, for London had not ruled out a policy of flirting further with Mussolini.

Even so, Eden would give Rome no specific assurances on the question of recognizing the Italian empire in East Africa. He knew very well that the British press, aroused by the piracy and by Mussolini's boastful speeches, would protest any British initiative in that regard. Nor did he have any reason to think that France or the other Geneva powers would welcome any such initiative. Eden therefore refused to exchange Abyssinian recognition for an Italian presence at Nyon. Nevertheless, he persisted in the view that Italian cooperation at Nyon and a quick end to the piracy might hasten the restoration of cordial Anglo-Italian relations and lead to an early opening of conversations. He tacitly conceded the obvious point that Italian cooperation at Nyon to end the piracy would improve the prospects of eventual League action in regard to Abyssinia. On September 8 he instructed Ingram to express these sentiments to Ciano, as he had already done with Grandi, but Ciano had already decided not to send a representative to Nyon.[28] He had received that day yet another hostile note from the Soviets, which lent further justification for his refusing the invitation to Nyon.[29]

The formal Italian note turning down the invitation arrived in London early Thursday afternoon, September 9, as Eden made his final preparations to travel first to Paris and then to Switzerland. It reported that the Italian government had been prepared to give an affirmative reply even before the formal invitation had arrived in Rome. But the Soviet note of September 6, it insisted, had caused the Italian government to change its mind, so that it would be necessary to "postpone any affirmative decision . . . until the incident created by the dispatch of the note of the Russian government . . . has been satisfactorily settled."[30] The note concluded with assurances that Rome, along with Berlin, stood ready to discuss the Nyon agenda in the Non-Intervention Committee.

A similar note from Berlin, arriving in Paris and London that same afternoon, indicated the German refusal to participate in the Nyon conference. It stressed German and Italian solidarity in turning down the invitation and, like the Italian note, proposed that the Mediterranean situation be considered in the Non-Intervention Committee rather than at a special international conference.[31] Since Berlin was expected to follow the Italian lead, neither Eden nor Delbos was surprised at the German refusal to attend the conference.

Ciano had therefore succeeded in maintaining a common front with Berlin on the question of Nyon, and because of the Soviet note, he had managed to evade the invitation to participate in the conference. He learned, moreover, that the British had penetrated Italian naval codes. On September 12, the Reich's foreign minister, Baron Constantin von Neurath, sent a confidential wire to the German chargé d'affaires in Rome: "Please inform Ciano personally that it appears from a statement made to me by the British Ambassador here that the British have intercepted and deciphered radio messages of Italian submarines operating in the Mediterranean."[32] It seems that ambassador to Berlin Arthur Henderson had spoken carelessly in a way to put vital British intelligence at risk. Ciano, though, had failed to wreck the Nyon conference, which would move forward as scheduled with neither Italy nor Germany attending, just as Delbos had preferred all along.

British and French Preparations for Nyon

Although Delbos and Eden shared a common concern to blunt Mediterranean piracy, French and British perspectives on the eve of the Nyon conference were not identical. Paris, having no confidence in the prospect of an enduring settlement with Rome, viewed Anglo-French naval cooperation as an end in itself. Delbos preferred to work with London at every step, rather than to undertake any unilateral action that might burden Anglo-French relations. Conversely, London was still thinking in terms of an eventual understanding with Rome, rather than with Paris, wishing to end the Mediterranean crisis with minimum damage to Anglo-Italian relations.

Despite their contrasting viewpoints, both Paris and London proceeded with preparations to use naval power to end the submarine menace. With British public opinion insisting upon stern measures, London had little choice but to keep open the option of using force. Accordingly, on September 3 Eden informed Cambon of British plans, which envisioned a joint agreement at Nyon to inform both Spanish parties that any submarine found submerged beyond Spanish territorial waters would be subject to attack. The participating powers would agree to confine their submarines within a ten-mile limit of their coasts. Any submarine found elsewhere in the Mediterranean would be subject to attack.[33]

With British intentions in hand, French preparations for the Nyon conference had been discussed in Paris on Monday, September 6, when Léon Blum, Delbos, and Admiral Jean François Darlan met in the company of selected ministers. After Delbos had summarized the events leading to the summoning of the conference, they discussed the option of linking the question of Mediterranean piracy to that of German and Italian withdrawal of their volunteers and to the opening of the French frontier to arms traffic. The dominant mood, however, was to avoid linkage and to work instead in close cooperation with Great Britain.[34]

When the discussion turned to the Mediterranean crisis, Darlan underscored the need to cooperate with Britain. He already had in mind a plan of operations based on the principle of Anglo-French naval cooperation. Should Britain and France unleash their naval power, he insisted, it would not be difficult to stop the piracy, which he thought was authored mainly by four Italian submarines, two on long-range missions and two that had been ceded to the Spanish Nationalists. He rejected the idea of forming an international fleet, which would be burdened by command problems. He did not, however, rule out a role for the navies of the smaller Mediterranean states. He did insist, however, that the British and French fleets be able to cooperate most effectively. His plan called for a system of surveillance zones in which warships under their own national commands would be assigned responsibility for specific areas of the Mediterranean. They would operate under the principle of mutual assistance, which would permit warships to enter the zones of another navy to pursue any aggressor and to lend support to each other. The cabinet, impressed with the plan, went ahead and approved it.[35] The French, therefore, would advance at Nyon Darlan's plan for surveillance zones rooted in the concept of mutual assistance most importantly between the Marine Nationale and the Royal Navy.

On September 7 Darlan drafted a brief note containing additional details of the proposed operation. Neutral shipping would be protected throughout the Mediterranean from surface, submarine, and air attack, but they would proceed into Spanish territorial waters at their own risk. Spanish surface ships would be allowed to attack each other, but any submarine or aerial aggressor whose nationality could not quickly be determined would be subject to attack. British ships, under the principle of reciprocity, would be permitted to operate in French coastal waters off Algeria. Darlan rejected the idea of a convoy system, which he thought would pose a spread of problems. It would be better, he thought, to route all shipping into clearly defined trade routes already made secure by warships assigned to protect them.[36]

Darlan ruled out the idea of an international naval command. Warships would remain under their own national command, even when they entered into the zone of another navy. It would be more efficient, he thought, for warships of different nationalities to cooperate at the tactical level in the pursuit of any aggressor that crossed over into another zone. Tactical cooperation should therefore be authorized in advance so that operations against a common enemy in a given zone would proceed on an automatic basis.[37]

Darlan's plan to neutralize friendly submarines resonated well with British plans. Since operations against "pirate" submarines would proceed throughout the Mediterranean, friendly submarines would be confined to specific designated zones near large naval bases, where they might proceed with their training without fear of being attacked. With friendly submarines therefore safely confined, any submarines found elsewhere in the Mediterranean would be considered unfriendly. The safe zones would be drawn in remote areas, distant from the busy trade routes. There would be, for example, no safe zones near Bizerte, where several trade routes converged. Nor would any nation's territorial waters constitute a safe zone, for "pirate" submarines might take refuge in them. Any submarine moving beyond its safe zone would proceed on the surface with clear markings in the company of a warship of the same nationality.[38]

When a summary of Darlan's proposal reached London later that same day, Captain T. S. V. Phillips, director of naval planning, noted that British and French plans ran generally along the same lines. The British, however, were uncomfortable with the French view to simultaneously confront aerial, surface, and submarine attacks on merchant shipping. In the British view, it would be better to isolate the submarine problem for immediate attention, to ensure a quick agreement, and better to deal with aerial and surface aggression later in separate categories. By this time the British had arrived independently at the French position for specific safe zones for friendly submarines, as opposed to zones extending throughout their territorial waters. On that same day, September 7, the Foreign Office accepted these views.[39] When the Nyon conference opened, the French and British naval commands were therefore beginning to close ranks at planning and operational levels. The two governments were together on the question of blunting the piracy, but their disagreements about forging afterward a Mediterranean settlement with Mussolini remained conveniently under the rug.

At the tactical level there remained the question of separating the problem of submarine aggression from that of aviation and surface ship aggression. The British were also aware of their naval weakness, particularly in terms of available destroyers. On September 7 Admiral Sir Ernle Chatfield explained to Eden that the Royal Navy could at best commit no more than thirty destroyers to the operation and that only fifteen of these could be on patrol at any one time. Since a single destroyer would be nearly useless against a submarine, the fifteen available ships would have to be divided into five or six groups operating in twos and threes. Chatfield explained further that large areas of the Mediterranean would still remain unprotected, that the French navy would have to play a major role in the patrol operation, and that the naval base at Algiers should be made available to the Royal Navy. He added that a time limit, renewable in perhaps a month, should be placed on the operation to ensure that British warships would not be committed indefinitely to fruitless patrol duty.[40]

In his Cabinet memorandum summarizing Chatfield's position, Eden noted his own view of the need to enlist the cooperation of Germany and Italy as soon as possible, should the two Axis powers not attend the conference.[41] Eden's desire to gain Axis cooperation seems out of step with the drift of events, particularly in view of his knowledge that Italian submarines were the main authors of the violence. Eden may have aimed only at appeasing Chamberlain, who wished to keep open the door to future Anglo-Italian conversations. Whatever his intentions, the memorandum raises the question of whether Eden had yet grasped fully the diplomatic advantage of closing with the French to the end of isolating Italy.

Mandate of Public Opinion

From the time news of the Nyon conference leaked to the press on September 2, and even before it was known whether Rome and Berlin would attend, British newspapers lent solid support to what they soon termed the "piracy conference." They did not, however, all take the same line, as some stressed Anglo-French solidarity and others collective action. On Monday, September 6, the *Daily Herald* took the lead to insist that prolonged negotiations and ideological squabbling could not be tolerated and that Britain and France must be prepared to act together should no agreement among the powers be reached.[42] On Tuesday and Wednesday, when it appeared that Rome and Berlin might not participate, the *Herald* pushed hard the same theme, urging bilateral Anglo-French action in any event.[43]

On Friday, September 10, the *Manchester Guardian* called for pursuit of a clear policy at Nyon, insisting, as did the *Herald*, that the proceedings not be allowed to bog down in political questions. The *Guardian*, however, put more emphasis on the need for broadly concerted naval measures. It did not, for example, rule out a role for Italy in helping to enforce an agreement should Rome not attend the conference.[44] The London *Times* deplored the defection of Germany and Italy but expressed the view that their absence made the conference even more necessary.[45] There was therefore broad agreement in the press that the conference should move forward, even in the absence of the two Axis powers.

When Eden arrived in Paris on the afternoon of September 9 to dine with Delbos at the Quai d'Orsay, he was no doubt aware that some French officials were unsure of the British resolve to take swift and effective action against the piracy.[46] Nevertheless, Eden and Delbos that same evening issued a joint statement stressing "complete agreement" between the French and British delegations on proposals to be presented to the conference.[47] As the two delegations traveled afterward to Geneva by night train, the British Eleventh Destroyer Division—the *Fury, Forester, Firedrake,* and *Fortune*—prepared to set sail for the Mediterranean.[48] At the same time, a division of French torpedo boats was placed on alert to join French naval forces already in the Mediterranean.[49] When the French and British delegations arrived in Geneva on the morning of Friday, September 10, to travel that same day to nearby Nyon, they had nearly all of their plans in place, and their naval forces were already preparing for whatever action might be demanded of them to suppress the piracy. The stage was set for Britain and France to combine their naval power to blunt fascist aggression in the Mediterranean.

Chapter 5

Solving a Mediterranean Problem

On Friday, September 10, when the French and British delegations arrived at Nyon, the French could justifiably harbor doubts as to whether the British were prepared to take energetic action against the Mediterranean piracy. Foreign Minister Yvon Delbos was well aware that statesmen in London still had hopes of reaching a general diplomatic settlement with Italy, whom everyone now knew to be the main author of the piracy. It was therefore easy for the French to worry that the British delegation might settle for weak solutions after all, at the expense of decisive naval action against fascist aggression in the Mediterranean.

But if the French harbored misgivings about British resolve, they could take comfort in the knowledge that public opinion in Britain remained stoutly in favor of firm measures. On the day that the British delegation arrived at Nyon, the *Manchester Guardian* urged British authorities to focus their attention on the single objective of arranging concerted naval measures to suppress lawlessness in the Mediterranean. The role of the British government, the editorial insisted, was to assure the other powers that the security of maritime traffic in the Mediterranean "is the sole aim of the Conference."[1] The *Daily Herald* spoke in a similar vein: "There must be no watering-down of the British draft plan to suppress the Mediterranean pirate ships." The editorial warned against any thought of quietly dropping plans of concerted naval action for fear of offending Germany and Italy, insisting that "if the Government were to weaken now, opinion at home would sag into confusion again, and Germany and Italy could hardly be blamed for drawing the obvious conclusions."[2] Clearly, a strong current of opinion in Britain demanded a stout determination to use armed force to suppress the piracy. It did not, however, anticipate the forging of an alliance with France. It aimed instead at solving a Mediterranean problem.

In step with the British press, Anthony Eden stood ready to cooperate with the French to confront head on the challenge of the piracy. In Geneva on the morning of September 10, the French and British delegations met privately to coordinate their plans. The idea was to deal swiftly with the main threat, that of submarine violence. The two delegations therefore agreed at once that the purpose of the conference would be to organize their naval forces in a manner to address promptly the pirate attacks. To this end, the French delegation accepted a British proposal that the main agenda would be the problem of submarine attacks, with the question of surface and aerial attacks to be considered at Geneva later that week. They further agreed that the Mediterranean would be divided into zones in which each fleet would operate under its own command. The zones would be constantly under review to address any changing circumstances. British and French submarines would be confined to restricted zones near their ports. Unaware that they were moving in the direction of an informal naval alliance, the French and British staffs began that same morning to iron out the details of these arrangements.[3]

The Opening Session

The first meeting of the Nyon conference, a plenary session attended by the public and the press, opened at four-thirty on the afternoon of September 10 at the Nyon town hall. Delbos headed the French delegation. Jean François Darlan, commander of the French fleet, stood at his side. Eden headed the British delegation, consisting of Admiral Sir Ernle Chatfield, chief of staff of the Royal Navy, and Sir Robert Vansittart, permanent undersecretary of state for foreign affairs. Maxim Litvinov, commissioner for foreign affairs, headed the Soviet delegation, and in attendance also were delegations from Bulgaria, Egypt, Greece, Romania, Turkey, and Yugoslavia.[4]

M. Schranz, mayor of Nyon, welcomed the delegates. After the courtesies had ended, he presided over the first action of the delegates, that of electing a president of the conference. In a move arranged in advance, Eden rose quickly to the floor and indicated that it was France that had taken the initiative to summon the conference. Accordingly, he nominated Delbos, who received the unanimous approval of the delegates. The French foreign minister then mounted the podium to take charge of the conference.[5]

Having thanked the mayor, Delbos moved directly to indicate the purpose of the conference—to suppress piracy and to enforce the rules of international law concerning the navigation of the Mediterranean. The unstable situation in that sea, he insisted, could not be permitted to continue any longer. Nor was it conceivable to allow navigation there to remain at the mercy of pirates, who respected no flag, who torpedoed merchant ships without warning, and who disregarded the 1936 protocol that had humanized the rules of undersea warfare.[6] He expressed regrets that Italy and Germany had declined their invitations on the grounds that the problem should be discussed in another arena. He insisted, however, that the piracy problem must be resolved quickly in a manner not to risk its being bogged down in the confusion attendant to discussions of nonintervention in the Spanish Civil War. He added that Mediterranean security was a matter vital to all of the governments represented at Nyon. The British and French governments, he insisted, had but two intentions: first, to end the piracy regime in the Mediterranean; and second, conceding a point to Eden, to restore a climate of conciliation in which Europe's pressing problems might find future discussion. He therefore urged the delegates to act quickly to adopt special measures to restore peaceful navigation in the Mediterranean.[7] He made no mention of any French motive to teach Mussolini a lesson.

If Delbos worried that Rome might decide at the last minute to send a delegation, his concern was surely eased by the blunt speech that Litvinov delivered toward the end of the public session. Having pledged Soviet cooperation at the conference, Litvinov deftly pointed an accusing finger at Italy as the author of the violence. "Everyone here," he insisted, "knows the object of this piracy, and what State is pursuing that piracy. Its name is on everyone's lips, although it cannot be pronounced in this hall."[8] Eden, perhaps embarrassed by Litvinov's blunt statement, rose to express regret at the absence of any state that might want to be helpful. Suggesting that much remained to be accomplished, he moved that the conference go into permanent committee to begin its work. The motion was approved unanimously, and the public session came to an end.[9]

The First Closed Session

Although the decisions of the permanent committee of the Nyon conference were released to the press after each meeting, the details of the deliberations remained confidential. However, these discussions are recorded in the minutes of the permanent committee housed in the French Naval Archives in Paris.[10] These minutes reveal that Litvinov attempted to dominate the session, raising meticulous objections to Anglo-French proposals, and that Eden and Delbos maneuvered astutely and tactfully in each case to carry the main points. In working harmoniously together, they preserved the spirit of unity among the delegations and set the stage for the British and French navies to seize control of the Mediterranean at the expense of Mussolini.

After Delbos had called the session to order, Eden took the floor, explaining that the aim of the conference was to organize naval forces to act in concert for the purpose of ending the violent and illegal acts that had disturbed navigation of the Mediterranean. He insisted that a convoy system would not work because it would require too many destroyer escorts. He then advanced the Anglo-French plan of dividing the Mediterranean into surveillance zones. Indicating that Britain and France were prepared to commit important assets to the enterprise, he suggested that it would be helpful to know how the eastern states would be able to participate in the operation.[11]

Litvinov, obviously aspiring to form a bloc among the eastern states, expressed his preference for an international fleet under a mixed leadership. Eden rose quickly to reply, explaining that the French and British naval commands had already discarded that option mainly on grounds that it would operate too slowly. The zoning system, he insisted, had the advantage of speedily addressing the piracy problem. Each navy, under its own command, he said, would be able to communicate better with its own ships. He added tactfully that the question raised by Litvinov ought nevertheless to be examined.[12]

The delegations from Turkey and Greece indicated that in the absence of their technical experts, they would have to submit the Anglo-French plan to their governments for a decision. Delbos answered that the plan ought not diminish the solidarity of the states represented there. He added that certain technical details might indeed have to await the arrival of the experts, but he suggested that the conference might want to make a list of these details and then move swiftly to address the larger issues. Speaking in support, Eden explained that the French and British navies would assume the entire responsibility of patrolling the area from Malta to Gibraltar and that these two navies stood ready to lend all possible naval assistance to the eastern states in their assigned zones. This system, he added, would enable the conference to end its work quickly and empower each state to take swift measures in its own zone.[13]

Eden's comments assumed that the French and British navies would cover patrol zones only to the west of Malta, leaving the eastern states with the main burden of patrolling the eastern basin of the Mediterranean. Quick to see the weakness of that system, Litvinov observed that it would create an imbalance with some zones better patrolled than others, which he thought would encourage the pirate submarines to shift their aggression to the poorly patrolled eastern Mediterranean. He added his opinion that a system of mixed command would provide a better balance in the patrol scheme. Yugoslavian delegate

Bojidar Pouritch observed that the British and French fleets would no doubt maintain a strong patrol in the west, but the smaller eastern navies would be able to patrol little more than their own territorial waters.[14]

At this point the conference appeared to have arrived at an impasse but for Tevfik Rustu Aras of Turkey, who offered objections to the creation of an international fleet. He would prefer the zone system, but it would be necessary, he thought, to know in advance how the governments would cooperate to stage an eastern patrol and what specific measures they intended to take. In a tactful way, Aras had asked exactly the right question, for it forced the French and British delegations to defend their commitment to lend assistance in the eastern Mediterranean. Delbos answered that the French and British fleets would lend every possible support. He cautioned, however, that it would be impossible to ensure full security to the entire Mediterranean and that it would be necessary to focus their naval power on the busiest and most endangered trade routes. Delbos insisted that the Anglo-French scheme was indeed the best solution, but he conceded that the conference might profit from a discussion of the zones and the level of naval forces necessary to render them effective.[15]

Admiral Chatfield, who had remained silent until this point, observed that it would be impossible to ensure surveillance of the entire Mediterranean because the number of warships available was insufficient to match the volume of trade. He insisted that a convoy system was out of the question and that the most urgent need was to put quickly into place a scheme that would work. The key, he insisted, was to keep all submarines out of the surveillance zones so that the naval patrols would not have to determine whether any given submarine was or was not an aggressor. The idea, he observed, was to reduce the attacks to a minimum. He indicated that the zones had been drawn to focus naval power on the areas where the attacks had been the most frequent, which was the western Mediterranean. He saw no reason why the zones might not be rearranged should the frequency of attacks shift to the eastern Mediterranean.[16]

Upon the suggestion of Delbos, the conference now considered whether it might be possible to move forward to approve in principle the system of surveillance zones, despite the several technical problems. Eden promised that maps indicating the exact limits of the zones would soon be distributed to the delegates. At that point Litvinov indicated his provisional acceptance in principle of the zones, but he asked whether it might be possible for the delegates to know the level of forces to be committed. Eden, no doubt relieved at Litvinov's concession, indicated that Britain and France intended to commit forty to fifty destroyers plus a number of other warships and aircraft to patrol the western basin of the Mediterranean. The delegates then voted to approve in principle the zone system as the basis of further discussion.[17]

The discussion now shifted to the text of the Anglo-French plan, which defined submarine aggression in terms of clauses in the 1930 London Naval Treaty requiring submarines in wartime to ensure the safety of the crews of merchant ships prior to attacking them. Rising quickly, Litvinov insisted that these clauses would serve only to legalize aggression against merchant ships in peacetime as long as the pirate submarine observed the wartime rules. He worried that the plan would serve only to humanize peacetime submarine aggression rather than to end it. After prolonged discussion of this point, it became clear that the document would have to be revised to clarify the conditions under which a submarine might be attacked.[18]

Following the distribution of maps, representatives of the eastern Mediterranean states complained about the zones assigned them. Obviously too large, these zones would stretch thin the naval assets of the smaller states. The question of the eastern zones, therefore, was deferred to the session scheduled for the next day. The first closed session ended early in the evening with the allocation of the eastern zones still undecided. In his statement to the press following the session, Delbos stressed the fact that important progress had been made, that a zone system had been adopted for the western Mediterranean, and that pirate submarines would be attacked. He added that a surveillance zone would be offered to Italy.[19]

The Dilemma of the Smaller States

The smaller eastern states—Yugoslavia, Greece, and Turkey—worked under the burden of a double threat to their security. Their navies were too small to contribute importantly to the proposed surveillance scheme. At the same time, geography placed them squarely between two stronger powers, the Soviet Union and Italy. The smaller states clearly had no interest in seeing Soviet destroyers in the Aegean Sea, nor did they stand to benefit from any naval confrontation with Italy. A clash between an Italian submarine and a Greek destroyer, for example, might easily escalate into an unwanted Italo-Greek war. On the other hand, the smaller states stood to benefit from a restoration of security in the Mediterranean that only Britain and France could ensure. From the perspective of the smaller states, the problem was to find a way to support the British and French naval initiatives without risking their relations with either Rome or Moscow.

At an informal meeting that evening, the eastern states made it clear that they would not cooperate with the Soviets to patrol Aegean waters. In his memoirs, Eden wrote that the mood of the eastern states "led to an altercation with the Russians and for an hour no progress was made."[20] Eden and Delbos could both see that the smaller states had no zeal for any arrangement to allow a Soviet intrusion into Aegean waters, which the Anglo-French plan would have permitted. In that informal session, the Nyon conference entered into a moment of crisis, but the confrontation anticipated a solution to the dilemma of the eastern states.

In a brief report to the Foreign Office late that evening, Eden summarized the events of the day.[21] Despite the rift that threatened to divide the eastern states, solid progress had been made regarding the western Mediterranean. The operational rules for confronting submarine aggression against neutral ship-ping had been clarified to permit counterattack, and the French and British naval staffs had agreed to isolate their own submarines in the Mediterranean. Most importantly, Delbos and Eden and their naval staffs had worked in har-mony to impress the conference with a display of Anglo-French solidarity and determination.

The Second Day of Nyon

The problems that had burdened the deliberations on the first day of Nyon were swiftly resolved on Saturday. When the delegations assembled that morn-ing, they quickly agreed that Britain and France would assume the burden of patrolling the entire Mediterranean and the Aegean Sea as well. The small states would patrol only their territorial waters, but they might be asked to assist British or French warships beyond those limits. More importantly, they would make certain designated ports available upon request by French and British warships. Eden explained the arrangement this way: "Britain and France would take over the brunt of the work in the western basin and in the Aegean as well. This was popular and during the morning of September 11th all agreed that instead of helping the smaller powers to patrol the Aegean, we should ask them to help us."[22]

This arrangement addressed directly the dilemma of the smaller states. It kept the Soviets out of the Aegean with minimum offense to their dignity. Since Soviet ships could in theory be asked to lend assistance in the Aegean, Litvinov was able to accept the scheme gracefully. Moreover, the arrangement significantly reduced the chances of a naval clash between Italy and any of the smaller powers. Finally, it confined the naval patrols of the smaller powers to nearby waters. The idea of asking the small states to lend naval assistance in the Aegean was largely a political fiction aimed at appeasing their relations with Italy. The French and British navies could not in any event expect important naval assistance from them. Their gaining access to the Aegean ports was a far more important concession, not only in a symbolic sense to underscore Italy's isolation, but also to make it possible for the British and French navies to stage patrols far beyond their home bases.

Nevertheless, the arrangement for the French and British navies to patrol the entire Mediterranean as well as the Aegean promised to stretch Anglo-French naval power to its limit. The original plan had required the commitment of forty to fifty destroyers, which Chatfield had assumed would be mainly British. But on Saturday morning Darlan offered to commit ten additional French destroyers so that the total Anglo-French commitment would be as many as sixty warships. The revised plan, with its heavier burden on Anglo-French naval power, would not have been workable without this additional French commitment. In his memoirs Eden explained, "Lord Chatfield and our naval experts had expected that most of the patrolling would fall to British warships. In the light of Laval's meagre efforts during the Abyssinian crisis, this was natural. However, Chatfield was surprised, and so was I, at the splendid contribution the French were prepared to make, which gave fresh impetus to our plans."[23]

The revised scheme required no basic changes in the original Anglo-French plan; rather, it amplified the possibilities inherent in it. The idea of extending Anglo-French naval power into the eastern Mediterranean was entirely spontaneous, not at all anticipated in advance. It was a product of the refusal of the small eastern states to participate in the zonal scheme and of the French commitment of additional assets. What is important, however, is that the new scheme gave international sanction to an interlude of Anglo-French domination of the entire Mediterranean. That was the most important strategic result of the Nyon conference. All of the states represented at Nyon, including the Soviet Union, had given their blessings to an arrangement empowering the Royal Navy and the Marine Nationale to call the signals throughout the Mediterranean at the expense of Italy. It was a brilliant strategic and diplomatic coup that held the promise of isolating Italy and imposing upon Rome a humiliating political setback. The question remained as to whether London would build upon the strategic advantage that Delbos and Eden had so skillfully negotiated.

When the Nyon states assembled again that Saturday afternoon in a final closed session, the business of the day had already been carefully programmed. Bojidar Pouritch of Yugoslavia, speaking for the Balkan Entente powers of Yugoslavia, Romania, Turkey, Greece, and Bulgaria, moved that the Riverian powers accept responsibility for patrolling their territorial waters and that Britain and France assume responsibility for opposing piracy in the waters beyond. The motion passed without discussion. The remainder of the session was given mainly to discussion of minor technical amendments to what would then become the Nyon Arrangement. At the end of the session, Victor Antonescu of Romania, speaking for the Balkan states and for all of the delegations, expressed his gratitude to Delbos, who, in his words, had "presided tactfully, skillfully, and loyally over the work of the Conference."[24] With those gracious remarks, the second closed session of the Nyon conference came to an end.

The Nyon Arrangement

The Nyon conference was notably successful, mainly in terms of the political and strategic advantages it accorded to the two leading naval powers. It was a rare triumph of Anglo-French diplomacy, marking the only time between the two world wars that French and British statesmen working together with their naval staffs seized the initiative to combine their naval power to the end of influencing the direction of European affairs. The work of the naval staffs was especially commendable, for it set the stage for the two navies to distribute and share their naval assets in a manner to amplify the full potential of their combined power.

Known as the Nyon Arrangement and dated September 14, 1937, the agreement among the nine powers appealed in its preamble to the 1930 London Naval Treaty, which had imposed by international agreement certain humane restrictions upon the operations of submarines in times of war. The Nyon Arrangement went one step further, authorizing in its preamble the exercise of "special collective measures against piratical acts by submarines" in times of peace.[25] It was a multilateral agreement that accorded the two leading naval powers a special authority to protect the collective security interests of all nine of the signatory states against submarine violence in the Mediterranean.

The arrangement authorized the participating powers to take action to protect all non-Spanish merchant ships in the Mediterranean. That action would consist of counterattacking and destroying any submarine found near an attack scene "in circumstances which give valid grounds for the belief that the submarine was guilty of the attack."[26] British and French warships would patrol the western basin of the Mediterranean and the territorial waters of each other, in accordance with a bilateral agreement to be concluded between the two governments. This important provision lent legitimacy to private Anglo-French naval consultation and coordination under the umbrella of the Nyon Arrangement. A large zone encompassing the Tyrrhenian Sea was reserved as a possible special arrangement to be offered to Italy, which the French had little choice but to accept gracefully. British and French warships patrolling the eastern basin of the Mediterranean would focus mainly on the major commercial routes, with the understanding that these zones might be revised according to necessity.[27]

With no more than sixty destroyers committed to the surveillance operation, the Anglo-French naval staffs understood from the beginning the futility of trying to patrol the entire Mediterranean. They would instead concentrate their assets along the most heavily traveled commercial routes in the hope of reducing pirate attacks to a minimum. The arrangement authorized the Nyon governments to advise their merchant shipping to follow certain clearly defined trade routes where protection might be provided.[28] Merchant ships were not required to follow those routes, nor was there any assurance that ships following them would be entirely secure. Nevertheless, the system amplified the level of protection along the main trade routes, within the limits of Anglo-French naval capabilities. The arrangement, including the patrol operations, was scheduled to enter into force on Monday, September 20.

In the meantime, on Tuesday, September 14, the Mediterranean conference came to an end when the delegates assembled in a final plenary session to sign the Nyon Arrangement. Opening the session, Delbos thanked the delegations for their spirit of collaboration and mutual good faith that had made it possible to conclude so promptly a workable agreement aimed at ending the intolerable acts of piracy in the Mediterranean. Litvinov also praised the work of the conference. Finally, Eden congratulated the chairman for the manner whereby he had conducted the business of the conference, and he added a word of thanks to the technical experts whose work had contributed importantly to the success of the conference. When the speeches were all finished, Delbos declared that the conference had come to an end.[29]

A Confidential Message from London

On that same Tuesday, September 14, two days after the essential work of the conference had ended, the British naval delegation at Nyon received a confidential message from naval intelligence in London. Addressed personally to Admiral Chatfield, it read:

> Personal for Chief of Naval Staff.
>
> Most secret information suggests that Italian submarines of Aegean patrol have been ordered to take no repetition no offensive action against units of any flag whatsoever. C. in C. Mediterranean and R.A. (D) have been informed.[30]

Housed in the Admiralty files at the Public Records Office in London, this document appears to be the controversial message informing Chatfield that the Italian government had called off its submarine campaign against neutral shipping. It is well known that British cryptanalysts had penetrated Italian naval codes, so historians of the Nyon conference have often believed that the British delegation knew from the beginning that Mussolini had already reined in his submarines. The date of the message, September 14, suggests, however, that the British delegation knew of Mussolini's retreat only after the main work of the conference had been finished.

Even if this message or similar information had been received earlier, there is no reason to expect that Eden and Chatfield would have acted differently at Nyon. Mussolini was fully capable of unleashing his submarines again, which indeed he did briefly, after a decent interval. Any indication of an Italian retreat would likely have been viewed at Nyon as nothing more than a tactical ploy on the part of Mussolini to weaken the work of the conference. Further, the withdrawal of Italian submarines would not have ended the threat of piracy, for Spanish submarines continued to operate in Mediterranean waters. And Mussolini could easily send additional submarines to Franco. It seems clear that the work of the conference was not significantly influenced by intelligence reports indicating that Mussolini had withdrawn his submarines.

Reaction of the Press

As the Nyon conference got under way, the French press was nearly unanimous in blaming Italy for the numerous submarine attacks in the Mediterranean. The British press echoed much the same sentiment, but in a more subdued way. In France, as in Britain, the political right remained suspicious of the Soviets, but when the finished work of the conference was made public, the mainstream press in both countries applauded its success. The French press spoke overwhelmingly in praise of the agreement. The newspapers of the political Left were especially outspoken, one of them observing that the combined Anglo-French fleets patrolling the Mediterranean served as "a warning to Mussolini that he was not going to have his own way in the Mediterranean forever." Another Paris daily wrote of Nyon as "a prelude to a stiffening of Franco-British diplomacy in the foreign field." For the most part, British editorials spoke favorably of including Italy in the patrol scheme on grounds that it might increase the chances of a future Anglo-French understanding in the Mediterranean. Overall, the French press applauded the prospect of Paris and London finally working together in concert, as the Nyon conference seemed to anticipate. The agreement whereby the French and British fleets would cooperate in the Mediterranean received especially favorable comment. But a pessimistic note was sounded by *Figaro*, which commented ominously, "England's firmness does not exclude her desire to negotiate with Italy."[31] Despite *Figaro*'s misgivings, the dominant theme running through the French press was praise of Anglo-French cooperation and the expectation that France and Britain might continue to work together politically and militarily in the interest of exerting a stronger influence on European affairs.

Although the British press applauded Anglo-French cooperation at Nyon, it tended more than the French to celebrate Nyon as a timely triumph of collective security to solve a particular problem. In an editorial on September 13, the *Daily Herald* stated that in one respect "Nyon was a model conference. It got through its work and produced its agreement in little more than 48 hours," adding, "France and Britain were, for once, completely in step with each other. Both were prepared for action and capable of just the sort of action needed to cope with this particular evil."[32] But on the sixteenth, the *Herald* broadened its focus, applauding Nyon instead as a triumph of collective action: "Warships of nine nations began to co-operate yesterday in a collective enterprise to maintain the freedom and security of the Mediterranean."[33]

Overall, the British press appears to have appreciated considerably less than the French the symbolic significance of British and French warships working in concert to police the Mediterranean. Nor is there much expression of the potential of Nyon for shaping future solidarity in Anglo-French relations. In contrast to the French, the British press focused sharply on the technical aspects of the arrangements, on the attitude of Italy, on the importance of keeping the Soviets out of the Mediterranean, and on the significance of Nyon as an example of the success of collective security, which discounted any enduring value of Anglo-French naval cooperation in seizing control of the Mediterranean at the expense of Italy.

These differences of opinion reflect basic foreign policy objectives, which were not the same in Paris and London. The fundamental assumption of French foreign policy under Delbos—that an Anglo-French entente was an end in itself—was not widely shared in Britain. In London, isolationist sentiment remained entrenched, which explains why the British press tended to applaud Anglo-French cooperation at Nyon in terms of its pragmatic value toward the solution to a particular crisis as opposed to any enduring value that might come of it. In fear of being dragged into a continental or Mediterranean war, London still preferred to keep France at arm's length. Nyon was therefore viewed as the triumph of collective security. If peace could be negotiated through collective arrangements, there would be no need for a risky French alliance, and London might accordingly keep open a spread of foreign policy options consistent with Britain's geographical isolation.

Frittering Away the Advantage

Among the British options remained that of an Anglo-Italian settlement, which London had not abandoned despite outrageous Italian submarine aggression and the brilliant Anglo-French breakthrough at Nyon. The idea of keeping Rome informed of events at Nyon and reserving a large surveillance zone for Italy was entirely of British origin, rather than French. Paris had no reason to appease Rome, but in the interest of building stronger Anglo-French relations, Delbos followed the British lead to accord Italy these concessions. The work of the Nyon conference was therefore reported promptly to Rome, but events had unfolded so swiftly that Mussolini and Ciano were caught by surprise at what for them was a major diplomatic and military setback compounded by the fact that Mussolini was scheduled to meet Hitler in Germany toward the end of September. He could hardly afford to meet the Führer in the wake of a major humiliation.

Mussolini learned of the Anglo-French success at Nyon late on September 11 by way of telephone calls from Renato Bova Scoppa, the Italian representative at Geneva. Ciano wrote in his diary that "the Duce is furious at the first news from Nyon."[34] When Ingram and Blondel arrived at the Foreign Ministry the next Monday afternoon, September 13, Ciano was already aware of the main provisions of the Nyon Arrangement, and he probably knew that the two diplomats would hand him an invitation to join the patrol scheme. Well prepared in advance, Ciano expressed his personal view that Italy could not accept such a small surveillance zone, one inconsistent with Italy's status as a great power. When Ciano observed that warships of nonadhering powers might be attacked in the Mediterranean, Blondel answered bluntly that "a grave situation certainly would then arise," and Ingram added "that it was all the more reason for Italy to adhere so as to avoid such a risk." Ciano answered that the invitation appeared to be a "take it or leave it" case, and Mussolini would certainly "leave it." The two diplomats denied that it was so, insisting that there was still room for Italian observations. But at that point, Ciano rejected the invitation, adding, "I am not asking for anything."[35] Later that evening Ingram wired London that "the whole attitude of Count Ciano was one of injured pride" and that he "is in an exalted and nervous frame of mind. Italian prestige seems to be the one thing at the moment that counts for him and Signor Mussolini."[36] It seems clear that Mussolini's visit to Berlin hinged upon the preservation of Italian prestige.

That evening Ciano wrote in his diary, "Ingram and Blondel have given us a copy of the Nyon decisions. I have prepared a reply in which, without advancing a claim to take part, I affirm our right to parity. It will certainly embarrass them. Either we co-operate, or their schemes fail and they are to blame. I am waiting for approval from Berlin before delivering my reply."[37] Ciano delivered his reply on September 15. An ambiguous statement, it complained about the small Italian zone and suggested that the Nyon scheme "appears inacceptable."[38]

Eden and Delbos therefore concluded that Rome had rejected the invitation to participate in the Nyon Arrangement. Ciano's awkward reply, clearly a tactical blunder, afforded Eden and Delbos the opportunity to exclude Italy altogether from the Nyon scheme, or at least to delay Italian participation long enough to spoil Mussolini's visit to Berlin. At that moment the negotiations with Italy entered into a decisive stage, but the British leadership failed to seize upon the opportunity that had fallen into their laps.

Ciano considered that the door to Italian participation remained open. That evening he wrote in his diary that Mussolini had arranged to deliver Franco four additional submarines. He added that Bova Scoppa "telephones from Geneva that Eden and Delbos are ready to accept our demands, but they would like us to take the first step. Impossible. We musn't move an inch. They will come to us." And next day he wrote that "they are awaiting a move from us, but they won't get one."[39] On Friday, the seventeenth, Ingram wired London that the Italian press continued to focus on the prestige question and that the door remained open for Italy to participate in the Nyon scheme once parity is granted. "The burning question," he reported, "is who is to make the next move and the Italian press leaves its readers to expect that it will not be Italy."[40]

In the meantime, on September 15, Bova Scoppa had approached M. Spitzmuller, first secretary to the French delegation at Geneva, to explore the attitude of the British and French governments. The Frenchman replied that the two governments would welcome Italian participation in the Nyon accords but that they had considered Ciano's curt reply a rejection of the invitation. He added that there was "no question of the signatories of the Nyon arrangement running after the Italian Government to get them to change their mind."[41] After consulting with Delbos, Spitzmuller suggested to Bova Scoppa that the French and British governments would consider any observations the Italian government might wish to make, but that such observations "should be clearly formulated and made through diplomatic channels."[42] That amounted to a renewal of the invitation for Italy to participate in the Nyon scheme, but on condition of an Italian initiative.

Confronted with a stiffening Anglo-French attitude and knowing that he soon would leave to meet Hitler, Mussolini reconsidered his position. Consequently, when Ciano received Ingram and Blondel on the nineteenth, the Italian caved in to the Anglo-French demand for an Italian initiative. Considerably more cordial than before, Ciano promised that once parity in the surveillance zones had been accorded, Italian participation in the Nyon

Arrangement would be assured. He then handed the two diplomats an official note clarifying the Italian position relative to the question of the equality of zones. In closing, Ciano stressed that he would be pleased to receive a positive reply prior to his departing for Germany with Mussolini on September 24.[43]

Obviously pleased at Ciano's changing mood, Ingram informed Eden immediately, suggesting early acceptance of the Italian note, prior to the departure of Mussolini and Ciano for Berlin, in the interest of keeping Italy out of the German camp and of keeping open the door to a future Anglo-Italian rapprochement.[44] Eden, still busy with League work at Geneva, responded on September 21, instructing Ingram to deliver to Ciano a proposal "that Naval experts of the three Powers should meet in Paris in the near future in order to explore practical modifications which it might be possible to make in the Nyon arrangements."[45] This amounted to an invitation for Mussolini to send an Italian representative to Paris.

Eden's prompt reply played directly into the hands of Mussolini, who would now visit Hitler with a diplomatic victory in his pocket. That evening, after Il Duce had approved the invitation to a technical conference, Ciano wrote in his diary that "it is a fine victory. From suspected pirates to policemen of the Mediterranean—and the Russians, whose ships we were sinking, excluded!" The next evening, he added, "The Duce, without saying so, showed that he is very pleased."[46]

Mussolini had every reason to be pleased, for Eden had failed to exploit fully the enormous diplomatic leverage Nyon had accorded him. His forcing Ciano to come to the table amounted to nothing more than a minor tactical victory. Had he refused to renew the invitation to Italy for technical discussions, as he might easily have done after Ciano had initially rejected them, or had he dragged out the negotiations on that point, Mussolini would have undertaken his visit to Germany in the wake of an embarrassing diplomatic setback.

Eden had frittered away an important diplomatic advantage, forfeiting a strategic victory that would have impressed both Rome and Berlin with Anglo-French resolve to dominate the Mediterranean at Italian expense. At that moment Anglo-French firmness and solidarity would have underscored Italian weakness in a language that Hitler would have understood. To be sure, Eden and Delbos had scored an impressive diplomatic victory at Nyon, but Eden's failure to exploit it fully on the eve of Mussolini's visit to Berlin diminished the negative impact it might have had on German-Italian relations.

At the same time, admitting Italy to the Nyon community appeased lingering concerns in the Admiralty that closer relations with France would risk dragging Britain into a Mediterranean war at a moment when the Royal Navy had only begun to rebuild its fleet. The Admiralty's concerns to keep the French at arm's length coincided with British public opinion that had applauded Nyon as a triumph of collective security to deal with an incident rather than a triumph of emerging Anglo-French solidarity. Even before the Nyon naval patrols got under way, the stage was being set for Chamberlain to renew his courtship with Mussolini.

Chapter 6

An Informal Naval Entente

The Nyon Arrangement marked only the beginning of the work to blunt fascist aggression in the Mediterranean. Returning to nearby Geneva, the nine Nyon powers quickly concluded a supplementary agreement governing collective measures to be undertaken against surface and aerial aggression. In addition, the Anglo-French naval staffs concluded an accord designed to coordinate their patrol operations in the Mediterranean. The Anglo-French Naval Staff Accord was key to the success of the Nyon Arrangement and to the conclusion of what amounted to an informal Anglo-French naval alliance at the operational level in the Mediterranean despite the Admiralty's misgivings about closer relations with France.

The other seven Nyon powers were not party to the Naval Staff Accord, nor was Italy. There remained, therefore, the task of organizing and launching the first Anglo-French naval and aerial operations, to be undertaken in accordance with the Naval Staff Accord. And finally, technical arrangements would have to be made to enter Italy into the Nyon patrol scheme in a way that would protect the cordial relations emerging among British and French naval officers and keep the Regia Marina isolated. Nyon was more than a challenge to fascist aggression in the Mediterranean. It also marked the opening of a productive era in Anglo-French naval relations at the level of planning and operations.

The Supplementary Agreement

From the beginning of the Nyon negotiations, London had insisted that the first round of discussions among the nine delegations be limited to the main threat, that of submarine aggression in the Mediterranean. The secondary question of aerial and surface aggression could be solved at another session. The nine delegations therefore departed Nyon and returned to Geneva, where the scheduled meeting of the League of Nations was just getting under way. Accordingly, the supplementary agreement was concluded at Geneva on September 17 with a swiftness equal to that of the initial accord.

The agreement, which entered into force immediately, authorized escort vessels in the Mediterranean to fire upon any aircraft attacking non-Spanish shipping, to resist any attack by surface vessels, and to summon assistance should that be necessary.[1] The agreement found special application in areas near the Strait of Sicily and in the western basin of the Mediterranean, where Italian and Spanish aircraft and destroyers had been visibly active. With no prior identification of the aggressor required, British and French warships were now free to offer swift resistance to any aggressor. The only identification required was that of the victim, whether or not it was Spanish. The agreement completed the legal process of according control of the Mediterranean to French and British naval power.

The Anglo-French Naval Staff Accord

In the meantime, the Anglo-French naval staffs meeting at Nyon on September 13 concluded an accord that lent substance to the Nyon Arrangement. Since the other seven states were not party to these negotiations, the Anglo-French Naval Staff Accord emerged as the main instrument whereby British and French warships exercised operational control of the Mediterranean traffic lanes. The accord divided the Mediterranean into five surveillance zones that matched the main trade routes in both the eastern and western basins, with the western basin receiving the higher level of protection. In addition, the accord provided for a measure of naval cooperation that exploited more fully the combined power of the two fleets. The accord was drafted by naval staff officers working under the authority of Admirals Jean François Darlan and Sir Ernle Chatfield.

Each of the five surveillance zones was anchored in a major French or British naval base. This arrangement took into account the operational range of the warships patrolling them in a manner to cover the main trading routes rather than the entire Mediterranean. There were two zones in the western basin. The British zone, anchored at Gibraltar, extended eastward to the Balearics and then south to Algiers to cover the main east–west traffic to and from the Strait of Gibraltar and the eastern coast of Spain. The French zone, anchored at Toulon and Marseilles, and also Algiers and Bizerte, covered north–south traffic between southern France and North Africa and traffic to the east of Algiers toward Sicily.[2]

In the eastern basin of the Mediterranean, British and French naval bases were not as well situated and not as numerous, so traffic off Greece and Turkey was not so easily covered. Malta, however, was admirably located to serve the British zone covering the Sicilian passage. The other British zone, covering the Aegean Sea north of the thirty-eighth parallel, was remote from the main British base at Alexandria. And a French zone, covering the remainder of the Aegean and the Ionian Sea off the western coast of Greece, was equally remote. Surveillance of these zones would depend heavily upon the use of Greek and Turkish harbors, which had been anticipated in the Nyon Arrangement.[3]

The zone scheme was not inflexible. British and French warships could cross into each other's zones in pursuit of an aggressor, and either navy could summon help from the other. In order to increase the level of protection, several of the main traffic arteries were modified in detail to match the patrol capabilities of the two navies. Although commercial shipping was not required to travel on the protected routes, these routes were recommended and given publicity. Nor was there any requirement for merchant ships to move in convoys. Given the heavy volume of traffic in the two basins and the shortage of destroyers, the scheme aimed at covering Mediterranean security needs selectively with a focus on the main shipping patterns.

The Naval Staff Accord contained provisions for Anglo-French naval cooperation and mutual assistance. French and British warships were authorized to put into each other's ports without prior notice, and the local naval command would offer full services to any visiting ship. For the most part this meant British ships entering French ports. Aircraft from either nation could fly over the other's territory without prior diplomatic authorization. Moreover, the accord brought British and French naval officers into consultation for the purpose of enforcing the terms of the Nyon Arrangement. Two admirals, one French and the other British, were assigned responsibility for operations, for keeping in close contact with each other, for exchanging information, for establishing guidelines for communications, and for simplifying the formalities of visitation and salutation. Each was to receive a liaison officer from the other service.[4] Vice-Admiral Jean-Pierre Esteva would command French operations, and Admiral Sir Dudley Pound, the British, both of them operating out of Oran, in North Africa, near the big French naval base at Mers el-Kébir.

The Nyon Arrangement and the Anglo-French Naval Staff Accord underscored what the French admiralty had understood for some time, that the British and French navies working together could dominate the Mediterranean and thereby influence European affairs from a position of strength. Although London was slow to arrive at that conclusion, Eden soon came around, writing Churchill on September 14 of his conviction that Anglo-French cooperation could be effective and "that the two Western democracies can still play a decisive part in European affairs."[5] Notwithstanding Eden's conceding a patrol zone to Italy, Nyon had upstaged Mussolini. It underscored the fact that Italy could not stand up to the combined might of the Royal Navy and the Marine Nationale and that the Mediterranean was the only place where the two western democracies could employ superior naval power in the service of diplomacy.

An Informal Anglo-French Naval Alliance

Having concluded the Naval Staff Accord at Nyon on September 13, the British and French staffs under Admirals Chatfield and René-Emile Godfroy met again, this time at Geneva on the afternoon of September 15. Their purpose was to seek agreement on operational details dealing mainly with attacks by surface ships and aircraft in the Mediterranean. These were vexing problems, for aggressor aircraft could not quickly be engaged by British or French aircraft, and aggressor surface ships might be more powerful than the destroyer patrol. They found no perfect solution to any of these problems, but the meeting was cordial and without important disagreement.[6] The work of patrolling the trade routes would therefore get under way with the British and French Mediterranean commands in step with each other.

Operating under what now amounted to an informal Anglo-French naval alliance in the Mediterranean, London and Paris quickly deployed there a strong offensive force. The Naval Staff Accord committed Britain to deploy thirty-five destroyers and France twenty-eight. On September 13, nine French destroyers prepared to depart Brest for Mediterranean duty.[7] By the twenty-fourth, British and French destroyers patrolling Mediterranean waters numbered close to fifty, about equally divided between the two navies. In addition, the Royal Navy deployed in supporting roles two battleships, three cruisers, and an aircraft carrier.[8] In the meantime, London and Paris had withdrawn their ships from their assignments under the Non-Intervention Committee.[9] With more than fifty warships on active patrol by the end of September, Britain and France had managed to combine their naval power in a manner to dominate the Mediterranean. On September 25, the German chargé d'affaires in Paris wired Berlin that "political and military cooperation in the Mediterranean, which Laval had avoided, has now become a fact."[10]

What now followed was a period of cordial Anglo-French naval relations in the Mediterranean at the command and operational levels. On September 18 Admirals Pound and Esteva met at Oran, and together they visited nearby Arzew. The visit was entirely cordial, with the French cooperating fully in support of British plans and operations. They arranged for British supply ships to be brought into Arzew to support the seaplanes soon to arrive there and for Oran to serve as the base for British destroyers operating in the western Mediterranean. Esteva informed Pound of French operational plans, which included numerous destroyer patrols with supporting aircraft based in both North Africa and France.[11] As a result of this meeting, Oran and Arzew quickly emerged as centers of British naval power in the Mediterranean. On that same day Esteva dispatched operational orders to all French Mediterranean commands, instructing them to lend every possible support to any British warship calling for assistance.[12]

The two navies easily cooperated with each other, exchanging information and codes, lending support to each other at sea and ashore, planning operations, attending to logistical problems, and exchanging social visits. In most of these activities, the British were the guests of the French, who provided the vitally needed ports to support British operations. French naval records indicate a continuous presence of British warships in French harbors during the months immediately following Nyon. British destroyers operated out of Oran, and a squadron of British seaplanes soon arrived at Arzew, where the battleship *Barham* and the aircraft carrier *Glorious* were regular visitors and where several hundred British support personnel were stationed. In early 1938 the battleship *Hood* visited Marseilles, as did dozens of other British warships in 1937 and early 1938.[13] Significantly, the British and the French navies were working as a team to patrol the Mediterranean, the British providing a little more than half of the naval assets and the French providing their share plus the bases essential to the needs of the Royal Navy.

In London the Admiralty moved swiftly to fulfill its responsibilities under the patrol scheme. By September 20, the date of the launching of the operation, there were eighteen destroyers and a destroyer leader operating out of Oran. They worked in two watches with nine destroyers always at sea. Additional destroyers would soon arrive from the Home Fleet so that there would be twenty-seven operating out of Oran and an additional five operating out of Malta.[14] From the beginning, the British were hard pressed to find enough destroyers to fulfill their commitments. What is more, their aerial support would have to await the transfer of float planes from the British Isles to Arzew. In contrast, the French easily shifted destroyers from the Bay of Biscay to the Mediterranean, and their aerial cover was in place from the start.[15] Despite the geographical problems facing the British, the two fleets were able to swiftly assemble a respectable force in the Mediterranean. But the patrol scheme would impose a heavier burden on the British than on the French, so the Admiralty would soon seek ways to reduce its commitment.

In the meantime, the British and French naval staffs made hurried preparations to receive the Italian naval staff for technical discussions in Paris to
open on September 27. The scheduling of this conference implied a revision of
the Nyon Arrangement and a symbolic role for the Italian navy in patrolling the
Mediterranean. But it did not envision an Italian entry into the Anglo-French
Naval Staff Accord.

The Italian Intrusion

Although the Anglo-French decision to permit Italy a role in the Mediterranean
patrol scheme obscured the brilliant diplomatic victory that Delbos and Eden
had won at Nyon, important sections of the British press applauded the decision. The London *Times* labeled it "a move forward," commenting that on the
whole "the balance of opinion is hopeful and much satisfaction is felt everywhere that matters should have taken this favourable turn before the departure
of Signor Mussolini for Germany."[16] That statement reflected the views of the
government. The French press took much the same position, hoping that the
meeting to include Italy in the Nyon Arrangement would ease tensions in the
Mediterranean.[17] In both countries the mainstream of public opinion seemed
willing to settle for an easing of Mediterranean tensions at the expense of any
larger objective of isolating Mussolini on the eve of his visit to Germany.

In London the Admiralty had supported all along the policy of Italian
participation in the Nyon scheme, thinking no doubt that Italian involvement would ease tensions in the Mediterranean and reduce the chances of
war breaking out there. The Admiralty was willing to recognize Italy's position
as a great Mediterranean power, but it would not accept Ciano's demand for
parity in the Mediterranean patrol.[18] The invitation to Rome, therefore, made
no mention of parity. In London's view, the Anglo-French-Italian conference
would be mainly a technical affair aimed at including Italian warships in the
Mediterranean patrol.[19]

The decision to revise the arrangement was, however, not popular among
the small Nyon allies in the eastern Mediterranean or with the Soviet Union.
The Greek government stoutly opposed any revisions that might permit Italian
warships to use Greek ports, insisting with London that "they were not prepared to give to Italy the same facilities which they gladly gave to the French
and British Navies."[20] Turkey and Yugoslavia adopted much the same attitude.
The Soviets objected on different grounds. Worried at the thought of sending their ships through an Italian zone, they insisted upon preserving a "red,
white, and blue" zone under Britain and France stretching the length of the
Mediterranean from the Black Sea to Spain.[21]

Clearly, the addition of Italy to the patrol scheme would pose delicate diplomatic problems. Delbos, therefore, proposed that a British officer be sent to Paris so that the French and British delegations might arrive at a common policy to deal with clashing Soviet and Italian expectations. Accordingly, Captain T. S. V. Phillips, director of plans for the Royal Navy, was sent to Paris in advance of the technical conference. Having managed British planning for the Nyon conference, Phillips was thoroughly familiar with the patrol scheme and the surveillance zones. London took care to conceal his mission from the press.[22]

Rushing on to Paris ahead of Vice-Admiral William James, head of the British delegation, Phillips discovered that Delbos had instructed the French delegation to support the Soviet proposal for an all Anglo-French trade route from the Black Sea to Spain. Phillips therefore accepted a French proposal to redraw the zones in a manner clearly intended to accommodate the Soviets without offending the Italians. By the terms of this arrangement, the British, French, and Italian zones would converge at Pantelleria, astride the main shipping route through the Malta Channel, which amounted to denying Italy any meaningful control of the important east–west trade route. Admiral James did not expect the Italian delegation to accept this arrangement.[23]

The Anglo-French-Italian naval staff conference opened in Paris at the Ministry of Marine on the Rue Royale on Monday afternoon, September 27. Hosted by the French delegation under Rear-Admiral Robert Godfroy, the initial session was surprisingly cordial. When the Italian delegation, headed by Admiral Wladimiro Pini, learned of the Anglo-French proposals, it offered no important objections. Pini suggested, however, that Italy be given control of one of the exits from the Mediterranean and a larger zone in the western basin. Admirals James and Godfroy, having no important objections, proposed an Italian zone anchored at Tobruk to stretch from Crete to Port Said at Suez, and another stretching in triangular fashion from Sardinia to the Balearics. No final agreement was reached, as the Italians requested time to study the proposals prior to the meeting scheduled for the next day. James wired the Admiralty that "we can only hope that they will not materially change their minds before then."[24]

James was to be disappointed. When the conference resumed on Tuesday morning, Pini upped the Italian demands in accordance with instructions from Mussolini. Now he insisted upon control of two portions of the main east–west trade route, one stretching a hundred miles in the Malta Channel and another in the Aegean Sea coinciding approximately with the French zone in that area. In addition, Pini demanded a larger zone west of Sardinia. But he was willing to settle for a diminished Aegean zone should Italy receive the more important concession in the Malta Channel. James thought the Italian demands to be reasonable. "The way out now," he wired London, "is to put pressure on the Russians to accept Italian proposal in Malta Channel Area. Russians in any case are receiving protection for their shipping and contributing nothing."[25]

The British delegation therefore leaned toward appeasing the Italians, rather than the Soviets, as did the French minister of marine, César Campinchi. That same evening, in the presence of Admiral James and British ambassador Sir Eric Phipps, French Prime Minister Camille Chautemps informed Delbos by telephone of the British position and gained approval of it. Accordingly, the French delegation would lend support the next day to the British proposal to redraw the zones in a manner to accord Italy control of a key section of the Malta Channel.[26] The stage had been set to hand Mussolini a modest diplomatic victory just as he departed for Germany.[27]

When the staff conference resumed Wednesday morning, the Italian delegation remained adamant in its most important demands. The Anglo-French delegations, unwilling to push the Italians too hard, concluded with Pini a generous agreement extending the Italian zone in the western basin from Sardinia to a point at the Balearics. Italy was also awarded a zone off the northwestern coast of Greece, but Italian warships would not use Greek ports. That zone was connected to another that extended in a point to Port Said and curled back to the coast of Libya. More importantly, Italy received a hundred miles of the trade route through the Malta Channel.[28] In his report to London early that afternoon, Phipps observed that any incident there would point either to Italian incompetency or breach of faith.[29]

The negotiations, however, had not come to an end. That afternoon, before the final documents had been signed, Delbos informed the British delegation that the Soviets now insisted upon an all Anglo-French trade route from the Black Sea to Port Said. That information came as an unpleasant surprise, for the agreement just concluded had awarded Italy control of a portion of that route. Later that day Godfroy and James tried dutifully to persuade Pini to accept a modification of the eastern zones. Predictably, Pini refused to budge, with the result that the eastern zones remained unchanged when the three delegations signed the final document the next day.[30]

Throughout the four days of the conference, the British and French delegations had caved in to the key Italian demands, handing Mussolini what amounted to a propaganda victory. On the other hand, the British and French naval delegations had stood together throughout the conference, which was more important than the details of the agreement. "After our conversations with Monsieur Chautemps last night," Phipps noted in his Wednesday report to London, "the French delegates showed themselves extremely conciliatory and the plan agreed upon follows the lines approved by the Admiralty yesterday."[31] At every step along the way the French delegation had followed the British lead. Despite the tactical victory Italy had won, Pini could not have missed the point that the British and French navies had stood together throughout the conference.

Anglo-French Naval Cooperation at Sea

The Paris agreement was scheduled to come into effect upon the signatures of the three contracting powers, but having gotten his way in Paris, Mussolini now had no reason to patrol any of his zones. Nevertheless, the French and British naval staffs moved forward to modify patrol operations in accordance with the agreement. Esteva and Pound received instructions from their respective admiralties, and preparations got under way for them to meet with an Italian admiral somewhere in the Mediterranean.[32] These arrangements moved slowly, however, so the meeting of the three admirals did not take place until late October.

Nevertheless, Pound and Esteva met on October 2 at Oran, where they discussed Italian participation in the patrol scheme. They readily agreed that exchange of liaison officers with the Italian navy would not be necessary or desirable and that simple codes or messages sent in clear would suffice for communications with Italian ships. Esteva made it clear that the French wished to have the least possible contact with the Italian navy and that they especially opposed the entry of Italian warships into French ports.[33] Pound, understanding the importance of French ports for British operations, had no interest in according to the Italians what the French had so generously conceded to the Royal Navy. It seems clear that the British and French Mediterranean commands wished to protect the special relationship emerging between the two navies and to keep the Regia Marina at arm's length.

The conference between the three Mediterranean commands finally took place on October 30 on board the British battleship *Barham* anchored off Bizerte, where Pound and Esteva received Italian admiral Romeo Bernotti. The Italian admiral could not have missed the point implicit in the scene, that a British battleship in a French port underscored the fact of Anglo-French solidarity in the Mediterranean at Italian expense. Perhaps for that reason, the meeting was without serious disagreements. The three admirals adopted what amounted to the agenda Pound and Esteva had agreed upon earlier at Oran. Bernotti made no demand for an exchange of liaison officers, nor did he request permission to enter Italian warships into French harbors. They ironed out certain operational details, among them the entry of thirty-six Italian warships and five squadrons of float planes to patrol the Italian zones beginning November 10.[34]

The meeting of the three admirals served only to amplify the special relationship that had been cultivated between the Royal Navy and the Marine Nationale. Whereas the Italian navy would relate to the British and French navies under the terms of the Paris agreement and the local arrangements just concluded, the British and French navies would continue to operate together under the confidential terms of the Anglo-French Naval Staff Accord concluded in the wake of the Nyon Arrangement.[35] The Italian navy remained isolated, excluded from the informal Mediterranean alliance that British and French diplomats and staff officers had forged at Nyon.

In the meantime, British and French destroyers continued to patrol the Mediterranean trade routes. But despite Anglo-French naval solidarity, Mussolini went ahead with his plans to authorize four of his submarines to remain under Spanish command. The Italian naval command, however, had no zeal to resume submarine piracy, which had been suspended in early September.[36] There were nevertheless good reasons for London and Paris to persist with the patrols. Mussolini might be tempted at any time to unleash his submarines again, and the Italian naval command could not easily restrain the four submarines sent to Franco.

Despite the apparent calm, the situation in the Mediterranean remained tense. There followed a number of disturbing incidents, among them a torpedo attack on the British destroyer *Basilisk*. Operating between Spain and Palma, the crew of the *Basilisk* was summoned to stations on October 4, when the ship's sonar device revealed what appeared to be a submarine. Minutes later crewmen reported a torpedo passing near the ship. The Second Destroyer Flotilla, summoned to the scene, launched a heavy depth charge attack, which produced no results. Although the incident was later written off as a false alarm, Pound in the meantime pressured the Spanish admiral at Palma to rein in his submarines. Pound would not attack them as long as they remained in place and caused no trouble; otherwise, he would destroy them with all the power at his disposal. For whatever reasons, there were no further submarine attacks recorded during the remainder of 1937. At the same time, Berlin prudently withdrew German submarines from the Mediterranean, no doubt in deference to the Anglo-French Mediterranean patrol.[37]

British Patrol Fatigue

The French naval command, enjoying a geographical advantage, was able to maintain regular patrol operations without undue wear to ships or stress to crews. But by early October the British had begun to feel the burden of sustained antisubmarine patrol, especially in Zone A north of Oran. Two destroyer flotillas had been transferred from home waters to the Mediterranean at the expense of the Home Fleet. There still were not enough destroyers to fulfill all of the British patrol commitments in the Mediterranean, however, so Pound took the risky step of reducing the patrol units from three ships to two. This redistribution of assets enabled him to maintain patrols with fewer destroyers. Nevertheless, British assets in the Mediterranean remained thin. There were, for example, no destroyers or British aircraft nearby when insurgent aircraft attacked the British merchant ship *Cervantes* in early October near the coast of Spain. There were no damages to the ship, but London could do nothing more than file an unofficial protest with the Franco government.[38]

British patrol operations also suffered under the burden of uncertain air support. British naval aviation had always lagged behind its full potential while it remained under the control of the Royal Air Force. Therefore, float planes covering the patrols operated under the Air Ministry, rather than the navy, and aircraft and aviation personnel sent to Arzew and Malta had to be transferred to naval command.[39] The float planes, moreover, operated far from their home bases, receiving essential supplies from the depot ship *Cyclops* anchored at Arzew. Not surprisingly, the aircraft soon began to suffer from mechanical fatigue, which limited their effectiveness in sustained search and support operations.

In contrast, French operations in the key zones enjoyed sustained air support from the beginning. Admiral Esteva had under his command, in addition to six divisions of destroyers, the seaplane carrier *Commandant-Teste* with its two squadrons of scouting and bombing seaplanes. He also commanded six large naval flying boats and several scouting seaplanes.[40] These aircraft had always operated out of French bases and under French naval command, so that Esteva escaped the bureaucratic and logistical problems that burdened Pound from the beginning of the patrols.

Esteva continued to maintain cordial relations with Pound, meeting with him frequently on HMS *Woolwich*, the British command ship anchored at Oran, and later on the *Cyclops*, at Arzew. At these meetings Esteva received the details of British patrol operations and their results. Pound kept him informed of British logistical problems and attendant plans to scale down operations. British and French naval officers grew accustomed to working together, and they sometimes exchanged social visits. Toward the end of November, just before the withdrawal of the *Woolwich*, more than a dozen British and French officers assembled on board the ship to share a hearty meal and to drink toasts in celebration of the cordial relations they had enjoyed since the conclusion of the Nyon Arrangement.[41]

By the middle of November the British naval and air patrols were becoming increasingly routine, without significant incidents, so Pound and air command at Arzew steadily reduced their frequency. Reconnaissance Wing No. 1 had been sent to the region for a term of six weeks, to be extended for another six weeks, which pushed the wing to the limits of its endurance. A prolonged stay would require considerably greater logistical support and new engines for the aircraft. Therefore, on November 15 Air Command inquired of the Admiralty as to when the wing might be withdrawn.[42]

The very next day Phillips raised with the Admiralty the question of when the patrols might be discontinued, with a small naval force remaining on the scene should the piracy be resumed. He suggested a target date of December 10 for the withdrawal of the naval patrols. But he noted that the air patrols, once withdrawn, could not be reestablished as quickly as the naval patrols, so at least one wing should remain in readiness should the patrols have to be resumed.[43] A week later Air Ministry made it clear that aircraft engines could not be maintained much longer at Arzew and that the unit would soon have to return to Britain for engine replacement and overhaul.[44]

Finally, after prolonged negotiations between the Admiralty and Air Ministry and in consultation with the Foreign Office, the decision was made in December to reduce to a minimum the level of the patrols. One air unit would be held in readiness to return to the Mediterranean should the piracy be resumed. Paris, while offering no objection, noted that French patrols would continue without important reduction.[45] The Italian government was not consulted in advance of the decision to reduce the patrols, but Pound informed Admiral Bernotti of it by telegram on January 2.[46] Accordingly, British patrols were reduced substantially and the air wings withdrawn in early January, with a squadron remaining in readiness at Arzew and another at Malta.

The Violence Renewed

The decision to scale down the patrols and Italian knowledge of it anticipated the violence that soon flared anew in the western Mediterranean in early 1938. On January 31 the British collier *Endymion* was torpedoed and sunk in the British zone off Cartagena by an unidentified submarine. Eleven crewmen were lost.[47] The *Endymion* was sailing on one of the recommended trade routes, unprotected since the reduction of the patrols. There were therefore no British warships in the area to attack or identify the aggressor submarine, which was thought to be Spanish rather than Italian.

Then, four days later, on February 4, Nationalist aircraft from Palma bombed and sank the British merchant ship *Alcira*. By this time seven destroyers had already departed Gibraltar to begin the process of restoring British naval power in Zone A. They were soon joined by the cruiser *Newcastle*, which departed Marseilles on February 2 to arrive off Palma on the seventh. At the same time four French destroyers were moved from southern France to waters off Barcelona, adding importantly to patrol operations in the French zone north and west of Palma.[48] These movements marked only the beginning of the restoration of British and French naval power in the two critical zones close to Spain. Other naval and air units would soon follow, until patrol operations in these zones were fully restored. The Anglo-French operational entente therefore continued into 1938.

Angered at the new aggression, London promptly dispatched a stern note to Franco, warning him that any submerged submarines found in the British zone outside Spanish territorial waters would be attacked and destroyed. Pound received more detailed orders, instructing him to destroy any submerged submarine and demand the surrender of any submarine found on the surface. Should the submarine refuse to surrender or should it attempt to submerge, it should be attacked and destroyed. Paris adopted these same measures so that any submerged submarine discovered anywhere in the Mediterranean would be attacked and destroyed.[49] Rome followed suit—not, however, in the interest of Mediterranean security but to head off any violent incident that might sidetrack high-level Anglo-Italian negotiations scheduled for early April.

Not surprisingly, therefore, the pirate attacks on Mediterranean shipping ended just as suddenly as they had begun. British naval power in Zone A was brought up to full strength, and regular patrols were continued. In March the patrols were increased to the maximum to prevent any incident that might disturb the Anglo-Italian diplomatic negotiations soon to get under way. In May, however, the patrols were again scaled down, mainly because there were not enough destroyers to maintain the patrols but also because the negotiations with Italy had finally been concluded.[50]

The End of the Nyon Arrangement

At the end of May the Admiralty notified Pound that the Foreign Office was approaching the Nyon powers with the view of discontinuing the patrols altogether. In June, however, the British merchant ship *Stanray* was attacked and damaged by unidentified aircraft, and another, the *African Trader*, was harassed by a Spanish warship. These incidents caused the Foreign Office to have second thoughts about ending the patrols, as did the Board of Trade, which stoutly insisted on maintaining British naval control of the shipping lanes. On June 24, therefore, the Admiralty informed Pound that the patrols would have to be continued at their present strength.[51]

During the spring and summer of 1938 the Mediterranean shipping routes remained relatively secure, with no important incidents reported. The Admiralty therefore began to think again in terms of reducing the patrol to a token force, or of ending them altogether. There remained an acute shortage of destroyers. With tensions emerging in eastern Europe, there was now little prospect of reinforcing the Mediterranean fleet with destroyers from the Home Fleet, and Air Ministry was anxious to withdraw its support altogether. But the Board of Trade refused to back off, insisting that the long absence of incidents argued for the efficiency of the Nyon patrols rather than their abandonment.[52]

That view was on target, for the success of the patrols was more a product of their threat to pirate submarines than to their actually attacking them, which in fact rarely occurred. The Nyon Arrangement therefore remained in effect, but as the Spanish Civil War wound down in late 1938 the patrols were ended altogether in the eastern Mediterranean and reduced to a bare minimum in the western basin. Finally, on April 6, 1939, after the Spanish conflict had ended, London notified Rome, Moscow, and the other concerned powers of British withdrawal from the Nyon Arrangement.[53] By this time Anglo-French naval planning for the war looming on the horizon had already gotten under way.

The Naval Lessons of Nyon

In many respects the naval operations attendant to the Nyon Arrangement anticipated the kind of war that the Royal Navy would have to fight at sea during the early years of World War II. The Nyon operations required the deployment of a very large number of destroyers to protect Mediterranean shipping lanes from only a handful of hostile submarines, surface ships, and aircraft. Italian and Spanish submarines prowling the Mediterranean in August of 1937 numbered perhaps half a dozen. But it required more than fifty British and French destroyers, supported by aircraft and larger ships, to defend the shipping lanes against them. This disproportionate ratio of offensive and defensive assets reflected important technological changes in naval warfare, now shifting from major surface actions to operations under the sea and above it as well.

The Nyon crisis reflected this shift in the patterns of naval warfare, clearly demonstrating the need for substantially more destroyers to counter the undersea threat. But British naval planners, preoccupied with fleet actions in the tradition of the Battle of Jutland and fearful of the emerging threat of Japanese naval power, rebuilt the fleet with balance toward the construction of heavy ships at the expense of destroyers. The Royal Navy therefore entered World War II still burdened with an acute shortage of destroyers. Despite the experiences of Nyon, the fleet of 1939 remained ill equipped to deal effectively with the closest and most urgent threat to British security, the German U-boat.

Anglo-French naval cooperation in the Mediterranean also thrust upon Paris and London the option of transforming the informal Nyon entente into a formal alliance, to match the emerging Axis alliance. Paris was ready to take that step. The burden of decision therefore rested with London, whose perspective on European and Mediterranean affairs did not coincide with that in Paris. The question in early 1938 was whether the Chamberlain government, with the Admiralty's support, would rebuild its foreign policy upon a new solidarity with France, or would it instead renew its courtship with Mussolini at the expense of the Nyon entente.

Chapter 7

From Nyon to Munich

The informal Mediterranean entente forged by the Nyon Arrangement meant one thing to the French and another to the English. In France it was widely applauded as the foundation of what might become a closer Anglo-French association, perhaps even an alliance, against the European Axis. In Britain, though, only Foreign Secretary Anthony Eden and a few others leaned in that direction. For the most part, London regarded Nyon as nothing more than a successful application of the principle of collective security in addressing a particular problem, that of piracy in the Mediterranean. That view was less risky than its alternative, which was to build upon the Nyon entente in a manner to amplify a common Anglo-French voice in international affairs.

Looming on the horizon in early 1938 was the German threat to Austria, where Hitler held the highest cards. Neither British nor French military capabilities extended into eastern Europe. At the same time the civil war dragged on in Spain, where Italian troops and equipment continued to benefit Franco. The Sino-Japanese war grew more threatening in Asia, but British and French military capabilities did not extend much beyond the Mediterranean. Their most flexible asset was sea power, but the Royal Navy was stretched thin in Asia as was the Marine Nationale. And sea power was largely irrelevant to the problem of German ambitions in eastern Europe. Given the realities of the international scene, the options in London were to isolate Mussolini with the threat of combined Anglo-French naval power in the Mediterranean or to flatter him with appeasement at the expense of closer relations with Paris.

The Need for Anglo-French Naval Cooperation

Swift Axis rearmament and the shifting balance of world naval power in 1936 and 1937 underscored the urgent need for Anglo-French naval cooperation. Although British and French naval power was stretched thin around the globe in 1937, the Royal Navy and the French fleet acting in concert could dominate the Mediterranean and defend selected Atlantic waters in fleet actions against either of the European Axis powers. Italy, with her fleet bottled up in the Mediterranean, and with Libya hanging like fruit to be picked, was vulnerable to combined Anglo-French naval power as Nyon had demonstrated. It seems clear that the Mediterranean was the area in which combined naval power was best suited to serve British and French diplomacy.

The stage was therefore set for London and Paris to exploit their advantage over Italy, the weakest of the Axis powers, and to focus their attention on the area where their diplomacy would enjoy the support of massive coercive power. The option that best matched their military and naval strength was to build upon the Nyon entente, bring their service staffs together for planning, avoid negotiations with either of the dictators, and maintain a strong naval presence in the Mediterranean. Winston Churchill understood the value of the Nyon entente. "Mussolini," he wrote to Eden on September 20, "only understands superior force, such as he is now confronted with in the Mediterranean." Italy, he added, "cannot resist an effective Anglo-French combination." Eden answered that eighty British and French destroyers patrolling the Mediterranean "has made a profound impression on opinion in Europe."[1]

Paris had felt the need for an Anglo-French alliance long before the Nyon crisis brought the two naval powers together in the Mediterranean, but the swiftly changing international scene in the mid-1930s led French naval strategists to underscore that need more than did their British opposites. A French parliamentary report of January 27, 1937, noting the weakness of the long-neglected Royal Navy, pointed to the urgent British need of French naval support.[2] At that moment British shipping routes remained vulnerable to the three German pocket battleships, whose speed and firepower were outmatched only by the five British and French battlecruisers. Should an Anglo-German war have broken out at that time, the *Dunkerque* and her sister ship, *Strasbourg*, soon to be commissioned, could lend important support to the *Hood*, *Repulse*, and *Renown* to the end of protecting the strategic advantage until the completion of the British naval construction program.

Another French report, originating in Admiral Darlan's headquarters and dated November 12, 1937, underscored the emerging threat of the three Axis powers to emphasize the need for a formal British alliance. Complaining about the episodic and untimely nature of Anglo-French military consultation, it insisted that the only way to organize any effective resistance to the Axis menace lay within the framework of a solid Anglo-French alliance under which the two states would relate to each other as allies.[3]

A different version of this theme was advanced in an article by the French general de Cuynac, published in a popular French journal that same month. Admitting that British and French perspectives on the problem of German intentions in eastern Europe were different, de Cuynac noted that Anglo-French interests ran parallel in the Far East and coincided exactly in the Mediterranean, where Italian ambitions threatened French and British security. He insisted that London and Paris must quickly close ranks, display solidarity, and bargain astutely to protect their common interests around the globe.[4]

In 1938 sentiment for a formal Anglo-French alliance continued to run strong in the French navy. An early 1938 document found in the personal files of Admiral Darlan reveals his growing concern about the emerging threat of the German navy, whose best ships had been carefully designed to prowl the vast expanse of ocean and prey upon French and British shipping. Darlan understood that the Kriegsmarine did not require tonnage equality with Britain and France to wage that kind of warfare, for only a few fast raiders at sea would require many times their number to hunt them down. It was a fundamental point that only one of the German pocket battleships prowling the Atlantic would demand the commitment of massive Anglo-French naval assets to protect the shipping lanes. To Darlan, the obvious solution was an Anglo-French alliance and the application of combined naval power to protect the shipping routes.[5]

Clearly, French naval opinion—and French public opinion as well—ran swift and deep in favor of Anglo-French solidarity and a formal alliance between the two democratic powers. In contrast, British opinion remained largely isolationist. And key British statesmen continued to think in terms of a Mediterranean settlement with Mussolini at the expense of a common Anglo-French diplomatic front based on naval power.

British Misgivings

With nearly a hundred British and French warships poised for action in the Mediterranean in November of 1937, the time had come when London and Paris might consider whether they could build further upon the Nyon entente. But in the view of the Admiralty, the weakness of the Royal Navy on the global scene demanded that at least one of the Axis powers be neutralized by diplomacy. Of the three Axis powers, Italy was the weakest and the one more likely to respond to diplomacy. It was therefore tempting for London to consider an independent policy, one that would forfeit the high trumps Eden and Yvon Delbos had won at Nyon and substitute for them a safer Anglo-Italian agreement to ensure Mediterranean stability. This view found support in the Admiralty, still worried that the French connection risked dragging the Royal Navy into an Italian war in waters vital to communications between Gibraltar and Singapore.

There were other reasons for keeping Paris at arm's length. Prime Minister Neville Chamberlain saw no need to close ranks with France, whose alliance with Czechoslovakia would risk dragging Britain into an unwinnable continental war. British public opinion remained opposed to any military commitment beyond the Rhineland provisions of the Locarno treaty, and no one wanted a repetition of the horrid bloodbath of 1914–18. British military strategists could easily see that the French alliance with Czechoslovakia was inconsistent with French military capabilities, which did not extend into eastern Europe. Moreover, British conservative leaders had no confidence in France's cozy relations with the Soviets. London therefore viewed French commitments in eastern Europe as more dangerous than useful. They cramped both British and French options and imposed a heavy burden on any efforts to build upon the Nyon entente.

In 1934 the main threat to German designs on Austria had been Italian military power. Although Hitler and Mussolini had closed ranks in 1936, London remained under the illusion that Rome might still be inclined to restrain German ambitions in Austria. In London the question was how to influence Mussolini in that direction and how at the same time to restrain him in Spain. Would London and Paris stand together to coerce Rome with the presence of combined Anglo-French naval power? Or would London instead back away from the Nyon entente and flirt with both Hitler and Mussolini in the hope of restraining them? Another option was to avoid negotiations with either of the dictators and consider with Paris whether the alliance with Czechoslovakia was worth its risks. In any event, neither London nor Paris had any vital interest in Austria, which lay directly in the shadow of the Reich and beyond French and British military capabilities.

Divisions in London

Notwithstanding his success at Nyon, Eden found himself increasingly isolated among government circles in London. He had no confidence in any further conversations with Mussolini, and he rightfully assumed Britain to be too weak to enter into conversations with Berlin about eastern Europe. At the same time, he favored closer relations with France, the opening of Anglo-French-Belgian military staff conversations, and swift military rearmament to lend London a stronger diplomatic voice in Europe.[6] Eden's perspective assumed that diplomacy in the absence of power had but limited value.

In contrast, Chamberlain stood eager to open conversations with both of the Axis dictators, one who he could easily threaten with naval power and the other whose military assets lay entirely beyond the reach of British naval and military capabilities. He appears to have made little distinction between the two diplomatic arenas. But he could easily see that bilateral negotiations with either of the Axis powers would be undertaken at the expense of Anglo-French solidarity. Nevertheless, Chamberlain was determined to push ahead with negotiations with Italy as well as with Germany, whose dominant military position in eastern Europe rendered irrelevant and presumptuous any British diplomatic initiative there.

His opportunity came in October 1937, when Hermann Göring invited Lord Halifax to be his guest at a sporting event. Chamberlain approved the visit, so Halifax rushed off to Germany in mid-November with the intent of wangling an interview with Hitler. Hitler, however, made clear to Halifax his opposition to any formal conversations with London. This meant that Berlin intended to call the signals in eastern Europe and that London ought to stand aside. Chamberlain, missing the point, clung to his hopes of negotiating with Berlin. The Halifax visit embarrassed Eden, weakened him in his role as foreign secretary, and undermined his French policy.[7]

Eden also found himself at odds with the British military chiefs. In early 1938 he circulated a Foreign Office paper recommending the opening of military and naval staff conversations with France and Belgium. He considered staff conversations to be vital to hasten the delivery of an expeditionary force to the continent should the Reich violate French or Belgian frontiers and to arrange for the French fleet to cover the Mediterranean if British warships were needed in Asia. According to Eden's memoirs, Chamberlain supported the proposal, but the chiefs of staff opposed it on the grounds of its being provocative to the Reich.[8]

The records of the Cabinet reveal, however, that Chamberlain had met earlier with the chiefs, agreeing with them that military staff consultations were not necessary and that a simple exchange of information at lower levels would suffice. Naval staff conversations would also be unnecessary, they agreed, since the cooperation of the French fleet could be arranged quickly in the event of a crisis with Japan.[9] These records reveal clearly that the Admiralty supported Chamberlain rather than Eden and that the Admiralty saw no reason to enter into consultations with France.

Eden and Chamberlain obviously differed on the value of the Nyon entente. Despite the notable Anglo-French naval success in the Mediterranean,

Chamberlain regarded the entire Nyon affair with misgivings. "We had a great success at Nyon," he wrote his sister, "but at the expense of Anglo-Italian relations." The Italians, he continued, refused to attend "and now with intense chagrin they see collaboration between the British and French fleets, of a kind never known before. . . . It would be amusing, if it were not also so dangerous."[10]

Chamberlain's comments reflect the widespread concerns in the Admiralty that the Nyon patrols risked dragging the Royal Navy into an Italian war. Unlike the Rue Royale, which viewed Italy as a potential enemy to be restrained by the threat of naval power, the Admiralty continued to expect the Foreign Office to neutralize Italy by diplomacy. Whereas the Rue Royale had few misgivings about fighting a Mediterranean war against Italy, the Admiralty preferred a peaceful Mediterranean to the end of keeping open naval communications between Gibraltar and Singapore. The Admiralty reasoned that a war in the Mediterranean might easily unleash Japanese aggression against British possessions in Asia. This being the case, Chamberlain's policy of appeasement to restore normal Anglo-Italian relations meshed neatly with strategic thinking in the Admiralty, which was worried that the French connection was more a burden than an asset in terms of British weakness in the balance of global naval power.

Chamberlain therefore discounted the diplomatic potential inherent in the Nyon entente. Instead of exploiting it, he awaited his chance to reopen negotiations with Rome. In early 1938 London knew that Mussolini had recently sent 10,000 additional Italian troops to Spain and that more were on the way.[11] Nevertheless, Chamberlain pressed Eden to open negotiations with Mussolini. Chamberlain and his foreign minister were clearly out of step with each other on Italian policy, and in February Eden resigned his office and was succeeded by Halifax. Chamberlain was now free to pursue his policy of appeasing Mussolini instead of restraining him with the threat of combined Anglo-French naval power.

Eden's departure anticipated the Anglo-Italian Accords of April 16, 1938, a benign agreement negotiated at the expense of the Nyon entente. The terms of the so-called Easter Accords are hardly noteworthy since they dealt mainly with peripheral issues and failed to solve the basic problem of Italian intervention in Spain. The accords, moreover, would not come into effect until Mussolini had begun the withdrawal of Italian volunteers. This provision amounted to tacit recognition of the volunteers because they remained in Spain under the agreement as long as Rome paid the price of deferring the benefits of the accords into the future when the volunteers would be withdrawn.[12] The accords eased Admiralty fears of being dragged into a naval war with Italy, but they also isolated France and frittered away any chance London and Paris might have had in the spring of 1938 to speak with a single voice.

French Naval Planning

With Chamberlain and the Admiralty keeping the French at arm's length, the Rue Royale had little choice but to move forward with its own naval planning. Admiral Darlan succeeded to the top French naval command at the beginning of 1937, at the moment when the global naval balance was beginning to shift decisively against the two European democracies. Since France could not count on the support of the Royal Navy, Darlan faced formidable planning problems. With French naval power badly overextended in 1937, he knew that France could not wage a successful naval war against all three Axis powers, nor uniquely against Japan. But it might be possible to mount successful operations against either Germany or Italy or perhaps against both of them. He therefore focused his attention on the role of the French navy in a war against Germany and Italy. Given the overextension of the French fleet, Darlan wrote off the French Empire in Asia as indefensible. This was the only realistic option, for Japanese naval power in Asia far exceeded the token French forces based at Hanoi.

Darlan therefore focused his attention on plans to serve French logistical needs in the event of a European war. His plan rested upon the prudent assumption that the main role of the navy would be to protect communications with French Africa, from which large manpower and other resources would have to be imported to sustain the military effort against Germany. He knew Italy to be capable of mounting surface and submarine operations against French shipping in the western Mediterranean. At that moment the German threat consisted mainly of fast surface raiders capable of attacking French shipping from West Africa and from more remote parts of the empire. In that case Darlan would have to divide his assets between two fronts against two widely separated enemies who could not however easily combine their naval power on either front. France held the geographical advantage of being able to shift fleet units easily between Mediterranean and the Atlantic waters as circumstances might demand.

Darlan could not, however, know in advance whether he would have to fight Germany, Italy, or the two simultaneously or whether he could count on the intervention of the Royal Navy at the outset. He subsequently assumed that Germany would be the first enemy and that Italy and Great Britain would remain neutral at the beginning of hostilities. Given that assumption, he concluded that French plans would have to be flexible, capable of swift adaptation in the event of British intervention at a later date.[13] His plan therefore assumed that the configuration of the war might easily change at any time after its outbreak.

These plans assumed that the initial German naval attacks would be directed against French maritime traffic off the coasts of West Africa and Morocco and would be conducted by fast surface raiders capable of striking French convoys and swiftly disappearing into the vast ocean expanses where supply ships lay in wait to nourish them. Should Italy enter the war at the outset, Darlan expected attacks against North Africa and against French communications across the Mediterranean. The Italian attacks, conducted by light surface craft, submarines, and perhaps aircraft, would threaten the vital traffic of reinforcements and supplies from North Africa to the military front in France.[14]

Since France's Atlantic ports were well suited to serve the interior, Darlan took special care to protect communications in the Bay of Biscay. Should Germany be the sole enemy, he would assign secondary units to protect the Mediterranean traffic lanes and the Strait of Gibraltar. His powerful High Seas Force, composed of France's newest and fastest ships, the *Dunkerque* and *Strasbourg*, would be stationed in Atlantic ports to blunt any German threat from the North Sea. In the event Italy entered the war, the Mediterranean squadron would be strengthened moderately with light ships to guard what would now become a lower volume of traffic in that area. He would keep his High Seas Force in the Atlantic to attack any German commerce raiders daring to prey upon French convoys. Expecting the enemy to be situated at the outset to attack French troop convoys, Darlan assigned highest priority to their protection. Units of the High Seas Force would provide escort. Should Italy remain neutral, French convoys would be routed through Gibraltar to ports in southern France.[15]

The plan called for all communications to be centered in Paris under Darlan, who would direct the scattered fleet units to prearranged locations. He would keep a tight grip on the High Seas Force. Reporting to Darlan would be two new commands, Commander-in-Chief South and Commander-in-Chief North, operating respectively out of Oran and Dunkirk. All other commands would remain unchanged, reporting directly to Darlan. Their forces and missions would vary according to whether France or Germany would enjoy the support of an ally. In the event of hostilities against Italy, or should Britain enter on the French side, important French assets would be shifted to the Mediterranean.[16]

Conservative and defensive, the plan aimed at protecting French shipping as opposed to seeking out the enemy for a decisive fleet action. The plan, however, suffered from a shortage of assets. Of necessity, it concentrated French naval power in Mediterranean and Atlantic waters north of Dakar. Scarcely anything was left for operations beyond Dakar, which is why he wrote off the Asian empire as indefensible.

An important staff study of November 1937 confirmed the point that the French navy was overextended, incapable of fulfilling its global mission. The study underscored the imperative of an Anglo-French alliance, but even that would not be enough, it continued, for London had waited too long to begin the reconstruction of the Royal Navy. Consequently, Germany and Japan would control vast expanses of ocean beyond the reach of combined Anglo-French naval power. With the British construction program just beginning, the study noted, the Royal Navy was stretched too thin to confront the German and Japanese fleets and simultaneously protect Anglo-French maritime communications stretching around the globe.[17]

Given the weakness of the French navy, which could not operate effectively beyond Dakar, Paris would have to concede to the Royal Navy the burden of protecting the remote parts of the empire. France could not defend Indochina. The best hope was that Japan would remain neutral, in which case combined Anglo-French naval power might be employed effectively in a European war against Germany and Italy. With the *Dunkerque* in service and the *Strasbourg* ready in 1938, the Marine Nationale was poised to lend important support to the Royal Navy, whose *Hood*, *Renown*, and *Repulse* were well suited to operate with the two French battlecruisers.

British Naval Rearmament

In 1937, when British rearmament finally got under way, there were acute shortages in every defense category—aviation, military, and naval. London therefore faced the vexing problem of massive rearmament under the burden of limited resources, with the added problem of finding a happy balance among the armed services. The defense of the homeland against air attack would assume highest priority, followed by naval rearmament to ensure the defense of the empire and of the traffic lanes connecting it with the British Isles. Military rearmament lagged behind that of the other two services. As for naval rearmament, the realignment of world naval power during 1936 and 1937 imposed a heavy burden, rendering British possessions in the Far East nearly as defenseless as the remote French colonies. The Royal Navy, however, was considerably larger than the French fleet, and the big naval base at Singapore could service important naval assets. So the Admiralty, unlike the Rue Royale, refused to write off the defense of Asia. The Admiralty therefore undertook the rebuilding of the Royal Navy with a global perspective that included a Japanese threat as opposed to the French view focused narrowly on Germany and Italy.

Crucial to British naval rearmament after 1936 was the question of the proper mix of vessel types to address the global balance of naval power. The most immediate threat was that of the German surface raiders, designed to prey upon merchant shipping vital to the life of the United Kingdom. By 1937 all three German pocket battleships—the *Deutschland*, *Admiral Scheer*, and *Graf Spee*—had long since been commissioned, and two other powerful raiders, the *Scharnhorst* and *Gneisenau*, had been launched but not yet commissioned.[18] To match them, the British would have to build cruisers and other heavy ships at the expense of destroyer construction. They would also have to be built in greater numbers since even one raider at sea would require multiple assets to hunt it down. Consequently, British naval rearmament would have to include construction of a prudent mix of battleships, cruisers, and aircraft carriers capable of chasing down and destroying the fast German commerce raiders.

At the same time the emerging threat of Japan imposed new construction problems. British naval planners had envisioned the light cruiser as ideal for imperial duty, but Japanese construction of heavy ships in the 1930s, including the twin giants *Yamato* and *Mushashi*, raised the prospect of Jutland-type fleet action in the Far East. But any battleships or heavy cruisers sent into Pacific waters would weaken Atlantic defenses against Germany as well as Mediterranean defenses against Italy. The Japanese threat in the Far East therefore caused British planners to consider a balance toward the construction of battleships and heavy cruisers at the expense of light cruisers and destroyers.

On the other hand, defense against submarine attack in Atlantic waters required smaller ships, especially destroyers. Although the German submarine fleet was not large in 1937, U-boats could be built quickly and in numbers far exceeding the three pocket battleships. As it turned out, the Reich would build 1,178 submarines during World War II.[19] The experience of World War I, moreover, had suggested that the submarine remained the most effective weapon against merchant shipping, a fact compounded by the Nyon patrols, which further suggested that Britain suffered from a serious shortage of destroyers. The shortage was amplified by the fact that only a portion of the destroyer fleet could be assigned to antisubmarine operations. Additional destroyers would have to be assigned to coastal defense, the empire, and the Home Fleet, whose heavy ships dared not venture from port without a strong destroyer escort. Given the acute shortage of destroyers, British antisubmarine capabilities would presumably demand massive construction of destroyers and other light warships during the 1930s.

Light warships were of course not the only weapons useful for antisubmarine warfare. Another was the airplane, but the Royal Air Force focused its attention on the construction of long-range strategic bombers and fighter aircraft to defend the homeland against air attack—at the expense of aircraft suitable for antisubmarine patrol. Nor was there any productive initiative to develop inexpensive naval aviation technology uniquely for antisubmarine operations. Consequently, British naval and military aviation continued into the late 1930s with aircraft and doctrine ill suited to address any U-boat threat, this despite the lessons of Nyon indicating clearly the value of the airplane to help chase down submarines.

Even before the 1936 London Naval Conference had gotten under way, the Admiralty Board and the Defense Requirements Committee (DRC) had begun to draft plans for massive naval rearmament. In early 1935 the board proposed to the DRC an ambitious construction program to cover the years between 1936, when the treaty limitations would expire, and 1942. A revised proposal, adopted by the DRC in October 1935, called for the construction of 12 capital ships, 4 aircraft carriers, 23 cruisers, 16 flotillas of destroyers (154 ships), 24 submarines, 37 sloops, and various auxiliary craft. The proposal also called for the renovation of 7 older battleships.[20] The failure of the 1936 disarmament conference opened the door for London to move forward with new naval construction on the basis of this long-range plan. But the plan, too ambitious in terms of resources, was scaled down more than once. The Treasury Department dragged its feet on granting the necessary credits, and British shipyards—many of them long since inactive and lacking skilled workers—were plagued with untimely delays.

Nevertheless, construction got under way in 1937. The 1936 and 1937 programs called for the construction of five new battleships. By the end of 1938 all five of them were under construction, and four more had been authorized under the 1938 and 1939 programs.[21] But the lead time in battleship construction was five to six years, and not all of them moved forward at the same pace. Consequently, neither the *King George V*, completed in 1940, nor the *Prince of Wales* in 1941, would be available when war broke out, in 1939.

British planners had assumed a minimum of eighty-eight cruisers to serve Britain's global needs. The 1938 construction program included 4 of the 6-inch *Fiji*-class cruisers and 3 of the 5.24-inch *Dido* class. In addition, the first of 10 heavy cruisers of the *Southampton*, *Gloucester*, and *Edinburgh* classes were already under construction. In 1938 42 cruisers were in service, and in 1939 19 others were under construction. When war broke out in September, the Royal Navy would have 56 cruisers in service, far short of the minimum requirement of 88 and fewer than half of the 120 cruisers in service in 1918.[22]

Significantly, British construction plans for destroyers badly underestimated the early wartime demand for convoy escorts. The sixteen celebrated

Tribal-class destroyers, constructed under the 1935 and 1936 programs, were larger ships in the range of 2,500 tons, similar to the French contre-torpilleurs.[23] They were designed primarily for fleet service rather than for convoy escort duty. There were no plans to build light destroyers of simple design to address the problem of convoy escort. In the view of the Admiralty, that kind of construction would be expensive and redundant, since overage destroyers unsuitable for fleet support could be assigned to convoy escort duty.[24] The Admiralty therefore saw no reason to construct quickly in large numbers the kinds of escort vessels the navy would desperately need early in World War II. They chose instead to use overage destroyers to fight submarines and to build heavy destroyers for fleet service in operations against German surface raiders.

The Admiralty, moreover, overestimated the value of the new Asdic sounding device to detect submerged submarines. With Asdics being installed on all new destroyers, it was widely believed that the submarine problem had been solved and that fewer escort ships would be required to protect shipping from undersea attack. The Royal Navy would later pay dearly for this error in judgment. Overconfident and obsessed with fleet actions against Japan and against German pocket battleships in the Atlantic, the Admiralty too easily accepted sharp cutbacks in the construction of destroyers and sloops.

Surprisingly, in the wake of the Nyon crisis, when the need for more destroyers had become obvious, the two destroyer flotillas included originally in the 1938 construction program were eliminated entirely. And the sixteen destroyers included in the 1939 program were all larger ships with construction schedules of nearly three years, as opposed to two for standard ships, which pushed their delivery dates later into the war. In late 1939, thirty-two destroyers were under construction, but only nine of them would be brought into service before the end of 1940.[25] Clearly, the absence of any destroyers from the 1938 program in favor of larger ones contributed importantly to the shortage of escort vessels in 1940 and 1941, when German U-boats took a heavy toll of British shipping.

The October 1938 report of the American naval attaché in London listed 115 British Commonwealth destroyers, of which 15 were in the service of Australia, Canada, or New Zealand.[26] This number stands in sharp contrast to the 443 British destroyers in service in 1918, most of which had been engaged in antisubmarine warfare.[27] By 1938 it was already too late to overcome the neglect of British destroyer construction during the twenty years since 1918. Should all of the late 1930s construction programs be completed on schedule, there still would be too few destroyers to serve the combined demands for fleet escort, imperial duty, coastal patrol, and convoy escort. The greater demand, as the Admiralty soon learned, would be for convoy escort, as it had been in World War I when the submarine threat turned out to be greater than that of surface raiders.

Therefore, when war broke out in 1939, British construction was skewed toward heavy ships to address the global imbalance at the expense of destroyers vital to waging a naval war against Germany. The five battleships tied up valuable construction resources that otherwise might have been committed to many times their number of destroyers and other light craft to address the U-boat menace. British naval planners had discounted the lessons of World War I as well as of Nyon, which had anticipated the main pattern of the next European naval war and the need for additional destroyers.

Anglo-French Naval Planning, 1936–38

Anglo-French naval planning attendant to the 1937 Nyon Arrangement had focused sharply on a regional crisis in the Mediterranean. Nyon ushered in an era of Anglo-French operational cooperation that served incidentally to promote better relations between the two navies. But Nyon implied no commitments beyond the Mediterranean. It was not a formal naval alliance. It was instead an informal entente that anticipated the conclusion later of a binding alliance involving larger commitments on the part of both navies.

Low-level Anglo-French military staff consultations had been intermittently in progress since April 1936, after the German reoccupation of the Rhineland. In these consultations, which also included Belgian representatives, London took care to limit narrowly the scope of the conversations and to maintain them at the lowest possible level—that of the service attachés. Discussions would be contained strictly within the bounds of British obligations under the Locarno treaty. The first discussions took place on April 15 and 17, 1936, in London to exchange information and to discuss technical matters, such as port facilities and defense forces that might be available in the event of an unprovoked German violation of Franco-Belgian frontiers. The consultations, London made clear, implied no political or military obligations on the part of the British government. They were instead intended only to exchange information in the event that higher-level negotiations then in progress with Germany on the Rhineland question should not find a satisfactory solution.

Following an opening session at the Admiralty, the representatives of the three services—naval, military, and aviation—met in separate sessions. British records indicate that the talks were useful and satisfactory from all viewpoints, and on April 18 the press was informed that successful discussions had taken place. There was talk of renewing the conversations, but in May the German military attaché in London hinted that further consultations might prompt his government to increase its military forces in the Rhineland. In the wake of this warning, official consultations were supplanted by informal contacts through standard attaché channels.[28] The efforts of Eden to reopen the conversations in early 1938 met with no success, but informal contacts at the attaché level continued.

British concern to move the discussions to a higher level mounted in March 1938, when German armies occupied Austria. The new crisis in eastern Europe created a delicate problem for British war planners, who wished to gain access to French airfields in the event that a German violation of the Franco-Belgian frontier would drag Britain into a war with the Reich. At that moment, however, Chamberlain was flirting with Mussolini in the interest of concluding a Mediterranean agreement. In these circumstances, the opening of high-level naval conversations with the French might put the Anglo-Italian conversations at risk, as the French surely would want to discuss fleet dispositions in the Mediterranean. The British therefore expected in the early spring of 1938 to limit any new staff consultations strictly to British obligations under the Locarno treaty and keep Anglo-French naval consultations in low profile.[29]

Nevertheless, Anglo-French naval consultations were resumed in June at the attaché level. But by the middle of the summer the great crisis attendant to the German threat to Czechoslovakia was already under way and tensions began to mount. When the crisis became acute in July and August, the naval consultations were moved to a higher level with the exchange of liaison officers. A French vice-admiral was assigned to the Admiralty and a British vice admiral to the Rue Royale. In these conversations the British delegation explained that the Royal Navy had no obligation to support the French navy in any war it might risk as a result of French fleet movements suggested in the consultations. The British made it clear, however, that the Royal Navy would request a redistribution of the French fleet in the event of an Anglo-German war and that administrative arrangements should be made in advance—arrangements that Darlan had already anticipated. The Admiralty concluded that the consultation had resulted in an exchange of information sufficient to coordinate Anglo-French fleet movements in the event of a war with Germany.[30] That brief conclusion does not, however, tell the full story of what went on behind the scenes in Paris, where the staff consultations appear to have nudged beyond that of informational exchange to a higher level of commitment.

The view from Paris helps to fill in the details. As the tensions mounted in August, French army reserve units were called up and sent to the frontier. At the same time, Darlan moved swiftly to mobilize the French fleet and to redistribute its units in accordance with the plans he had drafted in 1937. But

Darlan modified his plans at the peak of the crisis, on September 28, after he had received assurances of British naval cooperation in the event of war. These assurances appear to have been given during the last week of September in the course of the staff consultations. Accordingly, Darlan changed French plans in a manner intended to achieve maximum Anglo-French naval cooperation should war break out immediately. He knew the details of British fleet movements, so he adjusted his own plans to accommodate them.[31]

With assurances that the Royal Navy would protect the English Channel, Darlan substantially reduced the French naval forces in the Calais region in late September. He also organized his best ships into a new striking unit, the Raiding Force, intended to counter German surface raiders in the Atlantic. Finally, he shifted all of the remaining forces to the western Mediterranean, a move obviously intended to liberate British ships in that region for service elsewhere. All of these moves were undertaken on the assumption of British naval support immediately upon the outbreak of war.[32]

Darlan now moved to reorganize the French command and redistribute his naval units in accordance with the revised plan. He divided the main body of the fleet into five commands, all reporting directly to him. The Calais and Brest commands retained only a few small ships intended mainly for coastal patrol. He clearly would not have stripped away the defense of these vital areas without assurances that the Royal Navy would protect the French coast. A much larger squadron, commanded out of Toulon by Vice-Admiral Jean-Pierre Esteva, guarded the western basin of the Mediterranean mainly with destroyers stationed throughout the region. The High Seas Force, composed of three renovated battleships, ten cruisers, and twenty-four destroyers, was positioned to protect shipping from Africa to France. This squadron, with its command on board the heavy cruiser *Algèrie*, was capable of shifting its units for escort duty as the situation demanded. Finally, the Raiding Force was assembled from France's newest ships. Commanded by Vice-Admiral Marcel Gensoul on board the *Dunkerque*, it was supported by three *Gloire*-class cruisers and eight super destroyers. Fast and powerful, the Raiding Force was positioned to pursue and destroy German commerce raiders in the Atlantic.[33]

The pattern of this redistribution of French assets suggests that the staff consultations had moved beyond the official level of exchanging information to a level of commitment high enough that Darlan went ahead and revised his plans in a manner to amplify Anglo-French naval cooperation. The French documents do not prove conclusively that British staff officers gave Darlan specific assurances beyond the official limits of exchanging information, but it is clear that Darlan moved swiftly to redistribute his assets in a manner that assumed a high level of commitment on the part of the British naval staff.

Although the Munich crisis was settled peacefully at the end of September, Darlan maintained the French fleet in a state of readiness. The consultations assumed a lower profile as the tensions subsided, but in the meantime the French and British naval staffs had put in place specific measures to govern Anglo-French naval cooperation in the event of war against Germany. In the weeks after the Munich crisis, British naval officers assessed the results of the staff consultations. They concluded that sufficient information had been exchanged to manage an Anglo-French naval war against Germany. Nevertheless, they agreed that a war against Germany and Italy would require considerably more work and that the consultations would have to be elevated to a higher level.[34]

The Anglo-French staff consultations of 1938 had involved all three military services, so the naval consultations summarized herein constituted only one part of a larger planning operation. The consultations were limited officially to British continental commitments under the Locarno treaty. But the naval consultations had in fact assumed geographical dimensions considerably broader than that implied by the Locarno treaty. They spilled over into Mediterranean defense, to the strong Italian naval threat lurking in the background, and to the imperative of redistributing the combined assets of both navies at the outbreak of war. The 1938 consultations therefore anticipated the broad outlines of Anglo-French naval planning in 1939, the scope of which would extend far beyond the narrow confines of British commitments under the Locarno treaty.

Chapter 8

An Anglo-French Naval Alliance

While the scope of Anglo-French staff planning had been officially narrow during the Munich crisis, the changing international scene in 1939 would demand naval cooperation on a scale so vast as to require extensive planning at the highest levels. Planning could no longer be limited to British obligations under the Locarno treaty, for London now faced the prospect of being isolated to wage war against all three Axis powers. Anglo-French naval planning would therefore have to deal with strategic problems stretching around the globe.

Naval planning in 1939 was but one part of a broader spectrum of planning that included all three armed services—military, naval, and aviation—as well as intelligence services. Military, air, and intelligence planning would focus sharpest on the continent. But naval planning would assume broader dimensions aimed at protecting British and French imperial interests around the globe. These plans would assume the possibility of war with all three Axis powers. The naval staffs could see that the weakest of the Axis powers was Italy and that British and French naval power could be combined in the Mediterranean against Italy more easily than it could be combined against either Germany or Japan. Nevertheless, the assumptions of the two staffs about the role of combined naval power in the Mediterranean were not identical.

Toward High-Level Consultations

The occasion for the opening of high-level Anglo-French consultations arose in December 1938 when London received reports that France was poised to retreat from its military commitment in eastern Europe. These reports reflected indecision and divisions within the French government in late 1938, when Paris flirted with a spread of options that included the permanent settling of Franco-German differences. This initiative, championed by Foreign Minister Georges Bonnet, followed a similar initiative toward Italy that had reaped nothing but fascist contempt.[1]

Berlin was more receptive than Italy to the French overtures, which led finally to the Franco-German Declaration of Non-Aggression signed in Paris by Bonnet and German ambassador Joachim von Ribbentrop on December 6 recognizing the existing frontiers of the two states. Lacking in real commitment and making no statement about eastern Europe, the declaration nevertheless reflected a painful reappraisal of French diplomatic and defense options undertaken in the wake of the Munich crisis. Although the declaration resonated well enough with Chamberlain's policy of appeasement, London still had reason to be concerned since any Franco-German rapprochement risked isolating Great Britain in a world threatened by three Axis powers.

Given the presence of three hostile powers on France's borders—Germany, Italy, and Franco's Spain—Paris was tempted to settle differences with the strongest of them by conceding eastern Europe to the Reich rather than risking war in defense of Poland, Romania, or Czechoslovakia. While Bonnet was thinking of an enduring settlement with Berlin, other Frenchmen understood any withdrawal from eastern Europe as but a temporary modus vivendi, a realistic way to shift Berlin's attention away from France, to set the stage for a conflict between the Reich and the Soviets, and to defer the dreaded Franco-German war into the future.

Involved in these discussions, Admiral Darlan wrote privately on January 24, 1939, that "the war will last a long time . . . it will be exhausting. . . . We must avoid it. We must leave Germany free to act toward the east." He continued, "If she is engaged in the east, she would not want to turn this way for a long time."[2] From Darlan's perspective, the idea was to turn Germany against the Soviet Union, and thereby liberate France to defend her Mediterranean interests against Italy, or even to provoke Italy to war in the interest of solving the Mediterranean problem prior to any conflict with the Reich. In contrast, the military commander in chief, General Gamelin, wishing to concentrate all of his assets against Germany rather than divide them along two fronts, insisted upon keeping Italy neutral. Gamelin had already backed away from the idea of withdrawing French military commitments to eastern Europe on the grounds of its being inconsistent with France's role as a great power. So Premier Edouard Daladier discarded for the moment both initiatives, that of withdrawing from eastern Europe and that of provoking Italy to war.[3] Nevertheless, the initiative of abandoning eastern Europe remained an option as long as France made no public commitment to defend the region.

Recent studies have suggested that the French military command, intent on manipulating London, had leaked reports of Paris being at the point of withdrawing from eastern Europe. Alarmed, the Cabinet promptly moved to consider whether it should revise its French policy in a manner to conclude an alliance. While these discussions among the British chiefs continued into January, reports from the same source of an impending German attack on the Netherlands raised the specter of an Anglo-German war, with France sitting on the sidelines. Taken together, these reports precipitated a war scare sufficient to prompt London to consider again the opening of staff consultations with France.[4]

When the Cabinet met on February 2, it concluded that any German attack against Holland would constitute a direct threat to British security and that failure to intervene would undermine British relations with the dominions. It further concluded that British relations with France had grown so close as to rise above legalities to the level of mutual commitments. The Cabinet therefore invited the chiefs of staff to enter into staff conversations with the French on a basis wider than that of the Locarno treaty, with the understanding that global planning would impose higher commitments than those of earlier consultations.[5]

The Numerical Balance of Power

Prior to the formal opening of the consultations in late March 1939, British naval officers hurriedly prepared reports and memoranda to set the agenda for the conversations and define their direction. These documents reveal the basic assumptions that guided the British delegation in the conversations with their French opposites. The strategic picture confronting British naval planners in 1939 was in many ways similar to that which had prompted Admiral Darlan to draft French naval plans in 1937. Like Darlan, British planners could not know in advance how many of the Axis powers would become enemies. Unlike Darlan in 1937, British planners in 1939 could assume the support of an important naval ally. Therefore, Anglo-French naval planning would address a range of contingencies, including a global naval war. In the worst case, a war against three Axis enemies, the combined total of Anglo-French assets would be stretched so thin that the Allies would be unable to defend their Asian empires against Japan. From the British perspective it was therefore important to find agreement on a fleet distribution to restrain Italy and Japan, and keep them neutral, so that the Entente might fight but one naval war, that against Germany in the Atlantic.

A key British planning memorandum of April 1939 compares the relative strength of the British and French navies by ship category with the navies of Germany, Italy, and Japan. A comparison by ship category provides a useful but by no means complete picture of relative naval strengths. The imperatives of geography, the fact of swiftly changing naval technology, and the emergence of new methods of warfare skewed the value of a simple ship count. Nevertheless, naval planning began with an inventory of assets.

The document lists twelve British and five French battleships available for service in 1939, matching exactly the seventeen battleships in the service of Germany, Italy, and Japan. There were in addition three other British battleships undergoing major repair or modernization at the time. Germany and Italy together had seven capital ships in service, which included the modern *Scharnhorst* and *Gneisenau*, the three commerce raiders of the *Deutschland* class, and two modern Italian battleships. The Allies would therefore enjoy a numerical margin over the combined German and Italian battleship fleets, and a comfortable margin over either German or Italian ships in this category. The Allied margin was increased by the addition of seven aircraft carriers, six British and one French, since neither Germany nor Italy had even one carrier. But in Asia, ten Japanese battleships and six aircraft carriers accorded Japan an overwhelming numerical advantage over the smaller British and French squadrons stationed at Singapore and Indochina.[6] Therefore, on a global scale the Allies enjoyed no important numerical advantage in capital ships. Moreover, all of the British battleships in service were older ships with none commissioned since the *Rodney* and *Nelson* in 1927. In contrast, seven of the German and Italian capital ships were of recent construction or modernization.

The distribution of heavy and light cruisers bore a similar pattern, with seventy-two British and French ships in service, and sixty-seven in the service of Germany, Italy, and Japan. But of the sixty-seven Axis cruisers, thirty-seven were Japanese, which accorded Japan a clear cruiser advantage in Asian waters. The Entente, however, enjoyed an important advantage of seventy-two to thirty cruisers over Italy and Germany. This margin, coupled with that of the capital ships, accorded the Allies a significant numerical advantage over the European Axis in terms of battleships, aircraft carriers, and cruisers. But the Entente enjoyed no advantage over Japan in these ship categories.

In terms of destroyers, the numerical advantage shifted to the three potential enemies. The Axis powers possessed 298 destroyers—126 Italian, 122 Japanese, and 50 German. Of the Axis total, 214 were modern ships, reflecting steady Italian and Japanese construction of light warships not restricted under the Washington treaty. In contrast, Britain and France had in service only 200 destroyers, of which 137 were modern. The Entente total, however, was amplified by 32 French contre-torpilleurs, ships approaching 3,000 tons that are best classified as heavy destroyers rather than light cruisers. The Entente therefore had 232 destroyers in service, 66 fewer than that of the three Axis powers but 56 more than that of Italy and Germany.[7] Still, in the event of a war against Japan, the Entente would enjoy no advantage in destroyers, for only a fraction of the Entente total could be released for service in Asia.

The three Axis powers enjoyed a large numerical advantage in submarines. Of the 224 Axis submarines, Italy had in service 105; Japan, 62; and Germany, 57. In turn the Allies had in service 137 submarines, 80 French and 57 English, which fell 25 short of the 162 undersea craft in the service of Italy and Germany.[8] But since submarines rarely fight against each other, the Entente-Axis submarine ratio is less relevant than that of submarines to destroyers. A major concern, however, was the large number of Italian submarines operating in narrow Mediterranean waters vital to British communications between Gibraltar and Singapore.

The configuration of heavy and light ships indicated earlier confronted British naval planners with a range of problems, the most important of which were related to the rise of Japan as a major naval power. Assessing the broad strategic problem, they noted that "it would be hard to choose a worse geographical combination of enemies."[9] The figures suggested that a war against the European Axis and Japan would stretch Allied naval assets to the limit. British heavy ships at Alexandria would have to be moved swiftly to Singapore, thereby forfeiting British control of the eastern Mediterranean to Italy.[10] More than that, the Japanese advantage in aircraft carriers reduced importantly the value of British battleships at Alexandria, a fact not fully appreciated in 1939.

British planners considered that Japan, fearful of provoking Soviet or American intervention, would not likely enter the conflict at the outset. Should Japan remain neutral, the heavy units of the British and French fleets would enjoy an important numerical advantage over the European Axis in Atlantic and Mediterranean waters. Unlike Germany and Italy, whose fleets were separated by geography, the Entente could easily combine or distribute their assets in various patterns to wage war offensively or defensively according to the needs of the moment. And, significantly, they could distribute their assets in a manner to discourage the entry of Italy and Japan into an Entente-German war.

In view of Italian naval weakness in the face of combined Anglo-French naval power, British plans assumed Entente control of both ends of the Mediterranean and the greater part of the western basin. From bases at Alexandria, Gibraltar, and elsewhere, Entente warships could shut down Italian commerce from the Atlantic and the Red Sea. On the other hand, the strong Italian position in the central Mediterranean threatened Malta and British communications with the Near East so that shipping to Egypt would have to be diverted to the longer Capetown route.[11] Nevertheless, the advantage in the Mediterranean lay clearly with the Allies, whose combined naval power was capable of crippling the Regia Marina, isolating Libya, and securing Entente communications in the Mediterranean.

On the military side, these plans conceded a German advantage over France on the continent, especially in terms of manpower resources. Significantly, British planners fully understood that Germany could not be defeated on the military front in northern France, but they assumed that French fortifications were capable of containing the initial German onslaught. They therefore assumed a war of long duration and the need to lend France important logistical support even though they also observed that Italy, the weakest link in the Axis alliance, might in time be defeated by an overwhelming combination of Anglo-French naval power.[12] But the plans did not call for a combined attack on the Italian fleet at the outset of war or of provoking Italy to war. They observed instead that Italy might "in time" be defeated by naval power. The Admiralty's concern to avoid an Italian war coincided with the view of the French military command, and with Chamberlain, but not with the French naval command.

The Strategic Naval Balance

Not surprisingly, the British planning memoranda prepared prior to the opening of Anglo-French naval conversations expressed satisfaction with the Allied numerical superiority over Germany and Italy in terms of heavy warships—battleships, battlecruisers, cruisers, and aircraft carriers. In terms of traditional naval doctrine, which assigned great value to heavy ships, the Allied numerical margin was indeed impressive. Although German and Italian construction schedules were slightly ahead of their British and French counterparts, the Entente margin promised to remain favorable in the long term as seven additional British and French battleships were scheduled for completion in the early 1940s. The overwhelming numerical margin in heavy ships was sufficient to protect the British Isles from invasion, for the German navy was not designed to launch major amphibious operations. Nor was it large enough to challenge combined Anglo-French naval power to a major fleet action such as the 1916 Battle of Jutland. And whereas Great Britain and France could easily combine heavy naval assets in the North Sea or Atlantic waters, geography precluded any chance of the heavy ships of the Regia Marina and the Kriegsmarine operating together in any important combination.

The Admiralty thus reasoned that the Germans would likely wage a different kind of naval war, that of commerce raiding, for which all five of their modern heavy ships—the *Scharnhorst, Gneisenau*, and the three *Deutschland*-class battlecruisers—were specifically designed. Given this kind of warfare, the Anglo-French numerical margin in heavy ships is less impressive but nevertheless decisive. Although one or two enemy raiders at sea would tie up many times their number to chase them down, the loss of one or two raiders would significantly reduce the German ability to sustain much longer that kind of warfare. The loss of two of the German surface raiders, for example, would reduce by 40 percent the Reich's assets in that category. In contrast, the loss of two of the Entente's twenty battleships would reduce Anglo-French capabilities by 10 percent, leaving 90 percent of them in place to deal with the three remaining German surface raiders. The giant German battleship *Bismarck* was scheduled to enter into service in 1940, but by that time at least one of the British *George V*–class battleships would be available to match it. The Entente was therefore prepared well enough to address the problem of the German surface raiders, whose numbers were too small to pose a decisive threat.

On the other hand, the shortage of destroyers and escort vessels relative to enemy submarine strength in Atlantic waters posed a major problem. The slight Entente numerical superiority over the European Axis in terms of destroyers and lighter escort vessels was not strategically significant, for in the Atlantic these ships would not usually fight only against each other. British destroyers and escorts would instead be employed more often to counter enemy submarines or to lend support service elsewhere. But any effective defense against submarine attack upon Atlantic shipping would require a significantly larger numerical margin of destroyers and escort ships over enemy submarines. The British naval command understood that the demand for destroyers for fleet, empire, and coastal service would greatly reduce the number available for escort duty.[13] And the greater portion of the French destroyer fleet would have to be employed to protect Mediterranean commerce against Italian destroyers and submarines.

Fully aware of the shortage of destroyers, the British naval chiefs nevertheless underestimated the threat of German submarines, which at that time numbered 57 U-boats. Although they expected to suffer some losses, British planners concluded that "the number of German submarines available initially would not be so great as to present us with such a difficult problem as in the last war."[14] That conclusion, far off target in terms of the 1939 naval balance, overlooked the fact that Germany could produce submarines faster than Britain could produce destroyers. British planners estimated that 107 destroyers and other light ships would be required to escort convoys in the vicinity of the British Isles.[15] German U-boats were capable of striking targets over a vast expanse of ocean, though, and any defense against them in remote waters would require a numerical margin of destroyers and other escorts in multiples far exceeding the number of U-boats at sea in any given time. The shortage of destroyers, so obvious at the time of the Nyon crisis, would be amplified in 1940 and 1941. Certainly many more than the estimated 107 ships would be required in 1940 to protect Atlantic shipping against U-boat attack.

In the British view, the most urgent strategic problem was Japan, whose naval power in Asia clearly outdistanced that of the Royal Navy and, indeed, of the combined assets the two Entente navies could afford to send to Asia. Given the Japanese advantage in Asia, any success in waging war against Japan hinged upon stability in the Mediterranean, vital for the transfer of British naval assets to Singapore. The Japanese threat therefore raised the question in London as to whether even a winnable Italian war was worth the risk of tempting Tokyo to unleash its naval and military might against British and French possessions in the Far East.

Naval Consultations: The First Phase

The Munich Accord had eased the problem of the formal French military commitment to Czechoslovakia by substituting for it a weaker collective commitment. Munich also liberated Prime Minister Chamberlain to play again his only high card, that of appeasement in addressing the problem of German ambitions against the rump Czech state and Poland. Should he continue the policy of appeasing Germany, he would keep open the option of remaining neutral in the event of any German-Soviet confrontation over Poland. When German armies occupied the remainder of Czechoslovakia on March 15, 1939, Chamberlain might easily have remained silent, to isolate the Soviets and to keep both Berlin and Moscow guessing as to Entente intentions. But Chamberlain played his trump prematurely, announcing to Parliament on March 31 an Anglo-French guarantee to Poland. He had nothing more to offer the Soviets, whose interest now was to negotiate with Berlin to partition Poland and shift the burden of a German war to Britain and France. Anglo-French military and naval staff consultations had gotten under way just the day before, on March 30.

Since Chamberlain had frittered away his only high card, the Entente military chiefs could now anticipate the disastrous possibility of a German war without a strong ally in the East and of a prolonged struggle on the continent where the enemy held the military advantage.[16] Significantly, British defense planners now had no choice but to plan for a prolonged economic struggle with a naval blockade to deny the Reich the resources to wage war. Chamberlain's premature guarantee to Poland had tacitly redefined the impending war as first of all a naval conflict whose victory would hinge upon sea power to nourish military operations in northern France.

In a European war, the naval role of the Entente would be one of denying Germany access to the seas and of protecting vital shipping lanes to exploit the economic advantage the Entente enjoyed through their global trading network. Securing the trade routes was therefore high on the agenda of the first round of Anglo-French naval consultations that began in London at the Admiralty on March 30. The aims of the first meeting were to establish an agenda, exchange information, and pose questions for future discussion. The head of the French delegation, Admiral Jean-Léon Bourragué, chief of staff under Admiral Darlan, was assisted by the French naval attaché in London. Bourragué's opposite, Captain V. H. Danckwerts, served as director of plans for the Admiralty. Among his assistants was Captain Cedric S. Holland, the British naval attaché in Paris. Following the exchange of planning documents, the discussion quickly turned to the problem of German surface raiders. The French delegation had initially favored evasive routing, a way of dispersing ships in the vast expanse of ocean to avoid enemy raiders. When Danckwerts explained that the Royal Navy would instead employ a convoy system, Bourragué quickly fell in line with the British to draft joint plans for convoy escort. There followed a cordial and productive discussion of numerous other technical problems.[17]

The first session established a mood of cordiality and cooperation that carried over to subsequent sessions where the British delegation, representing the stronger naval power, would usually call the main signals. When there were disagreements, the French delegation would present its views tactfully and then concede the point to their British opposites. The discussions were not always easy, but they were conducted in a manner that combined respect and restraint to the end of maintaining cordial relations.

The discussions of March 31 proceeded on the assumption that Japan would remain neutral at the outset of any European war. The conversation, covering a broad range of contingencies, grew out of documents exchanged the day before indicating ship dispositions of the two navies. From these documents the French delegation could see that the Royal Navy was spread around the globe with the strongest part assigned to the Home Fleet operating mainly out of Scapa Flow, in northern Scotland. This powerful squadron—led by four battleships, two battlecruisers, and an aircraft carrier—was poised to cover the North Sea to interdict the exit of German surface raiders into the Atlantic. This squadron was reinforced by a Channel Force of two battleships, four cruisers, and eight destroyers based at Portland. Ships of the Local Home Commands, composed of numerous destroyers and various lighter ships, were based at ports around the British Isles for various service roles including that of trade protection. Another strong force, led by three battleships, an aircraft carrier, fourteen cruisers, and twenty-four destroyers, was based in the eastern Mediterranean at Alexandria for operations if necessary against either Italy or Japan. The remainder of the Royal Navy was scattered in ports around the globe from Gibraltar to Australia.[18]

In contrast, most of the French fleet was concentrated in Mediterranean or Atlantic waters on the Bay of Biscay. The lighter ships plus several old cruisers and battleships were based in the Mediterranean at Toulon, Bizerte, Algiers, and Mers el-Kébir. The heavier ships, led by the *Dunkerque* and *Strasbourg* and supported by fast cruisers and contre-torpilleurs, would operate out of Brest or Casablanca to cover the Atlantic approaches against German surface raiders.[19] It was obvious to the two commands that French fleet units could be shifted swiftly between Atlantic and Mediterranean waters according to need. The *Dunkerque* and *Strasbourg* might easily be combined with the *Hood*, *Renown*, or *Repulse* for service in the Atlantic as all of them were suitable for operations against enemy surface raiders. The two delegations, however, were unable to define exactly the operational relationship between the French Raiding Force and the Royal Navy. The British delegation raised the question of coordination at the tactical level, but Darlan, intent upon keeping a tight grip on his best ships, was unwilling to concede much authority to the French Atlantic command.

The discussions of March 31 bore heavily upon command and technical changes necessary to facilitate Anglo-French naval cooperation. They agreed, for example, to share port facilities and to provide mutual support and escort for ship movements whenever it might be necessary. These discussions were preliminary, however, with agreement in most cases tentative. The minutes of the March 31 sessions contain no hint of any discord or problems of communication. They agreed on an agenda for the next session, which included the coordination of plans for trade defense and for operations in the Mediterranean and Atlantic.[20]

A few weeks later, on April 12, the British chiefs of staff reviewed the report of the British delegation, which had recommended the full sharing of intelligence information with the French general staff. After consultations with the director of naval intelligence, the chiefs authorized the full sharing of information, but they would not disclose the most secret technical sources.[21] This meant that the British delegation would conceal from the French the fact of their having penetrated certain of the Axis codes. This precaution left open the option of withholding from the French any data that risked betraying the intelligence source.

The session of April 17, held at the Rue Royale in Paris, focused on the problem of protecting the three major convoy routes in the Atlantic. The convoys would assemble in Halifax, Nova Scotia; Kingston, West Indies; and Freetown, Sierra Leone. The plan called for a convoy to depart each of these ports every sixth day, so that one convoy would arrive in the English Channel every other day. The British command assumed that the submarine threat would be confined largely to the approaches to the home islands and that German surface raiders would be the main threat in more remote Atlantic waters. Therefore, two types of escorts would be necessary. The first would consist of heavier ships capable of engaging German surface raiders in distant waters and the second of light vessels equipped to engage enemy U-boats in waters closer to home. The lighter escorts would relieve the high seas escort at a point approximately three hundred miles west of Brest to cover the approaches to the Channel.[22]

The British delegation made it clear that French merchant ships could be included in convoys from Halifax and Kingston. This protection would accord an important benefit to the French, whose smaller navy was stretched too thin to provide adequate escort from all of its overseas connections. Still, the French fleet was fully capable of assisting the Royal Navy with Channel escorts. The British delegation therefore proposed that French merchant ships might be included in convoys originating at Sierra Leone if light French warships would assist with the Channel escorts. Since the initial planning assumed that convoy escorts would not be mixed, French warships would assume responsibility for escorting one in four of the convoys approaching the Channel. The convoys would arrive every other day, so the French navy would provide a Channel escort of four destroyers or torpedo boats every eighth day, easily within its capabilities. The French staff approved these arrangements a few days afterward.[23]

The conversations of April 17 touched on numerous other technical questions attendant to the protection of the shipping routes. It was agreed, for example, that no French or British submarines would operate in the Channel or the North Sea, so any submarine encountered there could be assumed hostile. The French navy, moreover, would protect British shipping in the western basin of the Mediterranean. As in the case of the earlier meetings, the British delegation took the lead. The French cooperated fully with the British initiatives, but some items received only tentative agreement pending the approval of Admiral Darlan. The minutes of the session contain no hint of any discord or problems of communication.[24]

Most of the unfinished business of the earlier meetings was finally wrapped up at the sessions of April 27–28 and May 3, which were held in London. They now officially agreed that the Mediterranean would be divided between the two navies. Nearly all of the French ships in the eastern basin would be withdrawn, as would most of the British ships in the western basin, including Gibraltar, where a light British squadron under British command would be retained to protect the western approaches to the strait. This meant that French ships would operate in and out of Gibraltar in greater force than the British. Although the exchange of liaison officers in the Mediterranean was not yet decided, the senior British command at Gibraltar and Malta was authorized to confer directly with the French naval command at Oran and Bizerte. But the French delegation insisted that coordination of operations between the two navies in the two basins of the Mediterranean be managed through the naval staffs in London and Paris rather than at the local level. The French, however, would soon back away from that demand. The two staffs also discussed offensive operations against Italy at the outbreak of war, but no agreement was reached on that point.[25]

In these discussions, the French delegation made clear its intention to maintain the powerful Raiding Force in Atlantic waters to operate against enemy surface raiders. Led by the *Dunkerque* and *Strasbourg*, this squadron would be based at Brest but might also operate out of Gibraltar, Casablanca, or Dakar, according to need. The two big ships would normally operate together to maximize their power. Since their movements would be controlled personally by Admiral Darlan, coordination with the Royal Navy would be arranged at the highest level, between the Admiralty in London and the Ministry of Marine in Paris, rather than at the local command. In the case of Atlantic operations, Darlan resisted liaison at the tactical level for fear of losing his grip on the operations of the Raiding Force. The French, however, finally conceded that the local French admiral in command of the Raiding Force would exchange information with his British opposite in the interest of maximizing efficiency of operations. It was further agreed that the Admiralty would communicate with the Rue Royale about arrangements for communications and liaison.[26]

During the course of these consultations the two staffs discussed and resolved numerous other problems involving the cooperation of the two navies. They defined, for example, the limits of air reconnaissance and naval operations in the approaches of the Channel, and they made arrangements for the planting of mines in the North Sea and near Dunkerque to close off the Channel to enemy submarines. They agreed upon the reciprocal use of their naval bases so that their ships might put into each other's ports without prior notice. They made arrangements for the sharing of codes, call signs, and recognition signals to facilitate communications between the two navies. The British, moreover, agreed to share with the French their Asdic sonar device, important in the search for enemy submarines. There remained, however, the delicate question of offensive operations in the Mediterranean against Italy, a topic that had been discussed only briefly. It was agreed that the two admiralties would exchange operational plans as the basis for further discussions relative to any war against Italy.[27] That decision set the stage for the second phase of the negotiations.

In the meantime, after Italian forces had struck into Albania on April 7, London and Paris extended additional military guarantees to Greece and Romania, and a little later London made a bilateral commitment to Turkey. It should be noted these commitments were less binding than that to Poland, and London gave no guarantee to Albania. The door therefore remained ajar for Chamberlain to persist with his appeasement of Mussolini and for the Admiralty to conclude agreements with France to neutralize Italy rather than to wage war against her.

Naval Consultations: The Second Phase

Despite the strong position the Italian navy enjoyed in the central Mediterranean to threaten Malta and communications with Alexandria, geography accorded the Entente navies the greater strategic advantage. The Entente controlled the two basins of the Mediterranean, trapping the Italian fleet between them. There was no way for the Regia Marina to break out of the Mediterranean. Italian sea communications with Ethiopia could easily be interdicted, and communications with Libya lay vulnerable to Allied attack from both east and west. Indeed, Libya itself emerged as a tempting target, especially to the French. The question was whether the Entente navies would combine to cripple the Italian fleet at the outset of hostilities or whether they would instead settle for a less aggressive strategy. There was also the chance that Italy would attempt to remain neutral at the outset of hostilities. Whatever Rome's intentions, Anglo-French naval planners had no choice but to assume Italian belligerency from the beginning and to plan accordingly. But there were no plans to provoke Italy to war. This is because the Admiralty wished to preserve the option of keeping Italy neutral rather than waging war in the Mediterranean.

As for Entente naval bases in the Mediterranean, the main problem lay in the absence of secure repair and docking facilities. Malta and Toulon both possessed full docking and repair facilities, but both of them lay within striking range of Italian air power. Alexandria and Gibraltar had only limited facilities, but they were well situated as operational bases. Bizerte was suitable as a repair and operational base for cruisers and light vessels. Algiers, Oran, and Marseilles, with only limited repair facilities, were nevertheless well suited as operational bases for heavy ships. There were extensive aviation facilities in Tunisia, but there were not enough aircraft available to exploit that advantage.[28] Nevertheless, the availability of numerous operational bases in the western basin accorded the Entente a decisive advantage over the Regia Marina.

In addition, the Royal Navy, with an aircraft carrier operating out of Alexandria, held an advantage in naval aviation over the Regia Marina, which had no aircraft carriers. But the importance of that advantage was not fully appreciated in 1939, as doctrines of naval aviation lagged behind its technology. Equally important, the Mediterranean Sea, much of which lay within range of land-based aviation, was not as friendly to aircraft carriers as were the vast waters of the Pacific Ocean. In the Mediterranean, the value of the British advantage would hinge upon how inventive the Royal Navy could be in matching the doctrine of naval aviation with the technological capabilities inherent in it as a weapons system.

The second phase of the naval consultations began on July 27 at Malta, where British admiral Sir Andrew Cunningham received French vice-admiral Emmanuel Ollive. These discussions assumed Italian belligerency at the outset of war with Germany. The two admirals quickly agreed upon a strategic policy of naval cooperation to render untenable the Italian positions in Libya and Ethiopia. The immediate objective was to cut all Italian maritime communications and to apply additional naval pressure upon Italy. When Cunningham stated that his mission included "bringing enemy naval forces to action wherever found," Ollive answered that "each ally had much the same tasks whilst between them lay the forces to be destroyed."[29]

But the Admiralty and the Rue Royale, in contrast to Cunningham and Ollive, were not in step on the question of an Italian war. While Cunningham and Ollive agreed that the best method of luring the enemy fleet to action was bombardment of enemy ports, Cunningham had orders not to attack Italian homeland ports until authorized to do so. Ollive's orders did not contain that restraint, so the French operational plans at the outset were more aggressive than the British.[30]

The British command, moreover, assumed separate operations in the two basins of the Mediterranean—the British in the east and the French in the west. The Admiralty did not intend for British and French warships to operate together as task forces. By this time, however, the French command had moved in the opposite direction, toward close operational cooperation in the Mediterranean. But Ollive had to settle for something less—that operations be timed in a manner to disperse enemy forces and to create opportunities for the other to exploit in the opposite basin. So instead of combining their forces, the two admirals agreed upon a demarcation line running between Malta and Tunisia to separate them.[31] As for interallied communications, it was decided that an exchange of liaison officers would not be necessary. These arrangements were not what the French had desired, but Ollive accepted them gracefully. What Ollive had offered, and what the Admiralty rejected, was French cooperation to combine Anglo-French naval assets in the Mediterranean to destroy the Regia Marina at the outset of hostilities.

Each command brought to the meeting specific plans to govern operations at the outset of war. Cunningham brought two plans, one more muscular than the other. Should the enemy have inflicted casualties among civilians, Cunningham would implement plan 1, which involved naval and carrier aviation attacks on Italian colonial ports. Staged out of Alexandria and requiring specific authorization from the Admiralty, these raids would be launched against Derna, Tobruk, and Benghazi in Libya and against Augusta and Catania on the eastern coast of Sicily. Plan 2, requiring no prior authorization, restricted British naval action to operations on the high seas and forbade attacks on Italian colonial ports. To be implemented in the event the enemy had not attacked civilian populations, it aimed at destroying Italian shipping in the eastern Mediterranean.[32] Neither of the British plans permitted attacks on Italian mainland ports.

The French plan, more aggressive than the British, contained no prohibition about attacking Italian mainland ports. Its first objective was to provide convoy protection for troop transports operating between North Africa and France. Beyond that, French warships of all types would seize the initiative in the Mediterranean. Submarines would take offensive action in an area stretching across the Ligurian and Tyrrhenian Seas. Other submarine units would attack Italian communications between Sicily and Libya. These attacks would be supplemented by light ships operating out of Bizerte to interrupt enemy traffic between Sicily and Libya. The French plan assumed the advantage of combined Anglo-French operations in the waters between Sicily and Libya. It also called for naval and aerial attacks on Italian port cities, including Genoa and Savona. Their targets would include shipping, harbors, oil tanks, and industrial works.[33]

Impressed with the French plans, Cunningham would have preferred a more aggressive strategy against Italy, but London would have none of it. Admiral Sir Dudley Pound, recently appointed First Sea Lord, had cautioned Cunningham about any plan to employ naval force to knock Italy quickly out of the war. Pound insisted that Italy could be defeated only by an invasion of her territory or by aerial bombardment and that aggressive naval action against her risked the loss of battleships, which would weaken British naval capabilities against Japan. Pound insisted instead upon a naval war of attrition against Italy—a war designed to wear Italy down by interrupting her naval communications, attacking her commerce, sinking her submarines, and only later attacking Libya and bombarding Italian ports.[34]

Pound was therefore opposed to any combined or concerted Anglo-French naval operation intended to strike a heavy blow against the Italian navy at the outset of hostilities. He favored instead restrained Mediterranean operations aimed mainly at avoiding loss of British battleships. His thinking reflected the Admiralty's perceptions about the purpose of the alliance, which assumed the role of Entente naval power in the Mediterranean to be one of restraining Italy and Japan, rather than one of defeating the Regia Marina.

Responding on July 26, Cunningham tactfully challenged Pound's cautious approach to Mediterranean war planning. He worried that Anglo-French planning had not been entirely satisfactory. "I had thought," he wrote, "that things were shaping up between the French and ourselves to go for the weak end of the Axis. I am not sure that the fault does not, to some extent, lie with ourselves." Cunningham insisted that Libya could easily be isolated and forced out of the war within six months, and that aggressive bombardment of Italian ports would impact heavily upon Italian morale. "But whether this view is correct or not," he added, "it appears to me to be the *only* plan before us which shows any signs of producing success for us and our Allies in the early stages." He went on to insist that "a policy of holding back the battlefleet would be a mistaken one." Commenting on the Ollive plan, Cunningham applauded the French proposal to launch aggressive naval attacks against Italian home ports. "In fact," he continued, "the French had decided upon an identical policy I had hoped was ours."[35] He added that he and Ollive were in full agreement that carefully concerted British and French attacks would disperse the Italians and significantly impact upon their morale. Cunningham, in full agreement with Ollive, was out of step with Pound on the question of concerted naval operations against Italy.

Meeting between Pound and Darlan

Although numerous details of Anglo-French naval war planning remained to be worked out, Pound received Darlan at Portsmouth on August 8 to enter into agreement on the strategic outlines of the plans. During the weeks prior to their meeting, Darlan and Pound had arrived at vastly different positions regarding how the naval war ought to be fought. Pound's policy of restraint in the Mediterranean contrasted sharply with Darlan's view of the Mediterranean as the decisive theater of operations where the crippling of the Regia Marina would fulfill a key strategic purpose of the alliance.

Darlan's staff directive of August 3 reveals that his strategic thinking had come into sharp focus. Darlan understood Germany to be the main enemy, but he saw clearly that there was no way to launch a naval attack against her. He believed, however, that the Axis could be reached through the Mediterranean. "It is therefore in the Mediterranean, especially in the central Mediterranean," he wrote, "that it is necessary to act. All other theatres are secondary."[36] Darlan knew that Germany would send her surface raiders into the Atlantic, but that threat did not worry him. He insisted that "the Atlantic has less importance than the Mediterranean. As soon as the question of the Mediterranean is settled, everything will be simplified. That will be particularly true for the Far East. In summary, the importance of operations in the Mediterranean will be predominant."[37]

Darlan's strategy therefore coincided with that of Cunningham rather than Pound. He focused on the Mediterranean, where the British and French navies working together held all of the high cards. Darlan envisioned an aggressive Anglo-French naval war against Italy with the goal of destroying the Italian fleet. With the Italian fleet no longer a threat, the Royal Navy would be free to commit its heaviest Mediterranean assets—those at Alexandria—to restrain Japan, and the greater part of the French fleet would be released to assist with the war against German commerce raiders in the Atlantic. The key was to destroy Italian naval power early in the war and to settle thereby the Mediterranean problem at the outset.

At the highest planning levels, therefore, the British and French naval commands were out of step with each other in terms of the purpose and capabilities of the alliance. Darlan, who viewed the alliance first as a tool to smash Italy, preferred combined operations and tight naval liaison down to the tactical level in the Mediterranean. In the Atlantic, though, he opposed tactical liaison in the interest of maintaining his firm grip on his Raiding Force. Pound, who viewed the alliance as an instrument to achieve a more efficient distribution of Entente naval assets, preferred tactical liaison in the Atlantic to orchestrate combined operations against German surface raiders. Conversely, in the Mediterranean he rejected French proposals for close cooperation at the tactical level.

The purpose of the August 8 meeting at Portsmouth between Pound and Darlan was to sign off on the agreements that had been hammered out by their planning staffs. These agreements were detailed and numerous, touching on contingencies stretching literally around the globe. They covered, for example, technical and operational problems related to minefields, aircraft search zones, defense of the English Channel, command organization, naval forces in the Red Sea, shipments of coal to France, new ship construction, harbor defenses, and defense of the Red Sea and French Indochina.[38]

The most urgent agreements concluded at Portsmouth were related to convoy protection and the defining of action zones. Tentative agreements reached earlier in London concerning convoy escort were confirmed. The powerful French Raiding Force would operate out of Brest for service in the Atlantic against enemy surface raiders since the *Dunkerque* and *Strasbourg* had been designed for that purpose. The North Sea and the remainder of the Atlantic would come under British responsibility. The two navies would share responsibilities for patrolling the Mediterranean, the French in the western basin and the British in the eastern. This meant that the British force at Alexandria would serve a dual role of restraining Italy and Japan simultaneously. Other technical and operational agreements provided for the use of each other's harbors and facilities and for the exchange of codes. To Darlan's disappointment, liaison officers in the Mediterranean would be exchanged only at high command levels.[39] Nevertheless, the meeting ended cordially, setting the stage for productive relations between Pound and Darlan during the war.

Clashing Mediterranean Strategies

Although the Admiralty and the Rue Royale had cooperated well enough to create the Entente, the prewar planning sessions failed to resolve basic differences between the two naval commands in terms of Mediterranean strategy. Pound's letter of August 18, 1939, to Cunningham sheds further light on the Admiralty's thinking about the opening stages of any war against Italy. Pound wrote that naval bombardments of Tobruk and other Libyan ports would be permissible. He objected, however, to any naval attack upon Italy itself on the grounds that the British fleet might be badly damaged. He would instead hold back any attack there until a time when it might be coordinated with an attack on the Italian fleet anchored at Taranto. He did not wish to prematurely risk the aircraft carrier *Glorious*, anchored at Alexandria, for its loss would sidetrack any aerial operation later in the war aimed at crippling the Regia Marina in a surprise attack.[40]

Pound had not ruled out an attack to cripple or destroy the Regia Marina. He had opted instead to hold that threat in reserve as a tool to be employed in a timely manner should Italy become a belligerent at the outset. He overestimated the power of British naval aviation at that early moment in the war, however, assuming an air raid at Taranto to be the equivalent of sustained Anglo-French naval operations to overwhelm the Regia Marina. What Pound most desired, and what the Admiralty and the British political command also desired, was Italian neutrality. Neither the naval nor the political leadership intended to provoke Italy to war. They aimed instead to keep Italy neutral and to continue the policy of appeasement toward Rome. In the meantime, British and French naval forces would patrol their separate Mediterranean zones in a manner to impress Rome with their power and simultaneously avoid any provocation that might interrupt naval communications between Gibraltar and Singapore.

The Admiralty and the Rue Royale therefore differed importantly in their Mediterranean strategy. Pound's cautious attitude and his concern to withhold

British assets betrayed the Admiralty's assumption of an auxiliary role for the French navy in the Mediterranean, one that assigned it a patrol zone to the end of liberating British ships for service elsewhere. That view discounted the tactical and strategic possibilities inherent in the alliance. In contrast, the Rue Royale appreciated the offensive capabilities of the two navies working together to cripple the Regia Marina, to isolate Libya, and to seize control of the Mediterranean at the outset of hostilities. French strategy assumed combined or concerted offensive operations against a weaker enemy to be the main naval advantage the Entente would enjoy early in the war.

The Italian naval command feared exactly the kind of war that Darlan had proposed to unleash. On May 18 Admiral Domenico Cavagnari, navy chief of staff, warned Mussolini that the Entente combination in the Mediterranean posed a naval threat at least double that of the strength of the Italian navy. Carrying the war to either end of the Mediterranean was out of the question, he insisted, and control even of the central Mediterranean would hinge upon Italian aerial domination that could not be ensured. And he admitted that there was little chance of maintaining naval communications between Italy and Libya.[41]

The Admiralty chose not to wage that kind of war. Worried at the rise of Japanese naval power in Asia, it settled for the safer strategy of distributing Anglo-French naval assets in a pattern to keep peace in the Mediterranean. In adopting that strategy, the Admiralty forfeited the option of striking at the outset a decisive blow against the weakest link in the Axis alliance.

Approach to War

As tensions mounted during the second half of August, the European powers postured their navies in a manner reflecting their plans and interests. Germany quickly seized the initiative. In late August the *Graf Spee* and *Deutschland* steamed toward the narrow waters east of the Shetland Islands approaching the North Atlantic, and several units of the Reich's U-boat fleet slipped into the North Sea. In mid-August the Royal Navy and the Royal Air Force held exercises to test Coastal Command's operational plans. Aerial patrols were sent to monitor German ship movements. By the end of August the ships of the Home Fleet had assumed their assigned wartime stations, and a powerful squadron under Admiral Sir Charles Forbes had begun patrolling the waters between the Shetlands and Norway.[42] But by this time the two German surface raiders had already entered the vast waters of the North Atlantic.

As war approached in late August, Mussolini opted for neutrality despite his alliance with Hitler. He chose neutrality because he expected the Entente to confront him with overwhelming naval and military power. In a message to Berlin on the twenty-fifth, Il Duce advanced prohibitive demands for Italy's entering the war, insisting that the Reich send at once "military supplies and materials to resist the attack which the French and English would predominately direct against us."[43] The next day he informed Hitler that "the French and British would attack Italy in full force by land, sea, and in the air, immediately war broke out."[44] Three days later German ambassador Hans Mackensen sent Berlin a precise explanation of Mussolini's motives, reporting that "in the event of war Italy would have to bear the whole brunt of a naval attack, because Germany is practically invulnerable, or only slightly vulnerable, thanks to her favorable geographical position."[45] Clearly, Mussolini backed away from war because he understood that the Regia Marina was too weak to challenge combined Anglo-French naval power in the Mediterranean.

In Paris, news of the August 23 Molotov-Ribbentrop Pact between Germany and the Soviet Union alerted Darlan to the possibility of immediate hostilities against Germany and perhaps Italy and Japan. During that last week of peace he met daily with his chiefs of staff, with Captain Cedric S. Holland, British naval attaché, always in attendance. Darlan warned French merchant ships at sea, ordered aerial surveillance of waters opposite French home and colonial ports, and instructed French naval attachés to report to their assigned posts with their British counterparts. By the end of the month the Marine Nationale was in a state of full alert.[46]

There remained the nagging question of how many enemies the Entente would have to fight. For obvious reasons, neither London nor Paris wanted a war with Japan. At the end of August, combined Anglo-French naval maneuvers were staged in the Far East to impress Tokyo with the fact of Entente solidarity.[47] In Rome, Mussolini waxed hot and cold between peace and war, trapped between the Axis alliance and overwhelming Entente naval power in the Mediterranean. Neutrality was inconsistent with his fascist dignity, but geography worked against him. News on August 23 of the German pact with the Soviets surprised and offended him, as he despised the Soviets. On that same day, under pressure from Ciano, he agreed upon a policy of working with London to seek a negotiated peace built around the transfer of Danzig to the Reich. But on August 26, with little thought to its diplomatic implications, he put the central Mediterranean naval command on full war footing. London and Paris undertook similar measures in accordance with Anglo-French plans. Halifax, however, took care the next day to assure Ciano, who noted in his diary the British assurances that "the precautionary measures taken in the Mediterranean must not be interpreted as a prelude to hostilities against us."[48]

But Mussolini, still out of step with Ciano, ordered additional defense measures, including overnight electrical blackouts of Rome.[49] The Entente might suspect that Rome was talking peace but preparing for war. Responding on August 31, London abruptly cut telephone communications with Rome. Ciano complained to Il Duce, who insisted that he would inform the Grand Council next day of Italy's intention to remain neutral. "Tomorrow may be too late," Ciano thought, "the English and French may by then have committed acts that render any such declaration very difficult."[50] Hurriedly, Ciano assured British ambassador Sir Percy Loraine that Italy would not go to war against Britain and France. The lights were turned on again, and communications were restored, but the affair had kindled in Ciano fears of an Entente naval strike against Italy.[51]

These fears were renewed in early September, after the outbreak of war on September 3, when London inquired about an unidentified submarine in the Mediterranean. Mussolini denied that the submarine was Italian, but the incident prompted Rome in desperation to propose a renewal of the Nyon Arrangement.[52] London had no interest in renewing Nyon, but on September 6 Loraine assured Ciano that the Royal Navy would take care to avoid incidents with Italian submarines.[53] With that assurance, London forfeited the opportunity to provoke a war against Italy at the outset of hostilities.

The Entente navies could easily have denied Mussolini his neutrality, but there was little chance of London's provoking an Italian war. Public opinion was against it. And, moreover, the events of August had imposed a heavy burden on Italo-German relations, setting the stage for Chamberlain to flirt again with Mussolini in the hope of luring him into the Entente camp. The war therefore erupted in early September with Mussolini standing on the sidelines.

While German armies rolled across Poland, the naval war in the Atlantic flared with similar violence. On September 3, the first day of the war, a German submarine sank the British passenger ship *Athena*, and London declared a blockade of the German coast. With the *Deutschland* and *Graf Spee* already at sea and with Nazi U-boats lurking in British home waters, the Admiralty focused its attention on the protection of near and distant trade routes. With Italy neutral, the Italian fleet lay in port at Taranto as a latent threat, tying up Entente assets that might have been employed elsewhere. In permitting Mussolini to remain neutral in 1939, the Entente backed away from the only war it was capable of winning.

Chapter 9

War on the Periphery

During the autumn of 1939 the Entente commands in London and Paris shared the vision of a war of *longue durée*, which assumed prolonged defensive warfare on the military front in northern France. They were for the most part confident of the strength of the Maginot Line, and they were prepared to move swiftly toward natural defensive positions in Belgium should the Reich strike from the north. The French military machine had been designed more for defense than offense, however, and when confronted with the fact of German military superiority on the continent, the Entente commands had no expectation of scoring a decisive victory on the French front when war broke out on September 3.

There was, however, an urgent need for victory in some quarter, for public opinion demanded it. Neither Neville Chamberlain nor Edouard Daladier enjoyed unanimous support on the home front, and they could not expect to survive politically in the absence of military success. From the beginning, therefore, London and Paris came to share the vision of shifting the focus of war from France to more remote areas. Historically, war on the periphery had been standard British strategy, but now it became attractive in Paris as a substitute for victories lacking on the main military front. War on the periphery would hinge heavily upon naval power, but the naval war quickly settled in waters closer to home, so consideration of remote adventures would have to wait its turn.

Problems of Naval Warfare

The main problem facing the Entente naval commands at the outbreak of war related to the fact that there was no good way to launch a naval war against Germany. The easiest targets were the Italian fleet and Libya. Winston Churchill, who returned to the Admiralty at the outbreak of war, underscored that point. "Our forces alone," he later wrote, "even without the French Navy and its fortified harbors, were sufficient to drive the Italian ships from the sea, and should secure complete naval command of the Mediterranean within two months and possibly sooner."[1] But London, unwilling to provoke Rome to war, accorded the Regia Marina a safe haven under the umbrella of neutrality.

In contrast, the German Kriegsmarine enjoyed important advantages that geography had denied the Regia Marina. The main German naval bases lay on the Baltic Sea beyond narrow waters easily defended or in secure ports such as Wilhelmshaven, on the North Sea. These ports were well suited to serve as bases from which to stage surface or undersea raids against shipping in the distant Atlantic or in British home waters. The naval war therefore unfolded in a predictable manner, with the Kriegsmarine seizing the initiative in a campaign against British shipping. German U-boats took up positions south of the British Isles and along the trade routes off the western coast of Spain. The surface raider *Deutschland*, already at sea, returned to German home waters, but the *Graf Spee* slipped unobserved into the distant Atlantic. The Reich's heaviest ships prudently avoided any fleet action against the much larger British Home Fleet.

In 1939 German submarines rarely ventured into the distant Atlantic. For the moment, therefore, the naval war unfolded mainly in waters south of the British Isles, where a small fleet of U-boats preyed upon a large volume of shipping. These early clashes at sea defined the main pattern of naval war that followed in Atlantic waters, and they gave rise to important problems whose solution would demand additional light assets and a suitable doctrine of antisubmarine warfare lacking at the outbreak of war. The Admiralty would soon learn by experience, for example, the heavy cost of sending big ships to fight submarines

During September Germany was able to station perhaps half a dozen U-boats on the approaches to the British home islands. The Entente began to organize convoys, according to plans, but in the first two weeks of September most merchantmen approached the British Isles independently. In two weeks the British suffered loss of 28 merchant ships, a total of 147,000 tons.[2] In terms of the total volume of trade, the losses were not enough to threaten the economic life of the British homeland. But the Reich had already begun construction of numerous tenders designed to nourish German raiders or submarines on the high seas, and German U-boat construction began to mount.[3] The stage was being set for a massive German U-boat offensive that would exploit the British shortage of light craft suitable for antisubmarine warfare.

British warships also came under attack, with important losses. Only two weeks into the war the aircraft carrier *Courageous*, on U-boat patrol in the Bristol Channel, was torpedoed and sunk by a German submarine. A month later the battleship *Royal Oak* met a similar fate when U-47 slipped undetected into the main British anchorage at Scapa Flow. The U-boat threat had become serious enough to render premature any plans to wage war on the periphery. With losses mounting, the Admiralty had good reason to focus its attention on the U-boat threat.

Anglo-French Naval Communications

Communications between the French and British naval commands early in the war unfolded at several levels, ranging from naval attaché and liaison contacts to high-level strategic planning under the authority of an inter-Allied war committee, which met as needed in London or Paris. Key players on the British side were the First Sea Lord, Admiral Sir Dudley Pound, and Captain Cedric Holland, the British naval liaison officer in France, later the head of the British naval mission there. Pound communicated regularly with Admiral Darlan, and Holland was often the intermediary in this correspondence. Popular and trusted among French officers, Holland was welcomed to the daily morning meetings of the French naval chiefs.

On the French side, Darlan called the main signals, but he regularly consulted his naval staff. Routine communications with him ran through his naval staff secretary, Captain Henri Ballande, a brilliant naval technician soon to take charge of the first bureau of French Maritime Forces, responsible for rationing to the fleet weapons, ammunition, and other scarce assets. Ballande reported to Admiral Maurice Le Luc, Darlan's chief of staff, but he also had access to Darlan. Also reporting to Le Luc were two deputy chiefs of staff, Captains Paul Auphan, responsible for strategic planning, and C. V. Négadelle, who covered technical matters. Holland came into regular contact with all of these officers and, with the exception of Auphan, held them in high regard.

After war broke out, Darlan shuttled between Paris and his alternate headquarters at Maintenon, about fifty miles southwest of Paris, where a vast network of telephone and telegraph lines converged. By the standards of that time, Maintenon was a marvel of naval communications. From his headquarters there, Darlan enjoyed direct cable communications with metropolitan and North African naval bases. Wireless facilities enabled him to communicate with ships at sea. In September Darlan transferred to Maintenon his naval staff and selected other services related to operations, planning, technology, and communications. Captain Holland also moved there, so Maintenon (code-named Marceau) emerged as a center of Anglo-French naval communications. Many of Holland's communications with London bear the code name Marceau.

Although the magnitude of the German submarine threat was not fully understood when war broke out in early September, Anglo-French naval communications during subsequent weeks reflect a growing concern at the shortage of antisubmarine assets. Darlan, responsible for patrolling Mediterranean traffic lanes, expressed his concern in a September 17 letter to Pound. "I am especially anxious," he wrote, "as regards traffic protection, because I feel very poor in A/S vessels."[4] He went on to request delivery to France of fifteen trawlers that had been ordered earlier. Pound, aware of British shortages, promptly answered that he could send only eight, adding that he "should like to leave the question of the other 7 until later when we see how things are going."[5]

Minor Tensions in the Alliance

Despite British inability to lend France much material support, communications between Pound and Darlan remained cordial. But routine problems sometimes burdened their good relations. In late October, for example, Darlan summoned Holland, informing him tactfully of a problem at Gibraltar, where French warships guarded the strait. The former British commander there had worked well with the French, Darlan said, but his replacement cooperated poorly, isolating himself so he could not be reached. Darlan confessed his misgivings about complaining directly to Admiral Pound lest it appear that he was asking the admiral to remove one of his flag officers. "But he did feel," Holland wrote Pound, "that it was necessary to bring this matter to your notice in some way as he considered a close co-operation in this area was so essential to the war effort."[6]

The British, in turn, sometimes found French officers to be uncooperative. In early November Darlan lent support to a British request for twelve French submarines to assist with the escorting of convoys from Halifax, subject to the approval of his staff. Holland felt sure that the French would cooperate, for he knew that Darlan favored the plan. Holland was therefore surprised when the French staff hedged on the request. Displeased, he wrote Pound that Captain Auphan "fought the scheme and carried the day with the result that at present only four are being sent. This only confirms the views I have previously sent you regarding this officer."[7] As it turned out, the French staff finally approved delivery of six submarines, for which Pound cordially thanked Darlan.[8] But Holland remained distrustful of Auphan.

Another awkward incident involved Darlan himself, who in early November received at Maintenon a British delegation headed by Winston Churchill, then First Lord of the Admiralty. The meeting was productive and for the most part cordial. Churchill was delighted at Darlan's promise to rush to completion the battleships *Richelieu* and *Jean Bart*, to counter the German *Bismarck*, scheduled to enter service prior to completion of the first *King George V*–class ships. But Churchill was piqued at the absence of his civilian counterpart, Minister of Marine César Campinchi, and with Darlan's insensitive explanation that under the French system the civilian minister is excluded from operational discussions. Although Churchill made no complaint, he was offended enough to mention the affront in his memoirs.[9] These tensions, however, were not serious enough to threaten the stability of the alliance.

Problems of Doctrine and Vision

Although the Entente had no good way to launch offensive naval operations against Germany, Churchill brought to the Admiralty an offensive mentality that poorly matched the kind of war the Reich had chosen to wage. The German submarine offensive early in the war focused on the heavy mercantile traffic near the British Isles. Prewar plans called for a convoy system, but Churchill, regarding escorts as defensive, pressed the Admiralty to find offensive solutions. The fundamental problem was the lack of a workable antisubmarine doctrine amplified by a shortage of destroyers and other small craft and by the failure of the Asdic sonar device to match its prewar expectations. In its frustration to find an offensive solution, the Admiralty hastened to prepare a series of visionary schemes out of step with the realities of modern naval warfare.

One of these, authored by Churchill during the first week of the war, reflects again the lack of an effective doctrine of antisubmarine warfare. The proposal called for the creation of hunting groups organized in a manner to seize the offensive initiative in the war at sea. Churchill initially expected to employ the concept against German surface raiders, but as the submarine menace became more serious early in the war he expanded it for operations against U-boats. At the center of each hunting group would be an aircraft carrier, escorted by lighter warships that included several destroyers. The idea was to use naval aviation to seek out enemy submarines and to send the destroyers to sink them.

The concept of employing aircraft carriers to destroy submarines proved to be a costly failure. The hunting groups rarely detected U-boats. There were not enough destroyers to serve both the hunting groups and the convoys, and aircraft carriers were too valuable to be risked in operations against submarines, a point underscored by the sinking of the *Courageous* in a submarine sweep. The loss of the *Courageous* was the product of poor naval aviation doctrine that misused valuable assets and failed to anticipate the need for smaller, inexpensive aircraft carriers. Better to withdraw the big carriers and assign the destroyers to convoy escort duty.[10]

Operation Catherine, another product of Churchill's fertile imagination, envisioned the use of armored battleships to break through the narrow waters between Denmark and Sweden to establish a base in the Baltic. Two or three *Royal Sovereign*–class battleships would be reinforced above with heavy steel plating and below with double steel bulges to protect them against torpedo attack. Minesweepers, destroyers, and submarines would clear the way for the battleships, to be followed by five cruisers, an aircraft carrier, a repair ship, and a host of tankers to provide fuel. The Scandinavian countries and the Soviet Union, impressed with this display of naval power, would presumably join the Allies and provide them naval bases in the Baltic.

Operation Catherine, a fanciful scheme full of technical and diplomatic problems, was wasteful and risky, courting disaster. Churchill vastly underestimated the effectiveness of air power against ships at sea, and he failed to understand that the Scandinavian states and the Soviets would not easily abandon their neutrality. Nor did he see that Catherine might provoke Germany to occupy Denmark. Pound opposed the project but dared not confront Churchill directly. Nevertheless, he patiently pointed out the numerous problems inherent in the operation, including the fact that it would stretch thin the assets of the Royal Navy elsewhere. The First Lord would not back off easily, though, so it was not until 1940 that preparations for Catherine were finally put to rest.[11]

French Plans for Peripheral Warfare

British naval planners in early 1939 expected to wage war in the Atlantic and to avoid a Mediterranean war. But General Maurice Gamelin and the French military command, surprised at the quick success of German armies against Poland, worried that the offensive might spill over into Romania and eventually into the Balkans. Accordingly, when the French War Committee met on September 8, the question arose as to whether it might be necessary to send military forces to the eastern Mediterranean, perhaps to Salonika, to establish a second front.[12] Although no decision was taken, the War Committee was considering whether to wage war in the Mediterranean, which was exactly what London had from the beginning intended to avoid.

When the French War Committee met again on September 20, it settled upon a proposal to send military aid to Turkey, Greece, and Yugoslavia to head off any German intervention in the Balkans. The proposal, like Operation Catherine, was full of problems. Any initiative in the Balkans risked provoking German intervention there rather than heading it off. And Darlan had warned that any French adventure in the eastern Mediterranean lay hostage to Italy, whose fleet might ambush vital communications through the central Mediterranean. The operation, therefore, hinged upon prior arrangements with Rome to ensure Italian neutrality. Innocently assuming that Mussolini might cooperate, the war committee agreed to move ahead with the plan. Paris would undertake a diplomatic initiative with Rome to explore the Italian attitude, and Daladier would request of London a meeting of the Supreme War Council for further discussions.[13]

When the Supreme War Council met in London two days later, French and British differences on war strategy came swiftly to the surface. Although the war was less than three weeks old, the Royal Navy was already overextended in its struggle with German U-boats in the Atlantic. So Daladier's proposal to expand the war into the Mediterranean hardly impressed the British chiefs. The lively discussion that followed served only to amplify Anglo-French differences. The Supreme War Council finally agreed to submit the proposal to the military staffs for study and to explore through diplomatic channels the attitudes of Italy and of Turkey.[14] This solution, a tactful way of putting the proposal on the shelf without undue embarrassment to the French ally, ought to have ended the matter.

The French, however, did not abandon the Balkan proposal, and in December, when the Supreme War Council met in Paris, the French chiefs brought it up again.[15] The council, however, made no decision to implement it. In the meantime, while talks with Rome and Ankara continued with no results, London and the British Mediterranean command continued to oppose the plan.[16] The British were therefore able to keep the proposal on the shelf without having to undergo the embarrassment of rejecting it outright at the expense of the alliance.

Problems in Naval Cooperation, 1939

During the last two months of 1939 the British naval chiefs pressed their French opposites for greater support in operations against German U-boats and surface raiders. Although a German raider of the *Deutschland* type was known to be at sea in October, the U-boat menace loomed as the greater threat. Late in the month the Admiralty requested the French command to provide destroyer reinforcements for British warships patrolling the waters west of Gibraltar. The French destroyers would have to be transferred to Gibraltar from Toulon, where they were employed to escort Mediterranean convoys and stand guard against any Italian aggression.[17]

When Holland presented the request to Auphan, however, the Frenchman rejected it outright, insisting that French destroyers were already mounting intermittent patrols west of Gibraltar. He added that the destroyers based at Toulon were being employed to escort troop convoys from North Africa and that none of these could be spared. Reporting back to London, Holland wrote, "I shall not let the matter drop but a refusal to any request has become so habitual with this Officer that now it may seem impossible for him to react in any other way."[18]

This problem and others were finally resolved on the morning of November 3, when Pound and his naval staff entered into discussions with the French staff at Maintenon. The meeting got off to a good start as Pound pledged further assistance and cooperation with the French navy. When the discussion moved to the question of French naval dispositions, Darlan overruled Auphan, agreeing to the transfer of six destroyers to establish a patrol west of Gibraltar. As the meeting continued, Holland saw that Darlan cooperated on every request the British made of him. Darlan agreed to make two old battleships available for convoy escort duty in the South Atlantic to lend added protection against German surface raiders, and he offered the services of the heavy cruiser *Suffren* to assist with the escorting of British convoys from Australia. He also arranged with the British chiefs to rotate their heavy ships in and out of the Dakar-Freetown area in sequence, so they could return to their home ports for routine maintenance.[19] This rotation, however, would have to be delayed, as these ships were already involved in joint naval operations to hunt down a German raider known to be somewhere in the South Atlantic.

Early in the war naval segregation in the Atlantic gave way to joint operations in key strategic areas where combining British and French assets would amplify Entente naval power. From Dakar, for example, the *Strasbourg* was joined with the British carrier *Hermes* to sweep waters between West Africa and the Antilles. Although the radius of action of the *Hermes* was less than that of the *Strasbourg*, reconnaissance aircraft from the carrier augmented the operational effectiveness of the fast French battlecruiser considerably beyond the capabilities of French naval aviation. Escorted by two heavy cruisers, *Algérie* and *Dupleix*, and five French destroyers based at Dakar, the *Hermes-Strasbourg* hunting group posed a strong threat to any German surface raider in central Atlantic waters.[20] This combined operation at the tactical level marked a productive departure from prewar planning that had assumed separate zones and segregated operations for the two navies in the Atlantic.

At the November 3 meeting at Maintenon, the French staff proposed matching the *Strasbourg* with the British carrier *Ark Royal*, based at Freetown, rather than with the *Hermes*. Darlan realized that the battlecruiser *Renown*, attached to the *Ark Royal*, was slower than the *Strasbourg,* and that the *Strasbourg* stood a better chance than the *Renown* of overtaking and engaging any German warship that the *Ark Royal's* aircraft might discover at points distant from the task force. Pound, however, insisted upon keeping the *Ark Royal* with the *Renown*. The French staff might have questioned Pound's judgment, but in the interest of Entente solidarity they graciously accepted the British view.[21] Pound's decision, however, was but a minor detail in what emerged otherwise as a brilliant example of Anglo-French cooperation in planning the destruction of the German raider *Graf Spee*.

The Glory Days of Anglo-French Naval Cooperation

Anglo-French naval planning proceeded with the eventual creation of nine hunting groups in the Atlantic, some of them composed of British and French warships operating together. The sinking in early October of three merchant ships near the Cape of Good Hope signaled the presence of an unidentified German pocket battleship in the South Atlantic. German naval strategy was to strike at widely divergent points for the purpose of spreading Entente assets thin. In pursuit of this strategy, and with the *Graf Spee* prowling the South Atlantic, the German naval command sent the battlecruisers *Gneisenau* and *Scharnhorst* through the Skagerrak into Atlantic waters off Norway, where on November 23 they sank the British merchant cruiser *Rawalpindi*.

This German initiative set the stage for another combined Anglo-French naval operation in the Atlantic. Within hours the *Hood* set sail from Plymouth to join its French counterpart, the *Dunkerque*, recently departed from Brest accompanied by two *Mogador*-class destroyers and the cruisers *Montcalm* and *Georges Leygues*—"Gorgeous Legs" to British sailors not fluent in French. The two battlecruisers with their escorts merged in the English Channel to intercept the enemy force. Although the two German raiders quickly retreated to home waters, this combined operation from November 25 to December 2 took the two Entente battlecruisers into waters as distant as Iceland. It also gave birth to warm camaraderie between the *Hood* and her French companion, the *Dunkerque*—"the friend of the *Hood*."[22]

The German initiative in northern waters failed to shift Entente attention away from the *Graf Spee*. The German raider, now in trouble, found itself isolated in the South Atlantic. In cooperation with the French naval command, the Admiralty reorganized Entente naval forces into a new pattern of hunting groups, two of which were composed of British and French warships working together to block the escape of the raider through the narrow Atlantic passage between Freetown and Pernambuco. Entente planners could assume that the *Graf Spee* would not risk passage through the well-defended waters off Dakar and Freetown. It would instead steam further to the west. Important

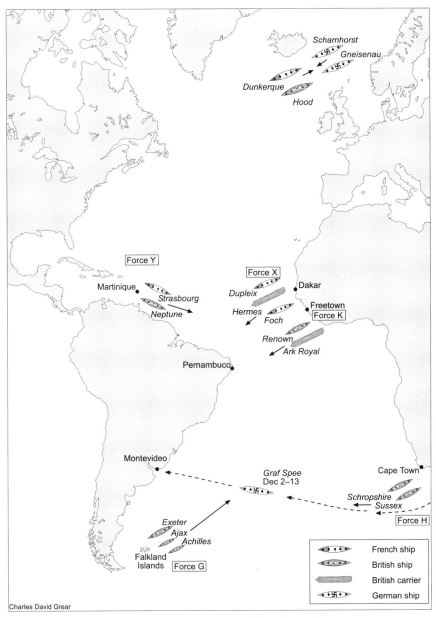

Map 1. Entente Strategy to Isolate the Graf Spee

to Entente strategy was Force X, led by the *Hermes*. Accompanied now by two French heavy cruisers, *Foch* and *Dupleix*, the *Hermes* steamed southwest from Dakar, where its aircraft mounted a wide search of mid-Atlantic waters. Lurking to the northwest in American waters was Force Y, consisting of six fast ships led by the *Strasbourg* and the British cruiser *Neptune*.[23] Should the *Graf Spee* steam northward toward the Antilles, it would encounter the *Strasbourg*, the Entente warship best suited to overtake the German raider and confront her with superior firepower. The plan obviously aimed at luring the *Graf Spee* into the presence of the *Strasbourg* and *Neptune*.

With a vast system of hunting groups in place, the search for the *Graf Spee* hinged upon her being sighted by aircraft or warships capable of closing or of maintaining contact until the arrival of a superior force. Apart from the combined Anglo-French forces built around the *Hermes* and the *Strasbourg*, there were other British hunting groups in the South Atlantic poised to close in on the German raider. In the mid-Atlantic, south of the *Hermes*, Force K, with the *Renown* and *Ark Royal*, covered vast expanses of mid-Atlantic waters. Force H, led by the cruisers *Sussex* and *Shropshire*, patrolled waters west of the Cape of Good Hope. There were additional forces, including the cruiser *Dorsetshire*, near the Cape. And Force G, with the heavy cruisers *Exeter* and *Cumberland* and light cruisers *Ajax* and *Achilles*, patrolled American waters near Uruguay. But the absence of the *Cumberland*, undergoing a refit in the Falklands, significantly weakened Force G, so it poorly matched the German raider with its 11-inch guns. Nevertheless, should the *Graf Spee* be sighted by Force G, it might be shadowed and finally confronted with powerful naval or carrier aviation forces capable of destroying it. Once the raider had been sighted, its chances of slipping back into home waters would be much diminished.

After the *Graf Spee* had sunk a British tanker in the Indian Ocean near Madagascar on November 15, she doubled back toward the South Atlantic, steaming far south of the Cape before she sank another ship, the *Doric Star*, on December 2. Commodore Henry Harwood, commander of Force G operating out of the Falklands, estimated that the German raider would appear off the River Plate on December 13 to prey upon the heavy commercial traffic in that area. He was on target, for early that morning the German raider appeared on the horizon. Captain Hans Langsdorff, commander of the *Graf Spee*, continued on course for another ten minutes, when he could have withdrawn in the hope of eluding the British squadron. Harwood, with the 8-inch cruiser *Exeter* and the 6-inch *Ajax* and *Achilles* but without the *Cumberland*, could also have avoided action, settling on a tactic of shadowing the raider until help arrived. He chose instead to close with the stronger ship. Maneuvering skillfully,

Harwood flanked the raider in a manner to divide the fire of her 11-inch guns. In the course of the battle, the *Exeter* was so badly damaged as to withdraw, with sixty-one crewmen dead. But the *Graf Spee*, also damaged, took refuge in the Uruguayan port of Montevideo. Four days later, as powerful Entente reinforcements closed in from several directions, the German raider scuttled herself in the river estuary. Langsdorff took his own life as the price to pay for losing his ship.

The heroic performance of Force G off the River Plate has long overshadowed the brilliant strategic planning that assembled a combination of British and French ships for the purpose of trapping the *Graf Spee* and confronting her with superior force. It seems ironic that Harwood's weak squadron, rather than Force K, with the *Ark Royal* and *Renown*, or Force Y, with *Strasbourg* and *Neptune*, should have played the decisive tactical card. It was, however, the larger strategic effort that had already doomed the German raider. Langsdorff finally scuttled his ship not because the *Ajax* and *Achilles* lay waiting off Montevideo, but because he knew that reinforcements operating out of British and French ports were fast approaching to confront him with superior power.

A New Strategic Picture

By the time that the British and French naval staffs met in London on December 20, the strategic situation had changed in the sense that the Entente had clearly demonstrated its ability to impose a heavy price upon enemy surface raiders operating in the Atlantic so that the naval war would soon shift into a pattern that amplified the role of smaller ships against U-boats. That change was not so obvious at the moment. As the meeting opened, Pound and Darlan exchanged friendly greetings. There were no important disagreements as they discussed a range of technical matters related mainly to repositioning their warships and rerouting convoys into waters that now had become more secure. Pound suggested the need to strengthen British forces in home waters to block the exits to the North Sea. Darlan readily agreed, promising that it might be possible for him to replace the two 6-inch cruisers assigned to the *Dunkerque* with 8-inch cruisers so that the French squadron would be better prepared to cooperate with British operations against any German raiders in northern waters. The meeting, which touched upon numerous other issues, was cordial and productive.[24]

The victorious operation against the *Graf Spee* remains the most notable example of Anglo-French naval cooperation of the war. Although the Royal Navy suffered the heavier losses and, indeed, took most of the credit, French ships and ports had played a key role in the strategic plan to track down the German raider. The operation also defined more clearly the limits of the surface raider as a weapon of economic warfare on the high seas. The threat of the *Graf Spee* prowling the Atlantic had provoked the Entente to commit in response a huge portion of its naval power, but the final outcome suggested that the costs of surface raiding were prohibitively high for a German fleet with too few raiders. The German surface fleet of 1939, including the *Scharnhorst* and *Gneisenau*, with their modest 11-inch guns, had been designed mainly to operate as commerce raiders. The destruction of the *Graf Spee*, 20 percent of the Reich's raiding force, signaled the high costs of continuing with that kind of warfare. The loss of the *Bismarck* in 1941 would underscore that message. In the meantime, the U-boat was fast emerging as a less expensive and more productive weapon than the surface raider.

Shifting Construction Priorities

Waging war against the submarine required an abundance of smaller and less expensive ships, of which the British had too few. Churchill had anticipated the U-boat threat early in the war, even before the German submarine offensive had gained momentum. With the war only in its third week, he reported in a memo to the War Cabinet that "we must expect a serious recrudescence of the U-Boat warfare during the summer and autumn of 1940."[25] Accordingly, he pushed steadily to suspend construction of the 16-inch battleships *Lion* and *Temeraire*, two unnamed battleships approved in 1939, and all other capital ships that could not be completed in 1941 so that greater emphasis could be placed on the construction of light vessels suited for antisubmarine warfare. Despite opposition from Pound, Churchill had his way. By the spring of 1940 British shipyards were changing gears to build more than a hundred destroyers, and more than twice that many corvettes, trawlers, and whalers suitable for antisubmarine patrol nearer to home ports.[26]

The British decision to cut back on the construction of capital ships was made easier by the fact that the French ally was rushing forward with construction of the *Richelieu* and *Jean Bart*, armed with 15-inch guns and scheduled for completion in the summer of 1940. In Britain, construction continued on the five 15-inch *King George V*–class battleships, so the Entente could expect seven new battleships to enter service by early 1942. But of the seven, only the two French ships were scheduled to enter service prior to the completion of the 15-inch German battleships *Bismarck* and *Tirpitz*. The British therefore expected the two French ships to cover the interval between the completion of the two German ships and the scheduled completion soon thereafter of the first two ships of the *George V* class.

The Reichsmarine of the Weimar Republic; German mariners with families at Swinemünde, 1931, on eve of maneuvers. AP Photo, National Archives and Records Administration

Modern ships of the Kriegsmarine; battle cruiser Deutschland, *sister ship of* Admiral Scheer *and* Admiral Graf Spee. AP Photo, National Archives and Records Administration

Spanish Nationalist submarine suspected of piracy in the Mediterranean, 1937.
AP Photo, National Archives and Records Administration

Sir Anthony Eden, 1938. Wide World Photo, National Archives
and Records Administration

Municipal Conference Hall, Nyon, Switzerland, site of the nine-power conference on piracy in the Mediterranean, September 1937. AP Photo, National Archives and Records Administration

Admiral Jean François Darlan, commander in chief of the French fleet, July 15, 1938. AP Photo, National Archives and Records Administration

British Prime Minister Neville Chamberlain, April 18, 1939. New York Times, National Archives and Records Administration

Captain Cedric Holland, British naval attaché to Paris, 1939–40. Courtesy of M. Hervé Grall, president of the Association des Anciens Marins et des Familles des Victimes de Mers-el-Kébir

Destruction of the German battle cruiser Graf Spee, December 1939. AP Photo, National Archives and Records Administration

French soldiers and mariners evacuated from Dunkirk, June 1940. Wide World Photo, National Archives and Records Administration

Admiral Sir Dudley Pound, at left, with American admiral Harold Stark. U.S. Naval Institute Photo Archive

Admiral Sir James Somerville. Courtesy of M. Hervé Grall, president of the Association des Anciens Marins et des Familles des Victimes de Mers-el-Kébir

French battle cruiser **Dunkerque.** AP Photo, National Archives and Records Administration

British battle cruiser **Hood.** U.S. Naval Institute Photo Archive

Obsolescent French battleship **Bretagne in 1913.** Courtesy of M. Hervé Grall, president of the Association des Anciens Marins et des Familles des Victimes de Mers-el-Kébir

French mariner guarding the battle cruisers Dunkerque *and* Strasbourg *at Mers el-Kébir prior to the British attack of July 3, 1940.* Courtesy of M. Hervé Grall, president of the Association des Anciens Marins et des Famillies des Victimes de Mers-el-Kébir

Flawed Strategies

Even though the French fleet had helped to track down the *Graf Spee*, the Royal Navy called the main signals in the operation that trapped the German raider at Montevideo. Whether that subordinate role influenced the attitude of Admiral Darlan is not certain, but it is clear that his morale began to sag toward the end of 1939. In his diary he complained about Communist propaganda that undermined morale on the home front and about the French military command, which he thought had prepared poorly for the war. He thought that the British, too, were unprepared, and that "after having done all they could for twenty years to prevent France having a navy, they are hanging onto my shirttail so that the French fleet will help them meet their responsibilities." He added, "We must conquer if we wish to remain free, and afterwards we will have to put down communism."[27] Darlan never expressed these views publicly—certainly not in the presence of the English—but he clearly had become frustrated at the army's inability to pursue the war aggressively, and he was growing resentful of his naval ally.

Distant events had already begun to nourish Darlan's anti-Bolshevism and lure him toward aggressive naval initiatives. With the Soviet invasion of Finland at the end of November 1939, the focus of war shifted abruptly to the East, far beyond the military or naval capabilities of either France or Great Britain. Nevertheless, news of heroic Finnish resistance against the larger Communist enemy stirred in France widespread emotions of anti-Bolshevism coupled with public demands upon Daladier to send military aid to Finland. Responding to this pressure, Darlan ordered Auphan to prepare studies with a spread of options to carry the war to the Soviets. Darlan was encouraged by confidential information that Mussolini, reportedly miffed at Hitler's cozy relations with the Kremlin, might also intervene in the war against the Soviets.[28]

Auphan's plans, in retrospect clearly out of touch with reality, reflect the pervasive anti-Bolshevism of the time and the widespread assumption of Soviet military weakness. The first option called for striking the Soviets through the Mediterranean by sending a strong naval and military force into the Black Sea to occupy Baku, with its rich oil deposits. The goal was to interrupt the flow of oil that nourished Soviet agriculture, so Soviet wheat shipments to Germany would come to a halt.[29] This plan, unrealistic and burdened with numerous technical and diplomatic problems, risked dragging the Soviet Union into the war against the Entente.

The second option also aimed at striking a blow at the German economy. The plan was to strike into northern Norway at Narvik and advance eastward to capture the rich Swedish mineral deposits at Gallivare that supplied the Reich with its main source of iron ore. From there the Allied armies would advance into Finland, where they presumably would find Italian volunteers eagerly fighting with the Finns against the Soviets.[30] At Daladier's insistence, Darlan grafted onto this plan an Allied attack on the Arctic port of Petsamo, recently occupied by the Soviets. The Soviets would be driven out, and the port returned to the Finns.[31]

Darlan reasoned that either of these plans would be less costly than an assault on the Siegfried Line or a prolonged naval blockade of the Reich. Oriented toward the Mediterranean, he favored the plan to attack the Caucasus, which would be easier to reach and might deprive Germany of vital oil supplies. He submitted these plans to Daladier on January 23, and the next day they decided to request a meeting of the Supreme War Council.[32] With aid to Finland at the top of the French agenda, the Black Sea strategy faded into the background.

Unlike the French, the British had little interest in aiding Finland. They were, however, concerned to seize the Swedish mines, and they had already drafted plans to that end. When the Supreme War Council met in Paris on February 5, it assigned highest priority to aiding Finland but in fact took action aimed at seizing the mines. Not surprisingly, the British sidetracked Daladier's Petsamo plan, which posed technical problems and also risked provoking a Soviet war. They pressed instead for an operation through Norway via Narvik to seize the Swedish mines. From there it might be possible to move into Finland, but there was no clear decision on that point. The Supreme War Council therefore settled upon the British plan and scheduled the operation for early March on the condition that Norway and Sweden permit entry of Allied armies onto their territory. Two British divisions scheduled for delivery to France were held back and trained instead for service in Norway.[33]

Not surprisingly, Norway and Sweden dragged their feet on the question of Allied entry into their territory. Nevertheless, Darlan continued French preparations for the operation until Daladier finally called it off on March 15, two days after Finnish resistance had ended. Four days later Daladier fell from power, to be succeeded by Paul Reynaud. For the next three weeks Allied plans for a Scandinavian operation shifted away from military intervention toward one of laying mines near the Norwegian coast where German merchant ships regularly exploited the safety of neutral territorial waters to deliver Swedish iron to Germany. In early April the Supreme War Council decided to go ahead with the mining project.[34] The minefields were planted as scheduled on April 8, and on the ninth German armies struck boldly into Denmark and Norway, not in response to the mining operation but in accordance with plans drafted earlier. The question now was whether the Allies would oppose the Germans on a distant front or whether they would instead seize the initiative closer to home.

A Wasteful War on the Periphery

The choice to oppose the aggression led to the outbreak of a wasteful war on the periphery. With German troops pouring into Denmark and Norway on April 9, the French War Cabinet met that morning to decide on a response, subject to the approval of the Supreme War Council scheduled to meet later in the day. Reynaud proposed a strike into Norway, which Darlan supported. But the admiral also proposed implementation of a contingent plan to advance into Belgium to establish strong defensive positions along the natural barrier of the Demer and Dyle Rivers. More practical than a counterattack in distant Norway, the Belgian option aimed at shortening the French defensive line opposite Germany. It was easily within Allied capabilities, and it could have been justified as a response to German aggression. The War Cabinet decided in principle to go forward with both plans.[35]

The Supreme War Council, meeting as scheduled in London that afternoon, promptly approved a counteroffensive in Norway. London had in fact already made that decision early that morning, for Norway lay within the British area of operations.[36] With the French delegation present during the afternoon session, the Supreme War Council went ahead to approve the Belgian option, but implementation of that plan was made contingent upon an invitation from Brussels. Subordinating the Belgian option to Brussels' approval amounted to shelving the operation, for Brussels was not likely to lend its approval.

Even before the Belgian option had been discussed that afternoon, London had earlier that morning entered the Entente into a Norwegian adventure at the far limits of its military and logistical capabilities. On the first day of hostilities, German forces swiftly seized key Norwegian ports from Oslo to Narvik in the far north. For several crucial hours the Admiralty assumed that German battlecruisers sighted in Norwegian waters were attempting a breakout into the North Atlantic. Accordingly, Admiral Sir Charles Forbes, commanding the Home Fleet at Scapa Flow, steamed his heavy ships on a course remote from the landings on the Norwegian coast. The Admiralty therefore missed its only chance to intervene in a timely manner to disperse the German operation. Although the Germans suffered important losses at the hand of Norwegian defenders, the landing operations were carried out successfully. At the same time German airborne forces seized key Norwegian airfields where German aircraft soon arrived in overwhelming numbers, setting the stage for German land-based aircraft to oppose any counterattack. From that point on, the Reich held a significant advantage in Norway.

The German advantage there was largely a matter of geography, which accorded it a logistical edge. German reinforcements and aircraft entered Norway swiftly by a short and secure route from Denmark, remote from the main British naval concentrations in the North Sea. Although the Kriegsmarine suffered heavy losses in a series of brisk fleet actions in the North Sea that included three cruisers and ten destroyers sunk and two battleships badly damaged, the Reich was nevertheless able to accumulate superior military and aerial assets in Norway. Once entrenched there, German military units enjoyed an advantage in mobility, and German aviation exploited the advantage of land bases supporting superior numbers of aircraft. From the very beginning, German air power dominated the skies over the beachheads and over the sea routes approaching them.

In contrast, geography imposed a heavy burden on the Entente, for Allied supply lines were longer and less secure than those of the enemy. French military forces destined for Norway proceeded from Brest, requiring twenty-seven ships to transport a light infantry division. Darlan calculated that he could send but one division per month.[37] The British in turn could send only eleven battalions, whereas the Germans delivered six full-strength divisions to Norway during the first few days of the campaign.[38] The Allied counteroffensive therefore moved against an enemy already on the scene with vastly superior forces and with land-based aircraft poised to attack any invasion attempt. The first French units arrived in Norway ten days after the first German landings. British forces had arrived a few days earlier. Landing north and south of Trondheim, at Namsos and Andalsnes, they came at once under heavy German aerial attack that blunted their effort to establish secure beachheads. British naval aviation was no match for German land-based aviation, so the beachheads had to be evacuated in early May. Later that month Allied troops seized Narvik, far to the north, but they were driven out after a few days of hard fighting.

The Norwegian operation was burdened by mismanagement, mainly on the part of the Admiralty, where Churchill called the main signals. The initial German offensive had been so swift that the Admiralty, having no occasion to plan effectively, resorted to piecemeal initiatives at Namsos, Andalsnes, and Narvik. All of them predictably fell victim to poor communications, faulty intelligence, indecisiveness, and a lack of clear operational doctrines. These initiatives were amphibious operations, but at that early stage of World War II the Admiralty had neither the doctrine nor the technology to support effective amphibious warfare. Consequently, troops sometimes entered into battle without their heavy equipment, and officers often proceeded with confusing or tentative orders.[39]

Despite the loss of the carrier *Courageous* in 1939, there still was no clear doctrine of naval aviation. Toward the end of the Scandinavian campaign, the carrier *Glorious* steamed south, well to the west of Narvik, with no observation aircraft in flight above, thereby breaking the most basic rule of carrier warfare. The Admiralty, moreover, had assigned only two destroyers to accompany her, so that the carrier had but slight protection against enemy gunships. Suddenly, on the afternoon of June 8, the *Glorious* stumbled upon the battlecruiser *Scharnhorst*, whose 11-inch guns promptly sank all three British ships.[40] The *Glorious* was the only fleet carrier sunk during World War II by an enemy battleship.

The French role in the Scandinavian campaign—important but long forgotten—was carried out with greater efficiency. French support of the British effort was managed mainly by Darlan, who shared Churchill's obsession with Narvik and the lure of the Swedish iron mines. Powerfully motivated to carry the fight to the enemy, Darlan cooperated energetically with his British counterparts, providing both naval and logistical support. With the Royal Navy heavily engaged in the North Sea, the French fleet lent support there and also assumed the main responsibility for guarding the western Mediterranean against any Italian aggression.

At the beginning of April, Darlan's Raiding Force, composed of his newest and heaviest ships, was at Mers el-Kébir, poised to discourage any Italian adventure or to intercept any German raider that might appear in the Atlantic. When the Scandinavian crisis broke out a few days later, Darlan ordered the Raiding Force to Brest, where it was situated to lend support in the North Sea. But in early May, uneasy about Italian intentions, he returned the squadron to the Mediterranean. When the Admiralty requested the intervention of other French ships in the Norwegian war, Darlan readily complied. By May 8 forty-three French warships were operating in the North Sea under overall British command. These included eight light cruisers, eighteen destroyers, thirteen submarines, and four lesser craft. These ships were employed to escort convoys, to deliver troops to Norway, and to attack German communications in Norwegian waters. There were also two divisions of destroyers on patrol under French command in waters off Belgium and Holland. One French destroyer, the *Bison*, was sunk in battle.[41]

Darlan also committed forty-five transport vessels for the delivery of French troops to British bases in northern Scotland, at Scapa Flow and the Clyde, where they would board British ships for deployment in Norway. Always efficient, Darlan managed to ship out of Brest by April 23 a division of sixteen thousand troops to augment the initial contingent of four thousand French troops that had already been deployed at Namsos. The first units of a second division departed Brest on April 26, but the British, unprepared to receive the French shipments, requested that the deliveries be slowed down. During the third week of April, French transports loaded with equipment were beginning to line up off the Clyde, as the port facilities there were inadequate to unload the transports promptly. In early May Darlan was ready to deliver a third division, but with the British still struggling to unload French transports, the delivery was cancelled. By that time Allied forces were being evacuated from Trondheim, so there was no need for additional French troops in that area. Darlan contemplated the delivery of the third division directly to Narvik, where the outcome had not yet been decided, but the distance from Brest to Narvik, three thousand kilometers, was beyond his logistical capabilities. The third division therefore remained in France.[42]

The Scandinavian campaign, though obviously mismanaged, failed because the Allies worked from the beginning at a logistical disadvantage. German supply lines were short and secure, so the Reich could deliver massive equipment and reinforcements to safe bases capable of interrupting Allied lines of supply near the coast. The British were therefore unable to deploy in Norway all of their assets, as the enemy's more modern land-based aircraft dominated the approaches to the landing areas. The Norwegian campaign was doomed from the beginning, for the Entente had chosen to fight in a remote area where the enemy enjoyed all of the logistical advantages.

The basic problem was that of poor strategic judgment. Entente war strategy matched poorly its logistical capabilities. In 1939 Allied war planners had assigned high priority to steady reinforcement of the French front. That strategy matched perfectly the Entente's logistical capabilities. It was designed to enlist the full industrial and manpower resources of the French and British empires to strengthen the main front. But Allied war planners allowed themselves to be drawn into a dead-end adventure on the periphery at the expense of reinforcing the military front in France.

The failure in Norway raised disturbing questions about the Entente's ability to wage war successfully. Darlan attributed the Norwegian fiasco to indecisiveness on the part of the Chamberlain government, burdened, he thought, by numerous committees; on the part of the Admiralty, which to him seemed flabby and irresolute; and finally upon his own government, with its sharp internal divisions. The French admiral always maintained a correct posture in the presence of his British opposites, but frustrated at London's refusal to wage war in the Mediterranean, he wrote privately on April 27 that "the British Admiralty, totally depressed, lacks offensive spirit." He further noted on May 3 that "the political situation, in France and England, is very troubled. The two governments are very shaken; that of Chamberlain because it is soft and hesitant, and that of Reynaud because it is divided, disorganized, and impotent."[43] Although Reynaud survived the Norwegian crisis, the Chamberlain government fell on

May 10, replaced by a national government under Churchill, who more than Chamberlain had been responsible for the Norwegian fiasco.

Tensions in the Alliance

In the meantime, Anglo-French naval relations began to suffer new tensions connected with the drafting of contingency plans for operations in the Mediterranean. The Scandinavian war was less than two weeks old when the Admiralty realized that the concentration of Entente assets in the North Sea undermined Mediterranean security needs. In April Anglo-Italian relations grew so tense that London feared that continuing the Norwegian campaign might provoke Mussolini to enter the war. Chamberlain clung tenaciously to appeasement as a means of keeping Italy neutral, but the Admiralty began to shift assets back to the Mediterranean. Darlan continued to cooperate with Pound, arranging in April for French battleships and destroyers to escort the *Royal Sovereign* and the *Malaya* from Malta to Alexandria.[44] Eager to wage war against Italy, Darlan drafted ambitious plans to seize Crete and other Mediterranean islands to the end of blunting any Italian aggression in the Balkans.

The Admiralty, however, reverted to a modified version of the original 1939 plan of maintaining naval strength in the Mediterranean to restrain Italy but not to wage war against her. Grafted onto the original plan was a sharply focused contingency plan to occupy Crete in the event of Italian aggression there. The Admiralty continued in the thought that any Mediterranean conflict might tempt Tokyo to unleash its naval power in Asia. Intent, therefore, upon avoiding a Mediterranean war, London responded cautiously to the looming Italian threat. The Admiralty continued to shift assets from the North Sea back to the Mediterranean, insisting with Rome that these ships were merely returning to their posts. Convoys approaching Suez from the east were rerouted around the Cape, and measures were taken to hasten the withdrawal of British merchant ships already in the Mediterranean. London clearly wished to avoid any incident that risked provoking Mussolini to war.[45]

On May 14, with Anglo-Italian relations at a boiling point, the British War Cabinet discussed options in the event of a Mediterranean war. The initial question was whether an Italian invasion of the Dalmatian coast would justify war. The minutes of the meeting indicate, however, that the War Cabinet was more concerned about Crete than Dalmatia and was satisfied that Anglo-French naval staff conversations aimed at seizing the island were already in progress. Orders were sent out that same day authorizing the British Mediterranean command to continue discussions at Alexandria with their French opposites.[46]

These plans were completed toward the end of May. British submarines were ordered to proceed ahead to warn of any Italian activity in the area. A battalion of British troops was designated to land on the island with twenty hours' notice, and a French contingent of three thousand men would arrive shortly thereafter. In the meantime, the British command at Alexandria would await the green light to launch the operation.[47] The implementation of these plans was contingent upon Italian aggression against the island.

Eager to wage war against Italy, Darlan welcomed the British proposal to consider a combined operation to occupy Crete, but he favored a larger operation, one involving multiple initiatives over much of the Aegean Sea. For this reason, the Admiralty staff was beginning to lose confidence in Darlan, commenting in private that his orders to the French Mediterranean command "did not appear to provide for sufficiently rapid action in the various contingencies that might arise."[48] They also questioned his strategic judgment, terming "imprudent" his suggestion that Allied forces also occupy the Aegean islands of Milos, Salamis, Navarino, and Argostoli.[49] More than that, the Admiralty was losing confidence in the entire top echelon of the French naval command, believing, as Pound wrote Cunningham on May 20, that "they have the wildest ideas in many respects and of imagining that they are in the last war and not this."[50]

Cunningham could see that Pound was referring to the advent of air power, which had played but a minor role in World War I naval operations, and to French proposals for risky Balkan adventures. The recent heavy losses in Norwegian waters no doubt reinforced Pound's strategic thinking and justified his defensive posture in the Mediterranean, where he could assume that land-based air power had amplified the risks of naval operations against coastal targets. So Pound went ahead with contingent plans for operations against Crete, vital to British communications between Gibraltar and Singapore, but he backed away from French plans for risky and provocative operations against Greek island or mainland targets such as Salonika.

Pound's cautious Mediterranean strategy was a product of prewar planning that had assigned the highest priority to keeping Italy neutral. Just as Darlan wished from the beginning to wage war against Italy, Pound wished to wage peace. And while Darlan flirted with useless offensive adventures in the Aegean, Pound persisted in the strategy of protecting communications between Gibraltar and Singapore. The control of Crete was vital to that strategy, and French adventures elsewhere in the Mediterranean would risk undermining it. The Admiralty had planned in 1939 to avoid provoking Italy even after the outbreak of a Mediterranean war. They therefore had no reason in the spring of 1940 to draft with the French any additional plans except for the occupation of Crete.

With the Admiralty therefore unwilling to plan further with the French, Darlan went ahead to draft his own plans, which he had in place for a swift response when Italy declared war on the Allies on June 10.[51] The French naval bombardment of Genoa three days later was therefore entirely of French initiative, and in accordance with prewar plans, the Royal Navy made no aggressive move against Italy at the outbreak of the Mediterranean war. Nor did the British occupy Crete until October, when the Italians finally threatened the island.

Farewell to a Good Friend

The Scandinavian war and broader problems of naval strategy had begun to erode confidence at the highest level of the alliance. The new tensions grew out of poor strategic judgment in waging the Norwegian war and of conflicting strategic objectives in the Mediterranean. Although everyone maintained a correct posture, the British and French naval commands at the highest levels had grown less confident of each other. But at the level of operations in the Atlantic, Anglo-French naval cooperation had prospered beyond that which prewar planning had expected. At Maintenon, despite the troublesome role of Auphan, a spirit of respect and amity reigned proud among French and British staff officers. French officers there had grown to admire and respect Captain Holland, who had served among them prior to the war as London's naval attaché at Paris and afterward as the chief of the British naval mission at Maintenon.

In early April French and British officers assembled at Maintenon to celebrate Holland's impending departure. They regretted his leaving, but they celebrated with him the good news of his promotion to command the carrier *Ark Royal*. Henri Balland, present at the celebration, later expressed praise of Holland's technical competence, his tactfulness, and his courtesy. "Each of us," he wrote, "regarded him as a personal friend."[52] As they raised their glasses in a toast to his promotion, they had no idea that his government would soon thrust him into an ugly new role that would shatter suddenly the warm relations they had all enjoyed.

Chapter 10

Twilight of the Anglo-French Naval Alliance

When the great German offensive opened on May 10, fifteen French and five British divisions advanced northward to take defensive positions behind Belgian rivers, the Demer and the Dyle, in accordance with previous plans. Five days later, just as General Maxime Weygand replaced Maurice Gamelin as French military commander in chief, strong German armored divisions broke through the thin French lines on the Meuse River near Sedan. By May 22 the powerful German offensive had reached the sea beyond Abbeville, isolating the entire Allied left flank in Belgium. The Entente's best option now was to cut the narrow corridor across northern France that nourished the German mechanized divisions with fuel. But the British and French attacks around Arras were poorly coordinated and quickly repulsed. From that point on the Allied military situation declined steadily so that by the middle of June the question was whether the French would continue in a hopeless struggle or instead approach the enemy to request armistice terms.

The German breakthrough on the French front was largely unrelated to naval operations. To be sure, the ill-advised Norwegian campaign had siphoned off assets that would have been better employed on the continent. The German breakthrough was, however, more importantly a matter of military doctrine whereby the Wehrmacht concentrated its armored assets at the moment when the French command distributed its tanks along the front in support of linear operations, as in 1918. Simultaneously, large concentrations of German aircraft lent closely coordinated tactical support to the military offensive. The German doctrinal advantage proved to be decisive.

Although the great crisis that followed was precipitated by military failures, the aftermath bore heavily upon Anglo-French naval relations and upon the stability of the Entente. From that point on the alliance entered into a crisis of confidence at the top level of command. This chapter examines the emerging tensions in the Entente mainly from a French perspective, for the winding down of the war and protecting the French fleet from the enemy was more a French than British undertaking.

Dunkirk Evacuation

When Lord John Gort, commander of the BEF (British Expeditionary Force), realized on May 25 that the Arras offensives had failed, he ordered the BEF to turn westward in a defensive maneuver intended to prevent his forces being trapped behind enemy lines. But that maneuver degenerated into a massive withdrawal toward the coast. On the twenty-eighth, Paul Auphan reported to Admiral Darlan from Dover that London had begun preparations to evacuate the BEF eight days earlier, on the twentieth. Darlan therefore concluded that the British had intended to evacuate the BEF without notifying their French ally.[1] Auphan's report was partly off target, for London had made no decision to withdraw until May 26, after Gort's failed attack against the corridor.[2] Nevertheless, the British had not taken care to notify their French ally of the preparations for an evacuation, so suspicion and mistrust emerged at the moment when British forces began to withdraw toward a beachhead forming around the port city of Dunkirk. This breakdown of communications led to misunderstandings at the expense of the solidarity of the alliance.

The beachhead, moreover, gave rise to further misunderstandings. The French military command intended to mount a vigorous defense of the beachhead, to buy time for Weygand to prepare strong defensive positions along the Somme River. But the British, according to Darlan, appeared not to understand the reasons for defending Dunkirk.[3] In a letter to his wife, Darlan wrote that "the British lion seems to sprout wings when it's a matter of getting back to the sea."[4] And he told Paul Reynaud that the British "wished at any price to precipitate the evacuation while leaving the French to defend the place."[5] By the end of May the evacuation of the BEF was already well under way at the moment when the French forces were preparing to defend the beachhead. Clearly, British and French plans concerning the beachhead were out of step with each other.

French support of the evacuation of the Entente armies began on May 28 after Darlan had received Auphan's notification of the British withdrawal. Moving quickly, the admiral created a separate command at Pas-de-Calais with the mission of sending French ships to the beachhead. He ordered Admiral Jean Abrial, commander north, to assist with the evacuation of British troops, who would arrive at the coast prior to their French allies. The British troops would therefore be evacuated first since they were nearest to the coast. When the Supreme War Council met in Paris on May 31, Churchill insisted that the armies be evacuated on equal terms, with the British forming the rear guard. That offer was little more than a gesture, however, for the French army was too far inland to be evacuated on equal terms. Therefore, the French army, rather than the British, formed the rear guard to protect the evacuation against German military units approaching the beachhead from several directions.

There were further tensions. On June 2, with the greater part of the British personnel already evacuated, London prepared to shut down the operation. But the first echelons of fifteen French divisions were now retreating toward the beachhead. Darlan, in a letter to Admiral Emmanuel Ollive, complained that he had to "kick the backside" of the British Admiralty for three days before the ally agreed to return for French troops arriving at the beaches.[6] The British did indeed evacuate more than 26,000 French troops, but the greater part of the French left flank, too far inland to reach the coast, was cut off and captured. The 26,000 French troops reaching the beachhead were moved directly to England, rather than to France, as the evacuation had been postured to ferry troops across the English Channel rather than down the coast, where they might have been reintegrated into the French army.

Notwithstanding the successful evacuation of the BEF, events moved swiftly toward a military collapse and ultimately to armistice agreements between France and the two European Axis powers. But the British leadership, confidant of its ability to defend the United Kingdom and the empire against Germany and Italy, was determined to continue in the war despite the objections of a small peace faction. By the middle of June, there was no question that the Anglo-French alliance was fast approaching a crisis. The question was whether the Entente would end peacefully or would it instead come crashing down in a violent clash of arms. Central to that question was the French fleet, now thrust to center stage to become the focus of Anglo-French political relations as France wound down the war and concluded armistice agreements first with Germany and then with Italy.

Winding Down the War

With strong German armies crossing the Somme at several points in early June, the French government abandoned Paris and moved first to Tours and then to Bordeaux. The Admiralty followed, relocating itself at Montbazon on June 12 and later at Rochefort, where Admiral Darlan continued to command naval operations. Even before Italy entered the war on the tenth, an armistice faction had emerged under Weygand and Marshal Philippe Pétain, hero of the previous war who had entered the government in May for the purpose of boosting morale and forging a spirit of unity. But Pétain and Weygand clashed sharply with Reynaud, who had promised the British in May that he would not seek a separate peace with the enemy. That promise bound Reynaud to wage war when French interests soon would demand an armistice. As French resistance became increasingly disorganized, Reynaud explored the possibility of mounting a stout defense in Brittany. But Weygand considered the so-called Breton Redoubt to be indefensible. Calling it "a joke in very bad taste," he, along with Pétain, continued to insist that the government request armistice terms.[7]

As the war wound down, London had no interest in seeing important French facilities near the coast come under the control of the advancing German armies. British demolition parties rushed to French channel ports to assist French naval engineers with the demolition of port facilities in danger of falling into enemy hands. Embarked by British destroyers, the demolition parties had orders to cooperate with their French counterparts and to destroy nothing without French permission except in cases where enemy forces were approaching. These parties had instructions to destroy any asset useful to the enemy, including fuel supplies, electrical power plants, dry docks, bridges, aviation facilities, repair facilities, service vessels in the harbors, and coastal artillery pieces that could not be evacuated.[8]

The systematic destruction of channel ports coincided with a French naval bombardment of the Italian port city of Genoa, launched during the night of June 13. This operation had been planned prior to the Italian entry into the war on June 10.[9] The damage to the Italian port was in no way decisive, but the raid sent a clear signal that the French fleet, in contrast to the army, had not been defeated. It remained a powerful fighting force capable of protecting communications between France and North Africa and of defending the western basin of the Mediterranean against the Italian enemy.

Nevertheless, the winding down of the war imposed impossible demands upon the Marine Nationale. With organized resistance on the military front coming to an end during the second week of June, Reynaud now had reason to regret his earlier pledge to make no separate peace with the enemy. He therefore proposed the option of continuing the war in North Africa, which assumed a massive naval evacuation of the army and its equipment. Reynaud appears not to have understood that the proposed operation, much larger and more complex than the Dunkirk evacuation, had by this time already ceased to be an option. The success of such a massive operation would depend upon careful planning, lengthy preparations, and early access to huge logistical support. It would require a swift and orderly withdrawal of scattered French military units to selected ports not yet destroyed or occupied by the enemy. And it assumed the rapid rerouting of dozens of widely scattered merchant vessels to the designated ports of embarkation. Further, it assumed careful Anglo-French naval planning to assemble convoys and to provide escort to distant African ports. For obvious reasons, an operation of such massive proportions could not be hastily improvised in the pattern of the Dunkirk evacuation.

Key to any evacuation was Admiral Darlan, who learned of the proposal on June 12 from General Charles de Gaulle, en route to London as assistant undersecretary of state for war. The general asked Darlan to study the problem of transporting 900,000 troops and 100,000 tons of supplies to Casablanca within 45 days.[10] Given the 45-day timetable, the project was not entirely unreasonable. But three days later, in a conference with Reynaud, Darlan discovered that the schedule had been reduced to 10 days. The admiral insisted on the impossibility of rallying 200 widely scattered ships to Bordeaux on such short notice. He indicated, however, that 10 transports then in the harbor could begin evacuation of 30,000 troops that same day. But Reynaud confessed that he could not assemble for evacuation even that many troops.[11]

It was therefore clear by mid-June that the bulk of the French army could not be assembled in French ports, much less evacuated to North Africa. And, moreover, any plans to continue the war from there would depend entirely upon the French fleet and the Royal Navy and upon whatever French military assets were already stationed in the region. Continuing the war from North Africa would have meant abandoning all of Metropolitan France to the enemy. Darlan could easily have moved the government to North Africa. Had Reynaud ordered Darlan on June 15 to evacuate the government, the admiral could hardly have refused. But Reynaud did not issue that order. He instead resigned from office the next day, to be succeeded by a new government under Marshal Pétain. The shift of power to the armistice faction imposed a heavy burden on Anglo-French naval relations, for any negotiations with the enemy risked the Reich's demanding delivery of the French fleet, just as the armistice of 1918 had required delivery of the German fleet to the victorious Allies.

Securing the Fleet

As early as the Dunkirk evacuation in late May, Darlan worried that his government might be tempted to sign an armistice at the expense of the navy, that politicians might be willing to deliver the fleet to the enemy in exchange for lenient armistice terms. Should it come to that, he would be thrust into a terrible crisis of conscience, one in which he would be forced to choose between his government and the fleet. Loyal by instinct, Darlan was not the type to commit treason. But he felt it his higher duty to keep the fleet from falling into the hands of the enemy, as his order of May 28 to Admiral Maurice Le Luc clearly indicates: "In case military events should lead to an armistice whose conditions would be imposed by the Germans and if those conditions should include delivery of the fleet, *I have no intention of executing that order*."[12] It seems clear that Darlan, from the beginning of the military crisis, had no intention of delivering the French fleet to either Axis enemy and that he would disobey any order from his government requiring its surrender.

Subsequent orders from Darlan reveal clearly his determination to protect the fleet from the enemy and to remain loyal to the British ally. The first of these, issued to Le Luc on June 15, prior to Darlan's departure from Rochefort, ordered French ships to take early measures to avoid falling into enemy hands, to flee to French colonial ports, or, significantly, to British ports, or to destroy themselves, in the case of any armistice terms risking French control of the fleet. This option would be executed upon receipt of new orders from the French Admiralty under the signature of "Xavier 377," so coded to underscore its authenticity as a valid order from Admiral Jean Xavier François Darlan. He ordered Le Luc to prepare to move the Admiralty to Marseilles, should that become necessary, and he indicated his intention to send the unfinished battleships *Jean Bart* and *Richelieu* to England no later than June 20.[13] Therefore, Darlan had by June 15 issued orders to protect his ships, and he clearly had not ruled out the option of bolting with the fleet to continue the war alongside the British ally should his government accept an armistice requiring delivery of the fleet to the enemy.

But when Darlan arrived in Bordeaux on Saturday, June 15, he began to shift toward the armistice faction—not out of political ambition, as has often been charged, but because he now realized that his government had plans to reject any armistice requiring the delivery of the fleet to the enemy. Even as he moved toward the armistice faction, Darlan still held the high card of bolting with the fleet. He would, however, not play that card until all other options had been exhausted. When the Reynaud government met that Saturday evening, the cabinet adopted a proposal to request an armistice with the private understanding that it would be rejected should the enemy demand the delivery of the fleet. With the fleet poised to continue the war, or to destroy itself if necessary, Darlan could see the advantages of awaiting the outcome of this final French diplomatic initiative.

The next day the Reynaud government fell, after London had released France from the commitment to continue the war, on condition that the fleet be sent to British ports pending the outcome of armistice negotiations. But the new Pétain government, formed late in the day of Sunday, June 16, had no intentions of entrusting the fleet to the English, nor by this time did Darlan, who could easily see that it would abort any chance of concluding an armistice with Germany. The new government immediately affirmed its resolve to reject any armistice requiring delivery of the fleet to the Axis.

At the same time, Darlan entered the Pétain government as minister of marine. This appointment, a signal to both London and Berlin, meant that France had no intention of negotiating a lenient armistice at the expense of the fleet, for Darlan's determination to keep the fleet under French control was by this time well known. Had the Pétain government intended to use the fleet as a bargaining chip in the armistice negotiations, it would never have promoted Darlan to a key cabinet rank. London, however, appears to have missed that important signal, concluding instead that the admiral had accepted the post as a reward for his coming over to the armistice faction, that he had chosen to nourish his political ambitions rather than to continue the war at the side of the British ally.[14] His motives, however, were considerably more complex than that. Darlan was, after all, a good Frenchman committed to protecting French interests as he understood them, rather than those of any foreign power.

Now that Darlan had committed himself to explore the possibility of an armistice, he no longer spoke of sending the fleet to English ports. He instead took measures to protect it against both the Axis and the British. On June 18, two days after his government had requested armistice terms of Berlin, he ordered French continental outposts to prepare for the withdrawal of all ships to French African ports and to destroy any ship at risk of being captured by the enemy.[15] Accordingly, the *Jean Bart* steamed to Casablanca and the *Richelieu* to Dakar rather than to British ports. Both ships were now safely beyond the grasp of either the Axis enemy or the British ally. Other French ships began to steam toward Oran, with its big harbor at nearby Mers el-Kébir. As a French delegation proceeded toward Tours on June 20 to receive the German armistice proposals, Darlan ordered his fleet to continue fighting, to disobey any foreign government—which would have included the British—and to abandon no ship to the enemy.[16]

With the main units of the French fleet now steaming to secure African ports, any German proposal requiring the surrender of the fleet would leave France in a position to drag its feet in the armistice negotiations, for draconian German demands upon the fleet might easily tempt the French to continue resistance in Africa and elsewhere in the empire. The German delegation could easily see that the surrender of the fleet to Germany would leave the French empire in North and West Africa largely defenseless against British aggression and that German and French interests coincided on the question of keeping the British out of French Africa.

When the British ambassador called on Darlan that same day, the admiral assured him that the fleet would remain French or perish, that he had "already taken the necessary precautions."[17] But he no longer spoke of delivering the fleet to the British or of continuing the war alongside them. He had instead decided to keep the fleet entirely under French control. This decision marked an important change in his thinking about the war. He had decided not to bolt with the fleet prematurely. He would instead await the German armistice terms in the expectation of keeping the fleet and the African empire safely under the control of his government, should the armistice terms not require the delivery of the fleet. Or, should the terms require its delivery, he would be in a position to insist in the cabinet that the surrender of the fleet or its self-destruction would amount to the partitioning of French Africa between Great Britain and Italy. Darlan could easily see that the fleet and the empire were not separate issues but were instead bound together in the same package. He could also see that sending the fleet to North and West African ports beyond the reach of either Axis enemy would keep alive a spread of options, all more attractive than that of scuttling the fleet.

The Armistice from the French Perspective

The German armistice proposal, received at Bordeaux late in the day of June 21, aimed at neutralizing the French fleet and the French empire, both of which lay beyond the grasp of German military or naval power. The Wehrmacht could easily have overrun all of France, but Germany could not so easily defeat the French fleet or occupy North Africa, secured by geography beyond a large body of water dominated by British naval power. Moreover, a German occupation of all of France would have risked provoking the navy to continue the war under a dissident French government in Africa. The armistice therefore provided for an unoccupied zone in southern France where the French government could be expected to maintain the neutrality of both the fleet and the empire while the war between the European Axis and Great Britain continued, presumably until London accepted the necessity of ending the war with a negotiated settlement.

The naval terms of the armistice, not at all what the French had desired, reflect the assumption in Berlin that the war was approaching an end and that Great Britain would soon seek terms of peace. Contained in Article 8, the naval terms required all units of the French fleet to return to their peacetime ports, where they would be disarmed and demobilized under German or Italian supervision. The German government pledged not to make use of any French ships except those required for coastal patrol and minesweeping. Nor would Germany make any claim on the fleet at the final settlement ending the war.

The terms required all French ships, except those assigned to colonial defense, to return to France.[18]

But these terms failed to take into account the possibility that London might after all continue in the war under the assumption that the Reich could not easily invade the British Isles. Nor did they take into account that French warships returning to their peacetime ports on the Bay of Biscay would come within the range of British land-based aviation. The armistice proposal therefore required the *Richelieu*, *Jean Bart*, *Dunkerque*, and *Strasbourg* along with their cruiser and destroyer escorts to enter into waters dominated by British naval and air power. The terms would set the stage for a clash between the French fleet and the Royal Navy, and they would leave North and West Africa with inadequate naval defenses against Italy and the former ally.

When the cabinet met late that night, Darlan spoke stoutly against the armistice, whose naval terms threatened to reverse his recent orders to rally the fleet to North and West African ports. Especially alarming were the clauses requiring his heaviest and newest units of the fleet to return to German-occupied Atlantic ports on the Bay of Biscay. This clause amounted to surrendering the fleet, for it created an opportunity for the former enemy to seize the ships by ruse or by force, especially after they had been disarmed and demobilized. Darlan had his way, as the cabinet voted to reject the terms requiring the return of the ships to their peacetime ports. Early the next morning the cabinet approved a Darlan proposal to disarm the warships and maintain them in North Africa with reduced crews.[19]

Later that same day the French armistice delegation at Tours proposed a series of amendments, including a provision to demobilize the fleet in French African ports rather than in German-occupied ports on the Bay of Biscay. They pointed out that any French warships demobilized in Atlantic ports would become easy targets of British airpower. General Wilhelm Keitel, head of the German delegation, rejected the French amendments, but he conceded that the question of protecting the fleet from air attack could be placed on the agenda of the armistice commission.[20] Keitel's concession was less than the French had desired, but implicit in it was the assumption that the heaviest units of the French fleet and their escorts would remain in North and West Africa pending the outcome of further negotiations. It also left open the door that the fleet might be demobilized in African ports or at Toulon in the unoccupied zone, which would have been a satisfactory solution to the French delegation.

In these negotiations, the French held a strong hand. With the ships already being demobilized in North Africa, any German demand in the armistice commission to return them to Atlantic ports would risk mutiny in the French navy and dissidence in the African empire. The navy was still full of fight, and sentiment against an armistice ran deep among French colonial officials. In Morocco, Resident General Auguste Noguès insisted upon continuing in the war.[21] Berlin clearly had no interest in provoking the French fleet and the empire back into the war on the side of the British, as this would serve only to encourage London to continue longer in the war.

Whether the French delegation at Tours fully appreciated the strategic advantage it enjoyed is not entirely clear. Nevertheless, it went ahead and accepted Keitel's concession in the expectation that the armistice commission would in the end permit the French fleet to be disarmed and demobilized in African ports beyond the reach of Axis military power and on the distant margin of British naval power. The French delegation in any event had no choice but to accept Keitel's concession, which meant that negotiations concerning the final disposition of the French fleet would continue for a time in two armistice commissions.

The question remains as to why the French government chose to conclude an armistice rather than to continue the war in North Africa behind a combination of French and British naval power, as London had desired. Darlan's order of June 22 to the fleet contains the answer. "Resistance in North Africa," he explained, "would be without any practical significance and would abandon the country to invasion without moral defense of the government. Little local support to wait for England or the United States."[22] Darlan made it clear that France could not expect the United States to intervene in the war for a very long time. The order no doubt reflects the dominant opinion in the French government at the time of the armistice.

It seems clear, then, that the question at Bordeaux was not whether combined French and British naval power might spearhead a successful defense of North Africa. It was instead a question of whether continuing the war in the colonies would serve any useful purpose. The French government chose the armistice because it believed that continued resistance in North Africa was pointless, that even a successful defense of the empire would offer no reasonable chance of returning later to drive the Axis enemy from France. That view, flawed with the advantage of hindsight, nevertheless appeared at the moment to be entirely reasonable. In 1940 there was no expectation that Great Britain could launch a cross-channel invasion to liberate France. Indeed, the expectation was much the opposite, that the Reich might launch an invasion of the British Isles. And the United States remained neutral with no sign that it had any intentions to enter into the European conflict. And even if the United States should eventually enter into the war, it would be many months and perhaps years before American armed forces would be strong enough to invade and liberate France.

The Franco-German armistice was signed on June 22. After a similar armistice with Italy had been signed on the twenty-fourth, Darlan issued new orders reflecting France's changing wartime posture. His coded order to the fleet later that day assumed that the naval clauses remained unsettled, subject to negotiations in the armistice commissions, and that he still might have to violate the armistice in the interest of protecting the moral integrity of the navy. The order summarized the naval clauses providing for the fleet to remain French and to be demobilized with reduced crews in home or colonial ports. Should the armistice commission rule otherwise, all French ships should steam to American ports without new orders. Failing this option, the ships should be scuttled to prevent the enemy seizing them. In this connection, Darlan repeated earlier orders for secret preparations to be undertaken to sabotage the ships so that neither the enemy nor the former ally might use them. In no case, he insisted, should any ship be left intact to the enemy, nor should any ship be used against Germany or Italy without further orders. Finally, he ordered that no French naval officer should in any event obey a foreign admiralty.[23]

It seems clear that by the last week of June Darlan had taken every possible measure keep the fleet and the empire beyond the grasp of the Axis. He had also given the Royal Navy and other British officials repeated assurances on this point, as we shall presently see. What he had no reason to suspect, however, was that the former ally, worried that the French fleet might be delivered to the enemy, was considering whether to await the full details of the armistice terms or instead to take immediate action to destroy the heavy ships of the French navy that lay in African harbors within reach of British naval power.

Chapter 11

Toward a Violent Solution

The end of organized French resistance in June 1940, soon after the Dunkirk evacuation, thrust London and Bordeaux into a final crisis centered upon naval power. British concerns about the French fleet emerged in June, when the powerful German offensive along the Somme signaled the possibility of a Franco-German armistice and after the War Cabinet had decided to continue in the war in the event of a French military collapse. The French fleet, powerful and undefeated, had played but a modest role in the continental war, but now it emerged in London as the main concern in any peace settlement. This chapter focuses on British concerns that an armistice to end the war on the continent might require France to deliver its fleet to the Axis enemy.

British Concerns and French Assurances

The French fleet held the key to the balance of naval power in the western Mediterranean. Should it fall into German or Italian hands, the Admiralty would have to decide whether to shift additional assets to the Mediterranean at the expense of vital Channel defenses against any German attempt to invade the British Isles. London had good reason to be concerned. But as the war approached its end, the main units of the French battle fleet lay beyond the German grasp, and it was dispersed in a manner that its heaviest units and their numerous surface and undersea escorts lay closer to the British than to the Axis orbit. These ships, however, were so scattered among numerous French African ports as to render impossible any British effort to seize or destroy more than a fraction of them. At the same time, numerous French auxiliary craft and some useful warships with their French crews lay in British home and colonial ports where they could be seized by force or with the threat of force. The distribution of the French fleet in both British and French ports therefore created for London a problem so complex as to find no easy military or diplomatic solution.

British concerns about the possible collapse of France date back to late May, at the time of the Dunkirk evacuation, when the chiefs of staff studied the question of whether the United Kingdom fighting alone could defend itself against German invasion and air attack. The staff report, concluding that high morale among British civilians and armed forces would outweigh German numerical superiority, amounted to a tacit decision on the part of the War Cabinet to continue in the war should France drop out of it.[1] Dated May 28, the report coincided exactly with Admiral Darlan's decision that same day to disobey any armistice requiring the delivery of the fleet to the enemy. At the end of May, therefore, as the war in France approached an end, the British and French governments had begun to move in different directions—the British toward rejecting an armistice altogether and the French toward accepting one should it not require the surrender of the fleet.

Darlan had already issued orders to protect the fleet, and he took care to lend assurances to the highest British authorities, the first on June 11, when he spoke briefly with Churchill at Briare. At that meeting of the Supreme War Council, Darlan heard that French resistance was nearing an end and that Britain would in any event continue in the war. The Prime Minister pulled the admiral aside: "Darlan, if you request an armistice it is not necessary for you to deliver your fleet to the Germans." Having already decided to disobey any orders to surrender the fleet, Darlan replied truthfully "there is no question about it . . . we would sink the fleet before we would deliver it."[2]

There is no question of the sincerity of Darlan's intention to destroy his ships in the interest of making them useless to the enemy. Soon thereafter German armies overrunning French naval bases along the Bay of Biscay discovered that the French ships stranded there—smaller craft, submarines undergoing repairs, and ships still under construction—had indeed been sabotaged in accordance with Darlan's orders. The destruction was so thorough that the Germans made no effort afterward to put these ships into service.[3] But Darlan had already ordered the heavier units of the fleet to the safety of African ports, where he hoped he would not have to destroy them.

The French Fleet to Center Stage

Although Darlan had already anticipated that Germany might demand the delivery of the French fleet as the price of an armistice, it was not until June 7 that London came fully to grips with the need to address that same question.

Late that Friday afternoon when Lord Maurice Hankey and Sir Alexander Cadogan, senior officials of the Foreign Office, confronted Admiral Sir Dudley Pound with the problem, the First Sea Lord thought only in terms of a military solution. Hankey and Cadogan advanced a number of diplomatic approaches, but Pound insisted repeatedly that the only practical solution was the destruction of the French fleet. He worried that the Germans would hold Paris hostage, that they would destroy the city should the French attempt to hold on to the fleet or deliver it to Britain. Hankey agreed, pointing out "how awkward it would be . . . if the Germans still threatened to destroy Paris unless we handed over the French Fleet."[4]

Pound, who had no desire at that moment to inherit the French fleet, pointed out that he could not in any event make use of it for some time, owing to the shortage of personnel, ammunition, and supplies. Pound repeated that "the only solution was to sink the French Fleet."[5] He conceded, however, that Admiral Darlan might be willing to scuttle the fleet rather than hand it over to the enemy. "If necessary," he added, "we would torpedo the French ships ourselves."[6] There seemed to be general agreement that the French fleet in British hands would be a liability rather than an asset. The meeting ended with the understanding that the Prime Minister and the First Lord of the Admiralty would be informed of the discussion and that efforts would be undertaken to contact Darlan, not to persuade him to deliver his fleet but to urge him to protect it from the enemy.

By the morning of June 15, however, when the War Cabinet met to discuss the military disaster unfolding in France, Pound had shifted his position. Messages from the British naval liaison officer in France had suggested that the French Admiralty, with the Reynaud government momentarily in disarray, might welcome British encouragement to send the heavy units of the French fleet to British ports. Accordingly, Pound reported instructions he had already sent to the liaison officer to encourage Darlan to send the *Richelieu* and *Jean Bart* to British home ports and the *Dunkerque* and *Strasbourg* to Gibraltar. The War Cabinet, having approved Pound's action, moved further to invite the French government to reestablish itself in the United Kingdom. At the end of the meeting, Churchill underscored the need to secure the French fleet, indicating that it might be necessary for him to discuss the matter personally with the French government at Bordeaux.[7] The Prime Minister clearly had not ruled out a high-level diplomatic solution.

But events moved faster than Churchill had expected. The next morning, Sunday the sixteenth, when the Bordeaux government requested release from its commitment to seek no separate peace, the War Cabinet considered a spread of options. Discussion turned at once toward the French fleet. After

Pound had explained Darlan's measures to secure it, several members spoke in favor of releasing France from its obligation. The idea was to lend encouragement to Reynaud, whose government had committed itself to refuse any armistice requiring delivery of the fleet. Others spoke of relaxing the obligation on condition of the fleet being sent safely to African ports pending receipt of armistice terms. These approaches, which matched well the needs of the Reynaud government, aimed at safeguarding the French fleet and keeping ajar the door for the French government to relocate in either England or the colonies should the Germans demand delivery of the fleet.[8]

Churchill, however, intervened sharply to persuade the War Cabinet to demand delivery of the fleet directly to British ports, pending receipt of armistice terms from the enemy.[9] Churchill's impulsive demand, arriving at Bordeaux shortly thereafter, served only to undermine Reynaud and help catapult the armistice faction to power later that Sunday afternoon, which is what the cooler heads in the Foreign Office had wished to avoid. The Prime Minister's hard-line solution reduced importantly any chances of the French government continuing in the war on the British side.

Nevertheless, negotiations continued briefly with Admiral Darlan when he received First Lord of the Admiralty H. V. Alexander and Admiral Pound at Bordeaux on Tuesday, June 18. Initiated by Pound and approved by Churchill, the meeting took place after the new government of Philippe Pétain had requested armistice terms but before the German reply had been received. It was important that the British delegation include Alexander, whose rank matched that of Darlan, recently appointed minister of marine. At this moment British concerns about the French fleet were urgent and authentic, for German armies swiftly approaching Brest and St. Nazaire threatened to seize the unfinished battleships *Richelieu* and *Jean Bart*, which were anchored in these ports. The purpose of the meeting, therefore, was to persuade Darlan to deliver these two ships to British ports before the Germans could seize them and to deliver the *Dunkerque* and *Strasbourg*, which were in the Mediterranean and not immediately threatened by the German military advance.

Darlan wrote in his diary that Pound invited him to send France's four capital ships to British ports. It would be a disaster, Pound said, if the Germans got hold of the French fleet. Darlan had already decided not to send any French ships to England. He answered, however, with solemn assurance "that there was by no means any question of delivering our fleet to Germany and if the armistice required its surrender, which would be contrary to honor, we would destroy the fleet." The fleet, he added, "will belong to no country but France." When Pound and Alexander commented favorably upon the French decision to hold on to the fleet, Darlan replied that it was for him "above all a question of honor."[10]

The British record of the meeting, more detailed than Darlan's brief notes, reveal the continuing good will and cooperation of the French admiral. The French navy, Darlan said, remained in the war and would continue to fight until the signing of an armistice, "but if the armistice terms were dishonorable to France, the Fleet would fight to the end and anything that escaped would go to a friendly country or would be destroyed." He would remain in France, he said, "unless he at any time found himself in the position of a rebel to the French Government of the day."[11] French merchant ships in Atlantic ports, he added, had already been ordered to steam to Great Britain.

As for the *Jean Bart*, Darlan suggested that the ship might have to be destroyed if it could not depart St. Nazaire before June 20, when low tides would prevent her leaving the harbor. But the *Richelieu*, he added, should already have departed Brest en route to Dakar. He suggested that the unfinished ship might have to be sent to the United States or Canada for its final construction, since sending it to a British port risked its being attacked by enemy aircraft. He went on to suggest a number of measures the two countries might undertake together to deny French assets to the enemy, among them a collaborative effort to destroy unfinished naval construction in Atlantic ports.[12] But as it turned out, they would not have to destroy the *Jean Bart*, which escaped St. Nazaire just ahead of the Germans and arrived at Casablanca before the armistice was signed.

Two days later, on June 20, Darlan gave similar assurances to British ambassador Sir Ronald Campbell and Colonial Minister Lord Lloyd, who inquired specifically about the French fleet. "I repeated to them," he wrote, "that it would remain French or else it would perish, and that I had already made all of the arrangements."[13] In two interviews, Darlan had made it clear that he was determined to safeguard his fleet. He had promised Pound and Alexander that he would disobey any order from his government to deliver it to the enemy, he had hinted that he might be forced finally to rebel against his government and bolt with the fleet, and he had already taken care to distribute the greater part of his fleet in African ports distant from the Axis orbit. Pound and Alexander could see that Darlan had kept open his options, that he wished to maintain good relations with the British, and that he remained open to further discussions with London on the question of the fleet.

The stage was therefore set for negotiations with Darlan about the security of the French fleet. Admiral Pound, Foreign Secretary Lord Halifax, and others in the War Cabinet assigned some value to that approach. Having interviewed Darlan on June 18, Pound had for the moment become more trustful of the

French admiral. When the War Cabinet assembled at 9:30 on Saturday morning, June 22, the news of the Franco-German armistice had not been received. Pound reported the disposition of the French fleet, indicating that the *Richelieu* and *Jean Bart* would shortly arrive, respectively, at Dakar and Casablanca, and that the *Jean Bart*, far from completion, had little fighting value. He added that the *Dunkerque* and *Strasbourg* were already at Oran and that two heavy cruisers at Alexandria had already been detained under British control. Another report indicated that Darlan had ordered Admiral Jean-Pierre Esteva, commander of the Mediterranean fleet, to continue fighting and to take orders from no foreign government. Pound answered that these measures accorded with Darlan's previous assurances to undertake every possible measure to safeguard British interests.[14] Given the distribution of the French fleet in ports beyond the Axis grasp, there seemed to be no need that Saturday morning to rush toward any violent measures to keep the French capital ships out of Axis hands.

But Churchill, already thinking in terms of an armed solution, expressed his lack of confidence in Darlan's assurances and urged the dispatch of British warships to Casablanca and Dakar to intercept the *Jean Bart* and *Richelieu* should they attempt to put out to sea. Although Darlan had ordered the *Jean Bart* and *Richelieu* to remote Atlantic harbors far beyond the German grasp and within the British orbit, Churchill worried that they might somehow join up with the German fleet in a manner that "might alter the whole course of the war."[15] He therefore urged the sending of a strong force to Dakar to lure the *Richelieu* into the British camp, or failing that, to launch an air attack against the ship. He assigned but nuisance value to the *Dunkerque* and *Strasbourg*, which he thought could not easily be destroyed behind their strong harbor defenses at Mers el-Kébir. Assuming a military solution to be premature, Halifax urged instead "that we should exhaust every means of persuasion before using force."[16]

There followed a long and confused discussion that ended in a decision to establish further contact with Darlan but also to contact local French naval commands in the interest of luring French ships to the British side. The War Cabinet appears not to have considered that local efforts to undermine Darlan's authority matched poorly a simultaneous approach to the French admiral. The War Cabinet decided that warships would be sent to prevent the departure of the battleships at Casablanca and Dakar, but the Cabinet backed away from Churchill's proposal to attack the *Richelieu*. Toward the end of the meeting, news arrived that France had signed an armistice with Germany, but the Cabinet knew nothing of its terms.[17]

With tensions mounting in London on Sunday, June 23, Pound addressed a letter to Darlan reminding him of British concern that the four French capital ships might fall into German hands and that Britain had released France to seek armistice terms only on the condition that the French fleet be delivered to British ports.[18] At the same time, Halifax summoned French ambassador Roger Cambon, explaining to him the urgent British concern that the French fleet might be delivered to the enemy. And Admiral Jean Odend'hal, head of the French naval mission in London, relayed to Bordeaux an urgent British request for an exact copy of the armistice's naval terms. The French reply, arriving the next day, gave no more than general assurances that the French fleet would be disarmed in French ports under the French flag and that the armistice terms did not threaten British interests.[19] The French refusal to share the details of the armistice terms did nothing to appease anxieties in London.

Before Darlan could reply to Pound's letter, British measures to take control of French ships in home harbors and at Alexandria caused the French admiral to question London's intentions. Darlan's suspicions were amplified by General de Gaulle's radio broadcast of June 18 encouraging the French empire to continue fighting and by British efforts to promote dissidence among French naval and colonial officers. On Sunday the admiral wrote in his diary that "Great Britain steps up its subversive effort among Frenchmen to prevent the government's signing an armistice: personal letters, flatteries, threats. They damage us through the radio. Their official and unofficial agents devote themselves to unscrupulous actions against our government. They are using General de Gaulle in that effort." The next day he concluded that "the British government continues its violent anti-French campaign and is trying to separate the colonies from the homeland."[20]

The Armistice from the British Perspective

In the meantime, the unofficial receipt of the German armistice terms, with their ambiguous naval clauses, nourished Churchill's misgivings about any diplomatic solution within the framework of an armistice. Article 8, containing the naval clauses, required the heavy units of the French fleet to return to their peacetime ports to be disarmed and demobilized under German supervision. The British chiefs, mistranslating the French word *controle* in article 8, assumed that the French fleet would be demobilized under German control rather than more accurately under German *supervision* or *inspection*. Accordingly, Churchill announced to the House of Commons that "from this text it is clear the French war vessels under this armistice pass into German or Italian control while fully armed."[21] More accurately, article 8 required the four newest French battleships and their escorts to return to harbors that the Germans had already occupied on the Bay of Biscay.

The French, however, assured London that any final decision on that point would be subject to a decision in the armistice commission at Wiesbaden. Darlan had already decided that he could not return his ships to ports on the Bay of Biscay, where British air and naval power might destroy them en route or upon their arrival. The French armistice delegation had made that point to their German opposites, but Bordeaux could give London no further assurances on that key item. That point, however, might easily have become the subject of further Anglo-French negotiations. In any such discussions, British domination of Atlantic waters would have dealt London all the high cards, for there was no way for Darlan to return his ships to their home ports without exposing them to the full wrath of British naval and air power. Remaining on the table, therefore, was the option of awaiting the decision of the armistice commission and holding in reserve the threat of British naval power in the interest of strengthening the French hand at Wiesbaden.

But Churchill had already lost all interest in negotiations with France. He no longer had any confidence in the Bordeaux government or in Darlan. Accordingly, he moved instead in the direction of local initiatives in French Africa and, in case they should fail, the use of force against the French warships. At the same time, he and the War Cabinet still clung to the hope that the French fleet and the French empire, or portions of them, might after all rally to the British rather than exiting the war.

With the armistice terms in hand, the Foreign Office continued to urge a policy of restraint and of maintaining communications with the French government. But opinion in the War Cabinet moved steadily in the opposite direction. In public announcements Churchill repeatedly referred to "the Bordeaux government," implying that it somehow lacked legitimacy and did not have the support of the French. The decline of formal diplomatic relations with the French government coincided with the mounting initiative at the local level to persuade French naval and colonial authorities in North and West Africa to break with their government, to continue in the war, and to rally their ships to British ports. At the same time British naval liaison officers and diplomatic officials in French Africa flooded London with reports of French ship crews and officers opposing the armistice and urging their superiors to rally their ships to the British cause.[22]

Since Darlan had already told Alexander and Pound that the French fleet would not be delivered to any foreign power, continuing negotiations with him on that point held little hope of Britain's gaining possession of the French fleet. Despite Pound's earlier insistence that Britain had no need for the French fleet, Churchill earnestly desired to possess its heaviest units. British concerns to possess French naval and imperial assets helps to explain why the War Cabinet ignored Darlan and turned instead to local French officials in Africa who they thought might after all rally to Britain the ships and territories under their command. During the final stages of the crisis in late June, the War Cabinet continued to flirt with the French fleet and simultaneously kept open the option of using force to destroy it.

In the meantime, the War Cabinet took the first step toward a military solution on Monday, June 24, when it issued orders to forbid the departure of French ships from British home ports and from other ports under British control. These included a large assortment of light ships at Plymouth and Portsmouth as well as Force X at Alexandria, which consisted of an old battleship, two heavy cruisers, two light cruisers, and several destroyers, under Admiral René-Emile Godfroy, who remained on good terms with his British opposite, Admiral Sir Andrew Cunningham. London had no choice but to detain these ships unilaterally without prior negotiations with Bordeaux, whose armistice relations with Germany required a fait accompli rather than negotiations to concede these ships to the British. Better just to go ahead and detain them. But the necessity of detaining these ships burdened any British communications with Bordeaux to address the more complex problem of the French warships beyond British control at Mers el-Kébir and Dakar. So the detention of the French ships played into the hands of Churchill at the expense of Halifax, who preferred a diplomatic solution to the problem of the French battle fleet.

In detaining the French ships without sending a polite explanation to Darlan, London forfeited whatever diplomatic advantage it might have enjoyed in the wake of the French admiral's friendly posture toward Pound and Alexander at the Bordeaux conference just a few days prior. Responding four days later to Pound's note of June 23, Darlan protested the British action to detain the French ships. At the same time, he insisted upon his "foremost desire not to widen the gap between Great Britain and France" and upon France's desire "to be treated not as an enemy but as a neutral power." And, in the words of Odend'hal, who transmitted the note, he reminded Pound "that there never was any question of such unfriendly treatment in the course of his conversations with you in Bordeaux."[23] Later that day, Darlan renewed his assurances and instructed Odend'hal to urge the Admiralty to withhold judgment on the French fleet until the negotiations in the armistice commission had been concluded. France, he explained, would try to persuade the commission to permit the French ships to remain in African ports.[24] Darlan's notes to Pound amounted to an invitation to continue communications at the highest levels of naval command. At the same time Churchill was moving the War Cabinet toward a violent solution.

The Naval Staff Report

The War Cabinet met three times on Monday, June 24. At the first session that morning, Pound reviewed a report of the naval staff addressing the problem of the French ships in the Mediterranean. Assuming the French fleet to be a difficult target, the naval staff report underscored the futility of using force to gain control of the French navy, which included a large fleet of submarines and surface ships scattered about in widely dispersed Mediterranean ports. The use of armed force against any French ships, it noted, would reduce the chances of gaining control of anything but a tiny fraction of the French fleet as the remainder of the navy would become actively hostile. The naval staff, however, recognized that the delivery of France's capital ships to the enemy would have disastrous consequences and that if force must at last be employed, it should be directed against the *Dunkerque* and *Strasbourg*, protected by strong shore batteries around Mers el-Kébir. Any successful operation against them, Pound insisted, would have to be launched at dawn as a surprise attack. He added that the operation would risk the loss of two British battleships, which would then make it difficult to deal afterward with the *Jean Bart* and *Richelieu*.[25]

Pound commented that the probable loss of two British capital ships seemed a high price to pay for the uncertain outcome of an attack upon the two French battlecruisers. "Admiral Darlan and other French Admirals," he added, "had maintained the consistent attitude that in no circumstances would the French Fleet be surrendered, and it would seem more likely that we should achieve our object by trusting these assurances, rather than by attempting to eliminate units of the French Fleet by force."[26] Pound then declared his opposition to any armed attack against the French fleet.

Pound's report, representing the professional position of the naval staff, advanced the essential point governing the larger strategic picture—namely, that the Royal Navy was incapable of destroying or capturing the French fleet and that an attack on any French ship in French ports would impose heavy burdens on the future. Entirely on target, the report nevertheless did nothing to convince Churchill to back away from the use of force, as he was already obsessed at the thought of attacking or seizing the French battleships.

In the long and confused discussion that followed, the War Cabinet momentarily backed away from any operation against the two French battlecruisers at Oran, noting that an armed attack on the recent ally would serve only to alienate the entire French Empire. Churchill agreed that an attack against the two ships would be costly and perhaps unsuccessful. So he shifted the discussion back to the *Jean Bart* and *Richelieu*, suggesting that they might easily be taken once they left the shelter of their ports. Finally, the War Cabinet agreed to defer for the moment any decision in regard to action against French naval units beyond British control.[27]

When the War Cabinet assembled again at noon, it learned that Admiral Esteva had received orders from Darlan that the French ships must in no event fall into German or Italian hands, that they must remain in French ports and as a last resort be scuttled. This news was consistent with the report that Pound had made in the morning session. But the Cabinet also learned that the British admiral at Gibraltar had been sent to Oran to confer with the French admiral there and to observe the berthing positions of the French ships at nearby Mers el-Kébir "in case it might be necessary to take drastic action against them."[28]

Word was also received that the HMS *Watchman* had arrived at Casablanca to keep an eye on the *Jean Bart* and that the heavy cruiser *Dorsetshire* had arrived in waters near Dakar. Now the War Cabinet instructed Pound to order Admiral Cunningham at Alexandria to detain the French squadron there. It also concluded that every measure should be taken to gain possession of the *Richelieu* and *Jean Bart* as well as the *Dunkerque* and *Strasbourg* or, should that not be possible, to make sure that all of them were scuttled.[29]

It seems clear that Churchill, despite Pound's sobering report earlier that morning, had managed behind the scenes to keep open the option of operations against the four heaviest units of the French fleet, either to seize or to destroy them. This would allow Churchill to turn the situation to his advantage, at the expense of Halifax and others in the War Cabinet who wished to avoid an armed clash with the French navy. Churchill appears to have ignored the professional perspective advanced that morning in the naval staff report.

Meeting again late that afternoon, the War Cabinet inched closer in the direction of using force against the French fleet. By this time the anxieties about the *Jean Bart* and *Richelieu* had subsided as they now had come under British surveillance. The discussion thus focused on the ships still in the Mediterranean, the *Dunkerque* and *Strasbourg* at Mers el-Kébir and numerous other French ships scattered around the Mediterranean. In the course of that discussion, Churchill insisted that "whatever assurances the French might have received from the Germans, we could not prevent the enemy obtaining possession of the ships unless they were either scuttled or taken in possession by us," and "if we were to stop the ships being handed over, we should have to act quickly."[30]

The War Cabinet discussed other options, but none of them addressed satisfactorily the perceived need for prompt action to neutralize the French fleet. Accordingly, the War Cabinet invited the Admiralty to prepare an appreciation as to what would be involved "if it was found necessary to take action by force against French warships not at present under our control."[31] In taking that measure, the War Cabinet had allowed itself to be rushed prematurely toward a naval action that risked creating more problems than it would solve.

By the end of that day the French squadron at Alexandria, the two battleships at Casablanca and Dakar, and the French ships at Portsmouth and Plymouth had all come under the restraining influence of British naval power. There was little chance that any French ships under Darlan's orders would be sent to Atlantic ports under German control, for British naval and air power could easily intercept them en route or attack them in port. London therefore held the highest strategic cards, and it enjoyed the advantage of Darlan's assurances. More importantly, the naval staff had already warned that the use of force in the Mediterranean would at best eliminate but a fraction of the French fleet and that at prohibitive strategic costs. It seems clear that French naval assets were distributed on June 24 in a pattern to demand patience and continued surveillance as opposed to any dramatic gesture that held little chance of success.

Toward a Violent Solution

In spite of the risks, the War Cabinet moved even further in the direction of using force but for reasons unrelated to the Franco-German armistice. On June 25 events at sea played directly into the hands of Churchill, now growing more impatient for swift naval action. At 2:15 p.m. on that Tuesday afternoon the *Richelieu* departed her refuge at Dakar and put out to sea. Responding promptly, the Admiralty ordered British warships in the area to close in with the view of capturing the French ship. The War Cabinet, overconfident of a capture, discussed whether the *Richelieu* should be returned to France after the war. But the next afternoon, when the *Dorsetshire* made contact with her, the French ship turned abruptly back toward Dakar.[32] Although the sortie of the *Richelieu* came to nothing, it nourished anxieties in the War Cabinet as to whether other French ships might attempt to leave port.[33] Those anxieties strengthened Churchill's hand.

Moving closer to the hard line taken by Churchill, Pound worried on June 26 that the still unknown terms of the Franco-Italian armistice might require the *Dunkerque* and *Strasbourg* to steam to French or Italian ports on the northern coast of the Mediterranean. Thus, the Franco-Italian armistice emerged as more threatening than the German. Whereas the Franco-German armistice required French ships to be demobilized and disarmed in ports within easy range of British naval and air power, the Italian armistice posed a risk that the two French battlecruisers might be moved to Toulon, closer to Italy and at the far limits of British offensive capabilities. Pound therefore ordered two British submarines to take up station outside of Oran.

Churchill was now ready to advance a specific proposal. When the War Cabinet met at noon on Thursday, the twenty-seventh, Pound had already come around to the Prime Minister's hard-line position. Their proposal was to plant magnetic mines in the channel leading into the harbor at Mers el-Kébir. This action would isolate the French squadron until July 3, the earliest date for the arrival of a strong British force, which would confront the French admiral with an ultimatum requiring him to demilitarize his ships or deliver them to British ports. Should he refuse, the British force would proceed to fire upon the French ships in the harbor. According to the record of the meeting, "THE PRIME MINISTER summed up the discussion as follows: He thought the War Cabinet had approved in principle that the operation proposed should take place on the 3rd July. It might be combined with further operations in the Mediterranean or with operations designed to secure the RICHELIEU and the JEAN BART."[34] Following discussion of details, the War Cabinet approved the operation and invited the Admiralty to arrange for its immediate implementation. The Admiralty hurriedly drafted plans to force a quick showdown with the French squadron at Alexandria, with French ships in British home ports, and most importantly with the squadron at Mers el-Kébir. The latter they labeled Operation Catapult.

Churchill and the Armistice Commissions

In the meantime, Pound still had not shut down his channel of communication with Darlan. The Admiralty had access to Admiral Odend'hal and the French naval mission in London, so an exchange of messages with Darlan remained an option. As the crisis mounted in late June, members of the War Cabinet had suggested more than once that contacts with Darlan might be helpful, but neither Churchill nor Pound took any initiative to solicit the cooperation of the French admiral. The Prime Minister clearly had no interest in contacting Darlan.

Communications between the Admiralty and Darlan nevertheless continued in the form of responses to urgent messages the French admiral had sent to Pound through Odend'hal. In late June, when Darlan protested the British detention of French ships at Alexandria and in British home ports, Pound "told Admiral Odend'hal quite bluntly that if the French ships under our control tried to get away we would fire upon them" and that "Admiral Darlan should realize that the only hope of France's resurrection lay in a British victory, and he should not allow any niceties of procedure at this time to jeopardize the success of our efforts."[35] Pound's message did nothing to renew communications with Darlan or with the French government.

Late on Monday afternoon, July 1, Vice-Admiral T. S. V. Phillips, vice chief of the naval staff, informed the War Cabinet of an urgent plea from

Darlan, forwarded by Odend'hal, to reserve judgment pending a decision in the German armistice commission at Wiesbaden, whose discussions concerning the French fleet were scheduled for that same day. Churchill could assume from that message that the armistice commission was at the point of making a decision. He brushed the message aside, though, insisting that "discussions as to the armistice conditions could not affect the real facts of the situation."[36]

The Axis armistice commissions, however, were already conceding points to the French delegations. On Sunday, June 30, when the French delegation at Wiesbaden inquired as to which ports the French fleet would be interned, the German commission delegated the question to an undercommission for naval affairs. Then on Wednesday, July 3, it delegated all questions concerning the French Mediterranean fleet to the Italian armistice commission at Turin.[37] The Italian commission had already on June 30 conceded that the French Mediterranean fleet would be interned at either Toulon or in North African ports, which hinted that the *Dunkerque* and *Strasbourg*, a part of the Atlantic fleet, might also be interned there rather than in German-occupied ports on the Bay of Biscay. Darlan, no doubt thinking that London would applaud that revision, promptly informed Odend'hal of the decision at Turin.[38] But the Admiralty grew even more alarmed, for it opened the door for the two French battlecruisers to be interned at Toulon, closer to the Axis than to the British orbit.

The question remains as to whether Churchill already knew of the Italian concession, and if so, why he would withhold that information from the War Cabinet. British naval intelligence appears to have read on Sunday, June 30, a message from the French Admiralty to Odend'hal that had been decrypted by a confidential cipher. This message, number 5202, reads as follows: "Italian Government authorize stationing of fleet in half-crew condition in Toulon and North African ports. I have firm hope that German Government, whose reply is awaited, will agree to same."[39] If the message had indeed been decrypted on July 1, Pound would have delivered it promptly to Churchill, who therefore would have learned during the day that the Italian armistice commission had conceded that the French ships might be interned at Oran and Toulon rather than at Cherbourg or Brest.

When the War Cabinet met at 6:00 p.m. that same Monday, only Churchill, Pound, and Phillips would have known of the secret cipher and of the message announcing the Italian concession to the French delegation. This information would no doubt have been of interest to the War Cabinet, where there remained latent misgivings about using force at Oran. But neither Pound nor Phillips would have felt free to mention the confidential message, for it would have betrayed the secret cipher. So Phillips could do no more than report Odend'hal's delivery of Darlan's plea to await an armistice decision, which had arrived by standard channels rather than the secret cipher. The minutes of the meeting contain no hint that the Italian armistice commission had already agreed that the French ships at Mers el-Kébir might remain there or that they might be interned at Toulon. In the meantime, during that same Monday afternoon, the secret cipher was suddenly shut down, so the military services were forbidden to receive encrypted messages from that source.[40] The reasons for shutting it down are not clear, but the suppression of that channel enabled Churchill to avoid a debate in the War Cabinet on the merits of the Italian concession.

It is clear that events in the armistice commissions were turning to the French advantage at the very moment when Churchill dismissed the commissions as irrelevant. In the wake of the Italian decision, the French Mediterranean fleet would remain beyond German reach, but whether it would be interned at Oran or instead at Toulon was not clear. The negotiations in the armistice commissions were therefore evolving in a direction to demand further contacts with Darlan. Odend'hal had already on June 29 relayed to the French Admiralty a message from Phillips insisting that interning the French ships at Toulon was in the British view unacceptable.[41] So Darlan might be pressured to keep the French squadron at Oran if London would but await the decision of the armistice commissions. But awaiting that decision was exactly what Churchill intended to avoid.

Chapter 12

Blunder at Mers el-Kébir

The British attack on the French squadron anchored at Mers el-Kébir on July 3, 1940, marked the sudden and violent end to more than a year of productive Anglo-French naval relations. With its planning orchestrated at every step by Winston Churchill, the attack was a product of the Prime Minister's obsession after the fall of France to unleash British naval might against the French battleship fleet. As it turned out, the operation was a tactical failure and a political disaster that rendered the Mediterranean naval balance more hostile than it had been prior to the attack.

Planning Operation Catapult

Operation Catapult, the attack on the French squadron at Mers el-Kébir, was but one of four separate naval operations launched against the French fleet in early July 1940. Plans for these operations were hurriedly drafted at the Admiralty in late June and early July, so hurriedly that important details received but scant attention. The initial proposal approved by the War Cabinet on June 27 had envisioned offensive operations at Mers el-Kébir; at Casablanca and Dakar, where the French battleships *Jean Bart* and *Richelieu*, respectively, lay in harbor; and at Alexandria, where a French squadron, Force X, commanded by Vice-Admiral René-Emile Godfroy, had already been detained by Admiral Sir Andrew Cunningham. The Mers el-Kébir operation was scheduled for July 3, the earliest date that a strong British squadron could arrive in waters opposite the harbor where the *Dunkerque* and *Strasbourg* lay at anchor.[1]

Certain important changes were made early in the planning stage. In the first instance, the seizure of French ships in British home ports was added to

182

the plan and scheduled for the predawn hours of July 3, just prior to the confrontation at Oran. There would be no attack on the unfinished *Jean Bart*, and the attack on the *Richelieu* would be delayed until after the Mers el-Kébir operation had been completed. Nor would the British attack French warships at Algiers, consisting of two strong cruiser squadrons and numerous lighter ships, since the harbor was remote and well defended. The operation at Oran would proceed without Britain's newest battleship, the *Nelson*, which was unable to reach Gibraltar until July 5. Insisting upon haste, Churchill was unwilling to wait even two more days for the *Nelson* to join the British squadron forming at Gibraltar. Called Force H, the squadron had been created on June 27 and placed under the command of Vice-Admiral Sir James Somerville.[2]

The most vexing problem—clearly defining the mission of Force H—related importantly to the terms of the ultimatum to be presented to the French naval command in the harbor. The terms would be drafted by Churchill and approved by the War Cabinet. There emerged, however, sharp disagreements between London, where Churchill insisted upon a quick display of force, and Gibraltar, where British naval officers had no zeal to attack the former ally. Moreover, there persisted in both London and Gibraltar the hope that the French ships might be lured into the British camp or be neutralized in a way to avoid a clash of arms.

The question of the terms of the ultimatum was discussed first at the noon meeting of the War Cabinet on Thursday, June 27, and more importantly during the late afternoon meeting of Monday, July 1. At the Thursday meeting a spread of alternatives was discussed briefly. These included demilitarization of the French ships under British supervision, French delivery of the ships to British ports, or the use of force against the ships should the commanding officers refuse to scuttle them.[3] These discussions were only preliminary, however, and would be continued upon receipt of a draft proposal that the Prime Minister would prepare over the weekend.

On Monday evening, July 1, when the War Cabinet received Churchill's draft, the discussion focused on the key question of whether the French admiral at Mers el-Kébir should be offered the option of demilitarizing his ships on the spot under British supervision. Churchill opposed that option on the grounds that any quick measure of demilitarization could be undone in short order. But Admiral Pound pointed out that demilitarization was precisely the measure that would appeal to the French admiral and that the ships could be demobilized and demilitarized in a short time by destroying their turbines and disarming their guns with oxyacetylene metal cutters. The minutes of the meeting indicate their compromising the point. The British would not offer that option but would accept it should the French admiral propose it.[4] The

War Cabinet also agreed that the details of the message to the French admiral and instructions to Admiral Somerville would be settled that same evening in a meeting of the Prime Minister and First Lord of the Admiralty H. V. Alexander.

Misgivings at Gibraltar

In the meantime, on June 27 Admiral Somerville received in London orders indicating that the first task of Force H would be "to secure the transfer, surrender or destruction of the French warships at Oran and Mers el-Kébir, so as to ensure that these ships did not fall into German or Italian hands." Later that day Pound and Alexander explained to him that while "every preparation was to be made to employ force in order to complete the task of Force H, it was hoped that the necessity would not arise."[5] Somerville rushed off to Gibraltar the next day, thinking that the French command at Oran probably would not resist the British demands.

But Somerville soon discovered that the Mediterranean command was out of step with London. En route to Gibraltar on Sunday, June 30, on board the light cruiser *Arethusa*, he received a message from Admiral Cunningham, commander of the Mediterranean fleet at Alexandria, expressing strong opposition to using force against French warships at either Alexandria or Oran. Arriving at Gibraltar shortly thereafter, Somerville promptly consulted Admiral Sir Dudley North, commander North Atlantic, who expressed "grave concern" at the use of force, which "should be avoided at all costs." North feared that using force against the French ships risked provoking a combined Spanish-German assault on Gibraltar, which would render the base useless. This view was endorsed moments later by the governor of Gibraltar.[6]

Later that Sunday evening Somerville summoned his senior officers to examine the Oran operation. They discussed the technical difficulties attendant to attacking the French ships, whose positions ruled out aerial torpedo attack. The only viable option was bombardment from the ships offshore, which risked heavy casualties among civilians. They considered whether a few warning rounds aimed to explode harmlessly in the harbor might induce the French officers and crews to abandon their ships prior to their final destruction. Somerville summarized the meeting as follows: "The view I held, and which was shared by others present at the meeting, was that it was highly improbable that the French would use force to resist our demands."[7]

After the meeting had ended, Admiral North again expressed to Somerville his strong opposition to the use of force against the French ships. Vice-Admiral Lionel Wells, commander of Force H aircraft carriers, expressed equally strong opposition, as did Captain Cedric Holland, recent naval attaché in Paris who had been rushed to Gibraltar to deliver the ultimatum to French vice-admiral

Marcel Gensoul at Mers el-Kébir. All three British officers "considered that there was little fear of the French allowing their ships to fall into German hands."[8]

During the next two days, while Somerville managed the numerous technical details attendant to Catapult, additional messages arrived from London concerning the terms to be presented to Admiral Gensoul Wednesday morning. Contained in several messages, the terms were incomplete and sometimes contradictory, reflecting confusion and indecision in London as to whether the terms should afford Gensoul greater opportunity to neutralize his ships in a way to avoid an armed clash. A message arriving around dawn on Monday, July 1, listed four terms: (1) to steam their ships to British harbors and continue to fight on the British side; (2) to bring their ships to a British port with crews to be repatriated and ships returned at the end of the war; (3) to demilitarize their ships to British satisfaction; or (4) to sink their ships.[9] This message was sent twelve hours prior to the meeting of the War Cabinet scheduled for 6:00 that evening.

Somerville could see that he was trapped between local opinion to avoid force and London's instructions to employ force if necessary. He knew that he would have to fire upon the French ships should Gensoul refuse all of the options. He therefore reported to the Admiralty the local opposition to the use of force on the grounds that it would alienate French people everywhere.[10] The report made it clear that opinion at Gibraltar ran deep against the use of force.

Somerville's message arrived in London prior to the 6:00 p.m. meeting of the War Cabinet, which would consider the Admiralty's supplementary instructions for Somerville and the Prime Minister's draft of terms to be presented to Admiral Gensoul. The minutes of that meeting bear no evidence that the Admiralty had shared Somerville's report with the War Cabinet.[11] The absence in the minutes of any reference to it suggests that the War Cabinet may not have known that Gibraltar was out of step with London on the question of using force against the former ally.

Somerville received on July 2 his basic instructions to arrive off Mers el-Kébir early on Wednesday, July 3, and to present the French admiral there with four options, summarized briefly as follows: (1) sail their ships out of the harbor and continue to fight the Axis on the British side; (2) sail with reduced crews to a British port with crews to be repatriated as desired and with ships to be returned at the end of the war or with compensation in case of damage to them; (3) sail with reduced crews to a French port in the West Indies to be demobilized or entrusted to the United States; or (4) scuttle their ships. Another option, to demobilize their ships in the harbor to British satisfaction within six hours, would be considered only if the French themselves should propose that solution. Finally, Somerville was ordered to use force against the French ships should the French admiral reject all of the options.[12] Significantly, demobilization of the French ships in the harbor, which had been included among the options the day before, was omitted from the final list.

Force H, which included the battlecruiser *Hood*, battleships *Valiant* and *Resolution*, aircraft carrier *Ark Royal*, and a supporting force of cruisers and destroyers, departed Gibraltar late Tuesday. Steaming ahead was the destroyer *Foxhound*, carrying Captain Holland, who personally knew many of the French naval officers at Mers el-Kébir. Holland's job was to present the ultimatum early Wednesday morning to Admiral Gensoul, on board the *Dunkerque*, still remembered in the Royal Navy as "the friend of the *Hood*."

Violence before Dawn

During the early morning hours of July 3, as Force H steamed toward Mers el-Kébir, armed British marines moved swiftly to seize the nearly two hundred French ships detained since the armistice at Portsmouth and Plymouth. Many of these ships had fought along with British ships in convoy operations and other duties. Others had fled France in June to escape approaching German armies. Many of them were smaller vessels—tankers, minesweepers, armed fishing ships—of varied military value. Among the larger vessels were the old battleships *Paris* and *Courbet*, both obsolete. There were, however, other ships of considerable military value, notably the large destroyers *Leopard* and *Le Triomphant*; the world's largest submarine, *Surcouf*; and several other submarines. Many of these ships were in poor condition or had been damaged, and their crews in many cases were homesick and demoralized.[13]

In view of the slight value and limited threat of these ships, the question remains as to why it was necessary to seize them prior to any action that might take place at Oran. The problem was not so much their value but rather their large numbers and their numerous officers and crew who could be expected to turn hostile following Operation Catapult. The War Cabinet, aware of Admiral Darlan's orders for French officers to scuttle their ships should a foreign power attempt to seize them, concluded on July 1 that "it was important to take steps to avoid the risk of these ships being sunk in our harbours."[14] The urgent need, therefore, was to separate the crews from their ships prior to Catapult and to bring the crews under British control in the interest of settling with them later. In keeping open the option of using force at Oran, the War Cabinet had good reasons to seize these ships prior to any confrontation there.

Armed British marines boarded the French ships under the cover of darkness early Wednesday morning, July 3, catching their officers and crews by surprise. Vice-Admiral L. M. G. Cayol, commanding at Plymouth, and Rear-Admiral Gaudin de Villaine, commanding at Portsmouth, had already been detained in London. The ships at Portsmouth were seized without bloodshed, but at Plymouth crewmen on board the *Surcouf* resisted, resulting in the deaths of three British marines and one French sailor, and there were several wounded on each side. Some of the French crews attempted to scuttle their ships or damage vital equipment to make them useless, as the War Cabinet had expected, but these efforts were largely unsuccessful.[15] By dawn the operation had been completed.

The Frenchmen were quickly moved to nearby encampments where the crews were separated from their officers. Given the choice of repatriation or remaining in the United Kingdom, about seven hundred of them accepted service in the Royal Navy, and sixteen hundred of them entered into the service of Charles de Gaulle, marking the beginnings of the Free French Navy. The great majority of them chose to return to France.[16]

A Pragmatic Settlement at Alexandria

In accordance with prewar planning, French warships had assumed responsibility for the western basin of the Mediterranean so that the British Mediterranean Fleet under Admiral Cunningham might operate out of Alexandria to cover the eastern basin and in case of emergency to rally to Asian waters. Cunningham's squadron operated regularly in cooperation with a smaller French squadron, Force X, consisting of cruisers and lighter ships under the command of Vice-Admiral Godfroy. Cunningham and Godfroy maintained friendly relations, and French ships often accompanied British ships on combat missions. On June 20 Cunningham reported to the Admiralty that the French cruisers "are full of fight, in these operations."[17]

On June 25, after Godfroy had received orders from Darlan to steam his ships to Beirut, Cunningham intervened on his own initiative to inform the French admiral that his ships must remain at Alexandria. London promptly approved. As tensions at Alexandria began to mount, Cunningham and Godfroy entered into delicate negotiations to avoid a clash of arms in the harbor. On June 27 Godfroy promised to discharge the fuel from his ships on condition that Cunningham promise not to seize them by force. The crisis might have ended at that point, but London ordered Cunningham to avoid any commitment not to seize them. The next day Cunningham wired the Admiralty urging restraint: "I would emphasize frank and cordial relations exist here and feel that more can be done by friendly negotiations than by threatening forcible measures. In any case the ships will not go to sea."[18]

Although the War Cabinet refused to back away, the Admiralty continued to search for a bloodless solution, flashing Cunningham on June 30 a long message requesting his opinion: "It is under consideration to seize French ships at Alexandria—simultaneously with operation at Oran. Earliest date for this operation is a.m. 3 July. Request your views as to best procedure to follow so as to achieve our purpose with minimum risk of bloodshed and hostilities on the part of the French."[19]

Cunningham's reply, indicating his strong opposition to the seizure of French ships anywhere, offered London a sensible alternative to the use of force. Questioning the purpose of seizing Godfroy's ships on the premise of keeping them out of Axis hands, he insisted that that had already been done. He suggested, moreover, that any attempt to seize the ships would likely fail, for in his view the French "would resist most vigorously and it would be more likely to result in ships scuttling themselves at their moorings before it could be prevented, unnecessary British and French casualties, and a harbour fouled with wrecks." Cunningham reminded London of the need to maintain friendly relations with the French in the Middle East, and he added that allowing matters to run their course at Alexandria would probably result in the French ships falling eventually into British hands for lack of food and pay. Finally, he turned to the question of using armed force at Oran. "I am very much against action there if it can possibly be avoided. . . . The effect may be to alienate the whole of the French element friendly to us and in particular I would mention the effect in North America where friendly attitudes may make a great difference in naval operations later on."[20]

London replied on Tuesday with a set of options that left the door ajar for a negotiated settlement, to be concluded by nightfall on Wednesday, July 3. These included the French ships being turned over to the British in the harbor, or their being demobilized in the harbor to remain there under British control with skeleton French crews, or finally their being scuttled at sea. Cunningham therefore entered into negotiations with Godfroy as scheduled, but he ignored both the deadline and the options, and Godfroy ignored orders from Darlan to bolt from the harbor. Accordingly, the two admirals concluded a settlement on Thursday whereby Godfroy would discharge the fuel from his tanks and disarm his ships in a way to make them harmless. Discussion for a reduction of crews would follow afterward.[21]

The two admirals had avoided a costly clash of arms at Alexandria, but the bloody confrontation that unfolded simultaneously at Oran caused Godfroy to turn cold and aloof. Finally, on July 30 the French admiral shared privately with Cunningham a tactful and moving message that the British admiral must have appreciated:

> I should be very sorry that you think my present reserve means a change in my feelings toward yourself. You must believe that those feelings are always the same. I think of you . . . with the same respect and sympathy as before and I have no reason to do otherwise. But I feel obligated to take

into account for some time the grief of officers and petty officers of my squadron who have lost sons or brothers at Oran and would perhaps be hurt if we behaved as if nothing had happened.[22]

The Mission of Captain Holland

When the *Foxhound* arrived in waters opposite Mers el-Kébir at dawn on Wednesday, July 3, the mission of Captain Holland was already burdened by London's hurried planning. The Admiralty's instructions to Somerville had innocently assumed that a British captain would gain ready access to a French admiral, that there would be negotiations, and that there would be ample time for British demobilization parties to board and disarm numerous French ships within six hours should the French admiral propose the disarmament option. But Admiral Gensoul, interpreting the first signal from the *Foxhound* as an ultimatum, refused to receive Holland. Even if the Admiralty had arranged for Holland to be accompanied by an officer of Gensoul's rank, the French admiral would still have had good reason to reject Holland and stall for time. London's first mistake was to assume that the French admiral would receive Holland promptly upon his arrival.

Holland, lacking instructions to the contrary, had flashed from the *Foxhound* at 7:09 a.m. an invitation in clear for the French ships in the harbor to join up with the British squadron offshore. This was one of the options that Somerville had proposed to the Admiralty on July 1, but it was intended to be sent in clear to the ships in the harbor only after Holland had delivered the options personally to Gensoul. The thought was that French officers and crews would now pressure their admiral to rally their ships to the British.[23]

But Holland had flashed the message prematurely, so French officers knew of the impending British threat before Holland could deliver his message to Gensoul. With an ultimatum already on the table, the element of confidence between Holland and Gensoul was compromised even before their negotiations had begun. Determined to gain time to prepare his ships for action or for flight, Gensoul refused Holland's request to see him personally, with the result that much of the day was spent in an awkward exchange of messages between Gensoul on board the *Dunkerque* and Holland on board a small boat anchored at the entrance of the harbor remote from the *Foxhound*.[24]

Holland's first personal contact was with an old French friend, Lieutenant Bernard Dufay, who arrived at the harbor entrance in a barge with the news of Gensoul's refusal to receive the British captain. Holland nevertheless insisted upon seeing the admiral. Gensoul again refused but finally agreed to receive Holland's message. Accordingly, Dufay delivered the package at about

9:30 a.m., returning later in the morning with Gensoul's reply, which contained assurances he would not deliver his ships to the Axis. But this also made clear the French intention to defend their ships should the British use force against them. Now Holland crossed over to the barge, where he and Dufay discussed the matter as old friends. At 10:50 a.m. Dufay returned to the *Dunkerque* carrying with him a copy of Holland's script, intended to guide his conversation with the French admiral.[25]

Returning at about 11:30 a.m., Dufay was accompanied by Captain Jules Danbé, chief of staff of the Force de Raid as well as friend of Holland and an officer of equal rank. Danbé delivered the admiral's reply, indicating again his intention to defend his ships. "Admiral Gensoul," the message continued, "draws to the attention of Admiral Somerville the fact that the first shot fired against us would have the practical result of immediately turning the whole French fleet against Great Britain."[26] Holland now returned to the *Foxhound*, commenting to his French friend as he turned to leave, "Let me say to you, as one officer to another, that were I in your place, my response would not have been different."[27]

In the meantime, the *Hood* received reports from reconnaissance aircraft indicating that the French ships were preparing to put out to sea. At 10:45 a.m. Somerville sent this news to the Admiralty, who replied with the suggestion to use magnetic mines to prevent the departure of the French ships. Accordingly, aircraft from the *Ark Royal* mined the harbor entrance at about 1:30 p.m.[28] This was the first of several tactical blunders, for only five mines were laid, not nearly enough to seal off the harbor.[29]

With the negotiations approaching a dead end, the Admiralty began to have second thoughts as whether to offer the option the War Cabinet had previously withheld, to demilitarize the French ships in the harbor. Late in the morning, therefore, Admiral Pound drafted a proposal to offer Gensoul the demilitarization option, but the War Cabinet promptly rejected it as a concession that the French would interpret as a sign of weakness.[30] So Pound's proposal was not sent. Instead, the Admiralty ordered Somerville to inform Gensoul that Force H would fire on the French ships should they attempt to bolt from the harbor.[31]

But Somerville had already informed Gensoul that he would not let the French ships leave the harbor unless the British terms were accepted, and toward noon he had raised with Gensoul the question of demilitarization, informing him by signal light of the action being taken by Admiral Godfroy to demilitarize his ships at Alexandria.[32] Gensoul could interpret this message as a hint that demilitarization of his ships had been added to the options, but he did not know that it was Somerville who had offered the option and that London had rejected it.

The Role of Darlan

Gensoul's first communication to the French Admiralty, a brief summary of events that omitted the option of steaming to American waters, was sent by telegram at 8:45 a.m.: "English force composed of three battleships, an aircraft carrier, cruisers and destroyers off Oran. Ultimatum sent: sink your ships within six hours or we will be compelled to use force against you. Reply: French warships will respond with force."[33] Gensoul then alerted his ships with the intent of returning British fire or, if he could gain more time, of bolting the harbor under cover of darkness.[34]

Gensoul's message caught the French Admiralty in a state of disarray, stretched out along highways between Nérac and Vichy. The message was first received at Nérac, where Darlan's chief of staff, Admiral Maurice Le Luc, relayed the message to his under chief of staff, Captain C. V. Négadelle, at Clermont-Ferrand with the greater part of the Admiralty staff. Darlan was beyond his reach, on the road approaching Clermont-Ferrand. So Négadelle approved on his own initiative Gensoul's decision to resist any British attack. He also ordered all French warships in the eastern Mediterranean to rally toward Oran, which meant that Gensoul could expect four heavy and four light cruisers at Algiers to steam toward Oran that same day.[35]

Toward noon Négadelle made contact with Darlan, who approved the captain's instructions to Gensoul. At 1:30 p.m., in a telephone conversation with Gensoul, Darlan learned of the British hint that demobilization of the ships might be an option. But he could see that accepting any of the British terms would likely provoke a German occupation of Vichy's free zone, so he had no choice but to rule out any compromise with the British. Instead he instructed Gensoul to expect reinforcements and to respond with force to any British attack; and he ordered Le Luc to notify the armistice commissions of the British threat. Darlan then rushed on to Vichy, two hours away, where the government of Marshal Pétain had begun to establish itself.[36]

According to British historian David Brown, Darlan rejected the demilitarization compromise and thus took "the final political decision on either side in some haste, without reference to political colleagues, and therefore cut himself off from personal control, and even up-to-date news, of the fate of 'his' fleet."[37] This view, however, serves only to shift the blame for the Mers el-Kébir disaster from the aggressor to the victim, from Churchill to Darlan, which hardly squares with the facts.

Holland and Gensoul

Early in the afternoon Somerville realized that he still had not given Gensoul a clear deadline as to when he intended to attack the French ships. Accordingly, at 2:00 p.m. he signaled his intention to open fire an hour later. Faced with a specific deadline, the French admiral now agreed to receive a British delegation, causing Somerville to postpone the deadline until 5:30. Since the *Foxhound* had moved to a more remote position, Holland did not board the *Dunkerque* until 4:15. As Holland passed the ships in the harbor, he noticed French crewmen standing respectfully at attention.[38]

Within minutes Holland was in the presence of Gensoul, who insisted again that the first shot fired would alienate the entire French navy and that he would sink his ships to prevent their falling into Axis hands. Holland said that the enemy might use treachery to seize the French ships, but Gensoul replied that the security measures already in place were adequate to protect them. Holland could not accept that answer. He explained that Somerville had already disobeyed his orders to use force upon the expiration of the first deadline and that he would have to open fire at the end of the 5:30 deadline. Now realizing that Somerville intended to use force very soon, Gensoul revealed to Holland a copy of Darlan's secret order to scuttle the ships or to send them to North America should the enemy try to seize them.[39]

Holland could see that Darlan's American option resembled the third option of the British ultimatum, to send the ships with reduced crews to a French Caribbean port or to the United States. But Gensoul insisted that the execution of Darlan's American option hinged upon a German violation of the armistice and that it was irrelevant to the British ultimatum. Gensoul stated that he had already begun to demobilize his ships by reducing their crews. By this time, however, it was already late afternoon, rather than early morning, when demobilization might have been explored with greater care. Taking his leave, Holland departed the *Dunkerque* at 5:25, just before the ultimatum expired. Passing through the harbor in his small craft, he heard the French warships summon their crews to battle stations. And as he passed the *Bretagne*, the watch officer on deck saluted him smartly.[40]

The Battle of Mers el-Kébir

The moment for Churchill's dramatic gesture had finally arrived. The Battle of Mers el-Kébir began after Somerville had received a signal from London to "settle matters quickly or you will have reinforcements to deal with."[41] Accordingly, at 5:54 p.m., Somerville unleashed his massive firepower upon the French squadron confined to the narrow waters of the harbor. The heaviest

French ships, the *Dunkerque* and *Strasbourg*, each mounted eight 13-inch guns pointed forward, but neither ship mounted guns pointing aft. Also anchored in the harbor were the old battleships *Bretagne* and *Provence*, the seaplane tender *Commandant-Teste*, and six contre-torpilleurs or fleet destroyers. The *Dunkerque* and *Strasbourg*, docked against the breakwater with their sterns toward the sea and their sixteen heavy guns turned inland, were poorly positioned to respond to the British attack.

Gensoul's best hope was to bolt from the harbor, despite the minefield at the entrance. The French destroyers led the flight. The first of them, the *Mogador*, another old friend of the *Hood*, was struck immediately by a large shot that blew off her stern, so she had to be beached near the harbor entrance. But the five other destroyers steamed safely past the *Mogador* through the minefield into the open sea. The *Dunkerque*, soon in position to follow, fired several salvoes, all of them short of the target, before finally being struck by four shells from the *Hood*. Unable to continue, the big ship was run aground to prevent her being sunk. The *Provence*, damaged and set afire, was beached short of the harbor entrance near the *Mogador*. The *Commandante-Teste* remained undamaged in the harbor, but *Bretagne,* suffering multiple hits, quickly capsized and sank with heavy loss of life.[42]

Somerville observed that the French ships in the harbor were able to fire off thirty-six salvoes, all of which fell short of Force H. After Gensoul had flashed repeated requests for the British to stop firing, Somerville ordered a cease-fire at 6:04 p.m. He then replied, "Unless I see your ships sinking, I will open fire again."[43] But neither he nor his aerial observers could see much in the harbor, which was covered with thick black smoke. In the meantime, fire from the French shore batteries prompted Somerville to change course toward the west with the intention of resuming fire on the harbor a short time later, after the French crews had abandoned their ships. Confident of the minefield, he was sure that all of the French warships remained in the harbor.

Suddenly, at 6:20, Somerville was jolted by a report that a *Dunkerque*-class battlecruiser had bolted the harbor and was steaming eastward.[44] The ship was the *Strasbourg*, which had followed the five contre-torpilleurs out of the harbor, already being swept of mines. The big ship evaded what was left of the minefield and sped into the open seas before aircraft from the *Ark Royal* finally spotted her. Somerville had thus let a battlecruiser and five fleet destroyers escape the harbor. In addition, two destroyers from Oran slipped past Force H to join what now became the *Strasbourg* group.[45]

Now the choice targets were at sea, rather than in the harbor, and Force H was steaming westward, opposite that of the *Strasbourg* group. Somerville would have to move quickly to close with the French ships before dark, but he

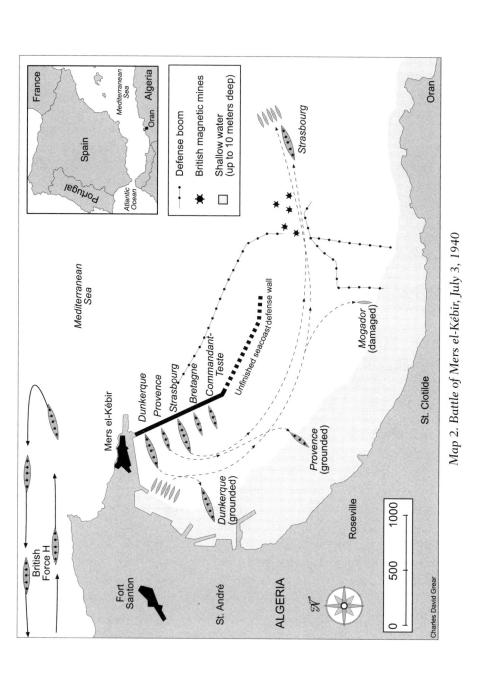

Map 2. Battle of Mers el-Kébir, July 3, 1940

wasted another ten minutes awaiting a confirmation of the escape of the French battlecruiser. It was not until 6:30 p.m. that he reversed course to give chase with the *Hood* and a screening force of cruisers, the *Arethusa* and *Enterprise*, and eleven destroyers. The slow battleships, *Valiant* and *Resolution*, fell behind. In the meantime, six Swordfish bombers from the *Ark Royal* attacked the *Strasbourg*, but they failed to score any hits. Later six Swordfish armed with torpedoes also missed their targets. Nevertheless, the *Hood*, slightly faster than the *Strasbourg*, had closed within twenty-five miles of the French ships by 8:20, when Somerville received reports that the French battlecruiser now had an escort of eleven destroyers.[46]

These reports prompted Somerville to break off the engagement at 8:20, the critical moment when the *Hood* and its screen of two cruisers and eleven destroyers were at the point of overtaking the *Strasbourg*, which had no guns aft to engage the *Hood*. Importantly, these reports suggested that additional destroyers had somehow arrived to reinforce the *Strasbourg* group. Somerville knew, moreover, that two strong cruiser squadrons from Algiers were steaming westward toward the *Strasbourg*. "From the reports received," he later wrote, "I calculated that the Algiers force, which included several 8-inch and 6-inch cruisers and destroyers, would probably meet *Strasbourg* shortly after 2100."[47] In his official report, Somerville listed several other reasons for his abandoning the chase, among them the fact that the approaching darkness would put his ships at a disadvantage, silhouetted against the twilight. The main reason, however, was his perception that the combined French force had become numerically superior to Force H.[48]

As it turned out, Somerville was mistaken in his thought that the Algiers force was at the point of joining the *Strasbourg* group, for the two French forces somehow missed their rendezvous, arriving separately at Toulon the next day.[49] Nevertheless, he was correct in his assumption that the *Strasbourg* group, reinforced at Toulon with eight additional cruisers and numerous destroyers, had become numerically superior to Force H. Importantly, London could now see that the British attack at Mers el-Kébir, far from destroying the French fleet, had served instead to bring together its scattered units into a powerful striking force at Toulon, beyond the reach of the Royal Navy and closer to the Axis orbit. The attack had achieved exactly what it had intended to prevent.

Subsequent attacks on French warships in July did little to change the Mediterranean naval balance, which had now become considerably more threatening to British interests. An aerial attack against the grounded *Dunkerque* on July 6, launched from the *Ark Royal*, inflicted more casualties and damaged the ship further, but not beyond repair. A similar attack at Dakar, launched on July 8 from the carrier *Hermes*, damaged the *Richelieu* in a manner to confine her to the harbor and to reduce the need of constant British surveillance. But the big French battleship had already been isolated well beyond the Axis grasp. In the meantime, French casualties at Mers el-Kébir had been heavy. A total of 1,297 French officers and crew had been killed, nearly a 1,000 from the ancient *Bretagne*, which exploded and capsized so quickly that few of the crew survived. Despite the high casualties, the attack had destroyed but a tiny fraction of the French fleet and turned the remainder of it into an enemy, just as the Admiralty report of July 24 had predicted.

Chapter 13

The Cover-Up and After

A merican memories of Mers el-Kébir are shaped overwhelmingly by a Churchillian perspective that matches poorly the facts. Americans who remember Mers el-Kébir, or have read about it, or have watched video documentaries of it usually applaud the attack as a regrettable but necessary British operation that destroyed the French fleet to head off its being delivered to the German enemy. No one would remember the operation as a tactical failure demanding a shabby cover-up and the fabrication of more than one myth to justify the attack and the motives behind it.

Reaction at Vichy and Gibraltar

The attack at Mers el-Kébir caught the French government in a state of disarray, just beginning to requisition hotels for office space at the resort town of Vichy, in the unoccupied zone of southern France. Admiral Darlan arrived there late that July 3 afternoon, full of anger and intent on revenge. On the next day, his anger mounted. Henri Ballande, a young naval aide of Darlan, observed that the admiral, known for his level-headedness, had lost his composure entirely. In a trembling voice he denounced the British, his brothers in arms who had betrayed him. More than once he insisted upon military reprisals, but cooler heads in the cabinet persuaded Marshal Pétain to settle instead for a token air raid on Gibraltar and the severing of diplomatic relations with London.[1] In response to the British attack, the German armistice commission at Wiesbaden suspended the naval clauses of the armistice agreement to liberate the French fleet now concentrated at Toulon to oppose any further British aggression.

British naval officers at Gibraltar responsible for executing Operation Catapult had from the beginning opposed the use of force, but they had entertained an innocent hope that the French command at Mers el-Kébir would in the end rally its ships to the British side or perhaps scuttle them in the harbor. But when the operation ended instead in a ghastly shedding of French blood, British officers looked back in disgust at what their government had demanded of them. There was overwhelming agreement among them that the operation was a moral and political blunder that would turn the entire French navy against them.

Captain Cedric Holland, with his friendly connections in the French navy, took it all personally, asking in protest to be relieved of his command of the *Ark Royal*. Overwhelmed with grief, he finally surrendered his command in 1941. Admiral Sir James Somerville, equally distressed, regretted profoundly that Catapult had ended so disastrously. In a series of letters to his wife over the following days, he poured out his feelings and explained his disgust about the affair. He termed it "a hateful business," one that left him and his officers feeling dirty and ashamed, depressed, and unclean. "It's all too bloody for words," he wrote, "and I curse the day I was landed with this appointment."[2]

Somerville's letter of July 6 reveals in graphic language the feeling of the officers and men around him at Gibraltar. "I hear from the Press that the French Government has severed diplomatic relations so what the hell have we gained by this monstrous business? I still simply can't understand how their minds are working at home. None of us can. It doesn't seem to worry the sailors at all as 'they never 'ad no use for them French bastards'. But to all of us Senior Officers it's simply incredible and revolting."[3]

At the same time, Somerville realized that he had failed to destroy the French squadron, as he confessed to his wife: "I feel sure I shall be blamed for bungling the job and I think I did. But to you I don't mind confessing I was halfhearted and you can't win an action that way." On July 4 he wrote, "In fact I shouldn't be surprised if I was relieved forthwith. I don't mind because it was an absolutely bloody business to shoot up these Frenchmen who showed the greatest gallantry. The truth is my heart wasn't in it."[4]

The Cover-Up

Somerville's comments make it clear that the operation was a failure that came nowhere close to destroying the French fleet. But Churchill did not hesitate to misrepresent the facts to the Parliament and the world. Although he did not know all of the details of Catapult by the next day, he understood that the operation had gone poorly, that a French battlecruiser and many other warships had escaped to Toulon, and that the operation had failed to destroy the French fleet. Nevertheless, he prepared a cynical cover-up intended to conceal the failure and turn it into a strategic victory.

Late in the day of July 4, the day after the attack, Sir Alexander Cadogan noted in his diary, "Result of naval operations yesterday not too good, but Winston was able to make a good enough showing in the House and had a good reception."[5] Cadogan's diary entry hints eloquently that the Prime Minister deliberately misrepresented the affair to the House of Commons, whose members celebrated the address with prolonged applause. The address to the Commons was but the first step in a larger cover-up that found its final expression in Churchill's postwar memoirs.

In the July 4 session of the Commons, Churchill advanced a skewed version of events in a way that gave birth to enduring myths about Mers el-Kébir. He cut through the complexities of the Franco-German armistice negotiations to leave the false impression that the armistice had already guaranteed the quick delivery of the French fleet to Germany and that the British attack had prevented it. He smoothed over the failures of the Mers el-Kébir operation to conceal the continuing threat of the strong French squadron that had rallied to Toulon, where the undamaged *Strasbourg* plus numerous cruisers and other warships were now closer to the Axis orbit than they had been prior to the attack. And in a presumptuous and outrageous claim about French motives, Churchill suggested that the French battlecruiser had rallied to Toulon for the specific purpose of putting itself under German control. He admitted that several cruisers at Algiers had also rallied to Toulon, but he pretended that the battlecruiser had been so badly damaged by British torpedoes as to be out of action for many months.[6]

Reporting in the same speech the seizure of approximately two hundred French ships in British ports, Churchill twisted the facts of a minor success in a way to obscure the larger failure of the Mers el-Kébir operation. He ignored the fact that the two ancient French battleships seized in British home ports were nearly useless, as were the bulk of the lighter ships, to leave the impression, as he intended, that "the greater part of the French fleet" had been brought under British control. In consequence, the press and the public wrongly assumed that the British had seized or destroyed the French navy, a view reflected in the dreadfully misleading headlines of July 5 in the *New York Times*: "BRITISH SEIZE OR SINK BULK OF FRENCH FLEET; THOSE RESISTING DEFEATED IN FURIOUS BATTLE." Here marks the origin of the myth that the attack at Mers el-Kébir had destroyed the French fleet.

Ten days later, in a July 14 radio address heard around the world, Churchill again skewed the facts, reporting that the Royal Navy had succeeded in its "sad duty of putting out of action for the duration of the war the capital ships of the French navy."[7] He admitted that French warships remained at Toulon and other French ports. Concerned now to appease Darlan, he promised that the Royal Navy would not attack these ships as long as they made no effort to bolt to Axis-controlled ports. But he concealed the fact that the *Strasbourg* had rallied undamaged to Toulon, which he would surely have learned by this time from intelligence reports.

In his postwar memoirs, Churchill perpetuated and amplified the myth that the attack had destroyed or neutralized the entire French navy, writing in 1949 that "the measures we had taken had removed the French Navy from major German calculations." Ignoring the unmistakable failure of the operation, he described it instead as "the elimination of the French Navy as an important factor almost in a single stroke by violent action."[8] And on the same page, Churchill advanced the outrageous claim that ordinary Frenchmen had applauded the British aggression, that French peasant families had buried their victim sons under the British flag. The attack in fact had precisely the opposite impact, inciting bitter Anglophobia among Frenchmen everywhere.

Moreover, despite Churchill's claim to the contrary, the attack left the greater part of the useful units of the French navy entirely undamaged. The most dangerous part of it—more than seventy submarines—had been untouched by the attack, and most of them lay beyond the British reach in scattered French and African ports, where Darlan might easily have unleashed them against British shipping. Instead of eliminating the French navy, as Churchill pretended in the cover-up, Mers el-Kébir created for the Royal Navy a strategic nightmare, an environment far more threatening than it had been prior to the attack.

Motives, Myths, and Burdens

The attack at Mers el-Kébir, a tactical blunder that burdened the Allied war effort with enduring political and strategic problems, raises the question of motives. Was Churchill motivated by the lofty motive to send a message to Washington, as British historians have suggested, or was he obsessed instead by the mundane concern to sink French battleships?

In his July 4 message to the Commons and later in his memoirs, Churchill justified the attack in terms of the political urgency of demonstrating British determination to continue in the war against the Axis. The attack did indeed make that point. But was that the reason for planning and launching the attack? In later years historians have suggested that Churchill intended specifically to impress President Franklin Roosevelt with the urgency of delivering to the British fifty overage American destroyers. Negotiations to that end were already in progress, but the president would require solid evidence of British determination to continue in the war against the Axis. So Churchill attacked the French fleet to make that point.[9] British historians have been quick to subscribe to this view, for it obscured the mundane motive of sinking French battleships and raised the discussion to a high diplomatic level consistent with Churchill's lofty reputation as a statesman.

That view, however, is no more than a myth, for the minutes of the War Cabinet prior to the July 27 decision suggest that Churchill was overwhelmingly motivated by nothing more than the thought of capturing or destroying the four modern French battleships. Obsessed with big gunships, Churchill insisted with the War Cabinet on June 22 that the question of the French capital ships was a matter vital to the safety of the British Empire, that the delivery of the *Jean Bart* and *Richelieu* to the enemy "might alter the whole course of the war."[10] Two days later the War Cabinet concluded "that we should do all in our power to get hold of the four big ships, *Richelieu, Jean Bart, Dunkerque,* and *Strasbourg.* If we could not get them into our possession, we should make sure that they were scuttled."[11] And after the attack had taken place, the War Cabinet made no mention of political motives but affirmed in its conclusions of July 6 "that our present policy had been designed to deal primarily with the four modern capital ships."[12]

In the War Cabinet debates prior to June 27, there had been no discussion of any motive to impress the Americans. In the session of Saturday, June 29, while Churchill was away at his country estate, the War Cabinet received a Foreign Office report that the American public would probably applaud any action against the French fleet.[13] Churchill surely read the minutes of that session upon his return to London on Sunday, but the minutes of the Sunday evening session that Churchill attended bear no evidence that he picked up on the political value of striking at the French fleet.[14] The minutes are nevertheless irrelevant to the question of motives, for the decision to launch the attack at Mers el-Kébir had been made three days earlier, on Thursday the twenty-seventh.

Finally, on July 3, while the attack at Mers el-Kébir was in progress, the War Cabinet received a telegram from the British ambassador in Washington indicating that President Roosevelt had assured him privately of American public approval of any British efforts to seize by force French ships stranded in British harbors.[15] The telegram said nothing about the use of force against French ships at Mers el-Kébir or in other French harbors. But Churchill could now conclude that the attack might after all have some political value, which explains his inserting the political motive into his speech the next day. But as in the case of Saturday's message, the decision to attack Mers el-Kébir had been made during the previous week, which suggests that the political motive was nothing but an afterthought.

A related myth, advanced in British and American television documentaries seventy years later, suggests that Roosevelt had lent prior approval of the attack at Mers el-Kébir, implying that the American government therefore shared responsibility for the aggression. The president was no doubt correct in his view that American public opinion would approve the British seizure of French ships at Portsmouth and Plymouth. It was therefore easy for the media to stretch the president's blessings to include also the attack at Mers el-Kébir. Although Roosevelt obviously opposed the delivery of any French warships to the Axis, he appears to have smiled upon nothing more than the seizure of French ships already in British harbors.[16]

If the July 3 attack at Mers el-Kébir had demonstrated British determination to persist in the war, as Churchill reported on the Commons next day, the question remains as to why it was then necessary to launch yet another attack on the *Dunkerque* on July 5 and another on the *Richelieu* at Dakar on July 8. And why did Churchill pressure Pound on July 7 to divert Force H to Casablanca "to dispose of the *Jean Bart*" after the Dakar operation had been completed?[17] The answer is perfectly clear. Churchill's intent was to sink French battleships because he thought they threatened British domination of the seas. That was exactly the point he made in his July 14 radio address.

If Churchill's goal was the staging of a display of British determination to fight on, it made more sense at the time to attack the Italian fleet or to launch an aerial attack on the German homeland, for either would have underscored at no political expense the British resolve to continue in the war. And either would have had the surplus value of demonstrating the British ability to wage war. In sum, the idea of staging Operation Catapult to demonstrate the British determination to fight on against the European Axis was but an afterthought, a justification for the aggression, and a part of the cover-up of a failed operation.

Frenchmen might have grudgingly accepted the detention of Force X at Alexandria or the seizure of French ships in British ports, for British interests clearly demanded these actions. But in choosing to use force against French warships at Mers el-Kébir and Dakar, Churchill gambled that British interests were better served by a macho naval adventure whose success or failure was sure to impose a heavy moral and strategic burden on the future war effort. The attack shattered British communications with the entire French naval command and with French administrative officials throughout the empire. It wrote off in one failed stroke the most useful parts of the French Empire, forfeiting any chance that French warships might rally on their own to the British side, that French West Africa might soon welcome a Gaullist occupation party, or that French separatists might conspire to lure North and West Africa out of the Vichy orbit. The attack instead embittered the entire French naval and colonial establishment, leaving Churchill with no better French connection than the troublesome Charles de Gaulle.

A More Threatening Strategic Picture

In the wake of the Mers el-Kébir attack, the Vichy government promptly severed diplomatic relations with the United Kingdom and entered into a period of uneasy neutrality between the warring powers. Although German armies occupied more than half of France, Vichy remained in control of French North Africa and French West Africa with its big port at Dakar. Vichy also remained in control of its fleet, whose surface units were capable of defending France's nearby colonies and whose submarines posed a potential threat to British shipping during the undeclared Franco-British war that followed in the summer of 1940, when the Admiralty was already burdened with a two-ocean naval war against Germany and Italy.

The fall of France imposed on the Royal Navy a new set of operational and strategic problems. It ended French naval support, thereby stretching even thinner the assets of the Royal Navy. German U-boats soon entrenched themselves in occupied French ports on the Bay of Biscay, to the advantage of the German blockade of the British Isles. And in the South Atlantic, British warships could no longer operate with French ships out of Dakar, nor could they use Dakar at all, so convoy escort operations against German surface raiders posed a greater challenge. In the Mediterranean, the Royal Navy no longer had access to French ports, nor did they enjoy any longer French naval support in the continuing war against Italy. And with the Regia Marina entrenched in the central Mediterranean, British communications between Gibraltar and Singapore were severed in a way to render the Alexandria squadron irrelevant in terms of restraining Japan.

The Anglo-Italian naval war therefore continued, marked importantly by the November 1940 naval aviation attack staged out of Alexandria to cripple heavy units of the Italian fleet anchored at Taranto. That operation stands as the fulfillment of Admiral Sir Dudley Pound's prewar plans to launch a timely surprise attack against the Regia Marina in its harbor. But the Taranto victory hardly touched the large Italian cruiser, submarine, and light surface fleets, nor did it sever Italian communications with Libya. The Taranto attack was an air raid that put three of six Italian battleships out of action. The raid, however, was but a pale substitute for the sustained assault that London had refused to unleash early in the war when combined Anglo-French naval power had been capable of smashing the Regia Marina.

The attack at Mers el-Kébir signaled to the French naval command that the main threat to French Africa had now become the former ally rather than the former enemy. With the naval clauses of the armistice now suspended, the *Strasbourg* squadron at Toulon could defend French North Africa against any further British aggression. The French Mediterranean fleet obviously could not defend Vichy's colonies in the Caribbean or Asia. The question instead was whether it could defend Dakar and the *Richelieu* against the former ally, now tempted to snipe at French colonies isolated at the far margin of Vichy's naval capabilities.

An Undeclared Anglo-French War

British interests turned swiftly toward West Africa, where the *Richelieu* and the colony itself seemed ripe for the picking. In August Churchill and the War Cabinet approved an operation whereby British warships would escort a Free French occupation force to West Africa, where a demoralized Vichy command at Dakar would presumably rally to de Gaulle without a fight. But should the Vichy forces offer resistance, the British escort would employ its heavy guns to support the landings of the Gaullist occupation force.[18]

The launching of Operation Menace, as it was called, was delayed several times, with the attack date finally scheduled for September 23. Menace would be staged from the British port of Freetown in Sierra Leone, about four hundred miles beyond Dakar. Two convoys departed the United Kingdom in late August while the main body of the British naval force steamed from Gibraltar in early September to join the convoys and form in the Atlantic a large task force destined for Freetown. The Anglo-Gaullist force would therefore steam past Dakar, refuel at Freetown, and afterward turn back to seize the Vichy port and hopefully the *Richelieu*.

In the meantime, Admiral Darlan had ordered three heavy cruisers of the *Georges Leygues* class and three *La Fantasque*–type super destroyers to Dakar with the intent of attacking French Equatorial Africa, where Libreville had rallied to de Gaulle. The French squadron slipped past Gibraltar on September 11, just ahead of a British squadron bolting the harbor to prevent the French ships from turning north toward German-occupied ports on the Bay of Biscay. But the French squadron turned instead toward Casablanca and then Dakar while the British force ahead of them steamed on past Dakar to Freetown.

The French operation to recapture Libreville began on September 15 when the 1920s vintage cruiser *Primaguet* departed Dakar escorting a tanker intended to nourish the three modern cruisers and their destroyer escorts scheduled to depart Dakar on September 18. The mission was aborted, however, when the *Primaguet* stumbled upon the British force returning from Freetown to attack Dakar. Two of the French cruisers, the *Georges Leygues* and *Montcalm*, returned to Dakar just ahead of the Anglo-Gaullist task force while the *Primaguet* and the remainder of the force slipped away to Casablanca.

When the British squadron appeared off Dakar on September 23, the Vichy French forces ashore were full of fight because the attack at Mers el-Kébir in July had turned sentiment in West Africa stoutly against the British. Governor-General Pierre Boisson, intently loyal to Vichy, promptly jailed two officers sent ashore that morning to negotiate the transfer of West Africa to de Gaulle. When the British warships opened fire early in the afternoon, the immobilized *Richelieu* with its 15-inch guns led the spirited French defense, supported by the *Georges Leygues* and *Montcalm* and by well-placed shore batteries that soon found easy targets. At the same time Gaullist forces landing at nearby Rufisque met with stubborn resistance.

The Battle of Dakar continued over two days, with the Vichy French suffering the loss of two submarines, a destroyer, and further damage to the *Richelieu*. But the Vichy forces scored a clear victory. Volleys from the shore batteries and from warships in the harbor found their mark repeatedly, damaging a destroyer and the battleships *Resolution* and *Barham*, and the heavy cruiser *Cumberland*. The battleship *Resolution*, flagship of the squadron, suffered heavy damage that rendered its main guns inoperable when a torpedo from the submarine *Beveziers* struck below the water line. The successful submarine attack was especially significant, a reminder that the attack at Mers el-Kébir had left untouched the most dangerous offensive arm of the French navy.

On September 25, when it became clear that Operation Menace had no chance of success, Admiral John Cunningham terminated the operation. Meanwhile, Darlan gained cabinet approval to launch aerial attacks on Gibraltar. These attacks, staged from Algeria and continuing until the British disengaged at Dakar, were less effective than symbolic of French capabilities. But significantly, the Vichy French had blunted the attack at Dakar and had launched air raids against Gibraltar to demonstrate their ability to fight back.

The Battle of Dakar is sometimes remembered as the French revenge for Mers el-Kébir. But, more importantly, it defined the main perimeters of Anglo-French naval relations until the French empire reentered the war in late 1942. London could now see that the French fleet and French Africa, far from being demoralized, were instead determined to defend themselves against Anglo-Gaullist aggression, that French airpower based in Africa was capable of harassing Gibraltar, and—significantly—that the French submarine fleet remained a potential threat to the Royal Navy and to British shipping. At the same time Darlan could see that the French navy was incapable of defending any part of the French empire beyond Dakar and that the power of its surface fleet beyond the western basin of the Mediterranean was marginal.

During the weeks following the clash of arms at Dakar, Anglo-French naval relations entered not surprisingly into a period of greater stability, reflecting the wartime realities of the moment. In October, when German U-boats took a heavy toll on British commerce, London had no interest in continuing with the undeclared naval war against Vichy or of committing important naval assets to enforce the blockade of the French Mediterranean coast. Churchill therefore took the initiative to find an informal diplomatic solution. These negotiations, pursued quietly through official and unofficial channels, finally resulted in a French commitment to restrain its naval power in exchange for a British concession to relax the blockade. Toward the end of 1940 French maritime traffic through Gibraltar increased steadily and soon became routine. At the same time, while the German U-boat war continued in the Atlantic, the French submarine fleet remained on the sidelines.

The Decline of the Marine Nationale

As the Royal Navy continued to wage war against the Kriegsmarine and the Regia Marina, and later the Imperial Japanese Navy, the units of the French fleet under Darlan's command remained interned in their Mediterranean and African ports under restrictions of the armistice, whose naval clauses had been reimposed. In early 1942, less than a year after the *Hood* had become a victim of the *Bismarck*, the patched-up *Dunkerque* slipped across the Mediterranean to join *Strasbourg* at Toulon. With the two ships now closer to the Axis orbit, the chances of their coming over to the Allies were much diminished. They were scuttled at Toulon in December 1942, along with more than ninety other French warships, when German armies entered Vichy's free zone in the wake of the Allied occupation of French North Africa.

In contrast, the greater part of the French navy remaining in Africa eventually joined the Allied war effort. The Alexandria squadron came over in 1943, as Cunningham had predicted in 1940. And both the *Jean Bart* and *Richelieu* fell into Allied hands in late 1942. The unfinished *Jean Bart*, caught up in the initial Allied assault at Casablanca in November, fell immediately to the Americans. But the ship was not completed in time for wartime service. The *Richelieu* remained at Dakar, beyond the reach of the Allied occupation and the successor French government at Algiers under Admiral Darlan. Nevertheless, it joined the war effort voluntarily in December when Darlan lured Governor-General Boisson and French West Africa into the Allied camp. The *Richelieu* was soon patched up and later completed in the United States in time to join the French Asian Fleet operating off Indochina with units of the British Pacific Fleet during the summer of 1945.

Ironically, the end of the war found French and British warships operating together against an Axis enemy, as the *Hood* and the *Dunkerque* had done at the beginning of the war in 1939. Their mission in 1945 was to stage a display of Anglo-French naval power to the end of justifying the postwar restoration of the British and French Asian empires. But in contrast to earlier cooperation, they did not operate alone against the Axis enemy. They operated instead in the shadow of the American Pacific Fleet, whose overwhelming power in naval aviation had already spearheaded the victory over Japan and had long since demoted the *Richelieu* and all battleships to lesser roles than that of the aircraft carrier.

Conclusions

Our review of relations between the two navies will benefit from a reminder that the British and French Empires after 1919 were the only ones among the five naval powers that stretched literally around the globe, that their defense depended importantly upon sea power, and that the imperial defense capabilities of the Royal Navy far outmatched those of the Marine Nationale. At the end of the Great War in 1918 the Royal Navy was the world's largest, but the Marine Nationale was too small and obsolescent to defend the French empire against any of the naval powers except Italy.

What Were the Main Trends?

There were two main trends framing Anglo-French naval relations between the wars, one local and the other global. The local trend was the steady renewal of French naval power and, in contrast, the British failure to rebuild the Royal Navy in a pattern to fulfill its combined European and Asian defense commitments. The rebuilding of the French navy proceeded steadily without serious interruption between the wars. On the other hand, the Royal Navy entered into a period of decline in the late 1920s, so the Admiralty chose to neutralize the weakest of its three potential enemies by diplomacy rather than by the threat of naval power.

The global trend was a shifting balance in world naval power that matured into the Axis alliance, thereby forging a new naval order supplanting the prior order shaped by the several naval arms control agreements. This new order found the Royal Navy isolated and overextended, unable to ensure the defense of British possessions in Asia. But the formation of the Axis alliance in 1936 and 1937 coincided with the high renaissance of French naval renewal, so an alliance to combine British and French naval power emerged as an imperative to address the global imbalance.

The Two Staffs Did Not Think in Identical Patterns

During the two decades between the wars, the British and French naval staffs had more in common than their troubled courtship might otherwise suggest. What they had in common was the responsibility to defend distant colonial possessions at the far limits of their naval capabilities. Yet as the wartime alliance broke down after 1918, the two staffs addressed their problems in different ways, reflecting their different geographical bases and their vastly dissimilar capabilities. The Admiralty thought in global terms befitting that of the world's strongest naval power; in contrast, the Rue Royale thought in regional terms matching the capabilities of a second tier naval power too weak to fulfill its distant defense commitments.

When the Rue Royale soon identified Italy as the most likely future enemy, French naval architects designed ships intended primarily for service in the Mediterranean. These were light ships often of innovative design—submarines, destroyers, and cruisers—rather than battleships. So the National Assembly voted generous credits to construct light ships, and French diplomats at the Washington Naval Conference protected France's right to rebuild its fleet to surpass Italy in all categories except capital ships.

During these two decades the Rue Royale easily identified its future enemies, Italy in the 1920s and Germany in the 1930s. French naval officers perceived the potential threat of Japan, but knowing the limitations of French naval power, they wrote off Asia as indefensible. With a narrow strategic focus, the Rue Royale began in the 1920s to rebuild the French fleet in a pattern to address the kind of war it expected to fight in the Mediterranean, for French Africa could be defended against Italy while Indochina lay beyond French defense capabilities. Although the French focus broadened in the 1930s to include the Atlantic, it remained nevertheless more regional than global.

In the case of the Admiralty, with its larger naval capabilities and its broader strategic focus, the problem of rebuilding the fleet to outmatch that of future enemies was more complex. The burdensome Ten-Year Rule imposed upon the navy by civilians implied that there were no enemies—a view close to target as long as Japan remained an ally. But when British statesmen at the Washington Naval Conference discarded the Japanese alliance, they also agreed to a definition of cruisers that served American and Japanese needs better than it did British. And the conference placed no quantitative limits on the construction of cruisers. So at the moment when the abrogation of the alliance turned Japan into a potential enemy, the Admiralty found itself committed to an expensive construction program that matched poorly its Asian defense responsibilities.

Prior to the Washington conference, the Admiralty had not ruled out the possibility of war with the United States. But Tokyo moved more aggressively than did Washington to rebuild its navy, and the Admiralty, in contrast to the Rue Royale, had never written off its Asian empire as indefensible. Japan therefore emerged in the 1920s as a potential threat to British imperial interests, and the Admiralty nudged closer to the Rue Royale, not because the French navy would be of much help in an Asian war but because the Admiralty needed a political ally in arms control negotiations with Washington. The 1928 Anglo-French Naval Staff Accord suggests that the two naval commands were more in step with each other than were their civilian governments. But these warm relations soon turned ambivalent.

Why an Ambivalent Anglo-French Naval Relationship?

The Anglo-French relationship became ambivalent because British political and naval authorities opted to appease Rome rather than to close ranks with Paris, whose continental commitments risked dragging Britain into a European war and whose rivalry with Italy risked provoking a war in waters between Gibraltar and Singapore. On the other hand, the emerging Japanese threat in Asia underscored the Admiralty's urgent need for a strong naval ally. So tensions between the demands of imperial defense and the obsession to avoid a continental or Mediterranean conflict shaped an ambivalent Anglo-French naval relationship.

The pattern of ambivalence emerged clearly in the 1937 Nyon crisis, when the Anglo-French Naval Staff Accord promoted increasingly cordial relations between British and French naval officers at local planning and operational levels. At the same time the Admiralty distanced itself from the Rue Royale for fear of being dragged into a Mediterranean war. Thus, the Admiralty joined Prime Minister Neville Chamberlain to appease Rome at the very moment when combined Anglo-French naval power had seized control of the Mediterranean at Italy's expense. The Admiralty therefore maintained a French connection in the Mediterranean at the level of operations and an Italian connection at the higher level of national policy. This ambivalence in Anglo-French naval relations reflected London's global perspective and the attendant strategy of relating to Rome from a posture of weakness rather than of strength.

Did Naval Power Serve British Foreign Policy?

The ambivalence inherent in Anglo-French naval relations coincided with a mounting idealism in British foreign policy after the departure of Eden in early 1938, so connections between diplomacy and power grew increasingly obscure. The question is whether naval power had much relevance to British diplomacy as tensions mounted after 1937.

The answer is that Chamberlain discounted the coercive value of massive Anglo-French naval power in the Mediterranean and simultaneously exaggerated British diplomatic influence in eastern Europe, which was beyond the limits of British military power. In 1938 Chamberlain appeased both Hitler and Mussolini, but appeasement matched British interests in eastern Europe better than it did in the Mediterranean, where combined Anglo-French naval power kept the door ajar for a spread of options to restrain Mussolini. Whereas the two Axis dictators thought uniquely in terms of power relationships, Chamberlain backed away from the option of exploiting appeasement as a ruthless substitute for Entente weakness in eastern Europe. Insensitive to power relationships, he abandoned appeasement on the continent and committed Britain to defend Poland prior to the time when the British and French defense staffs were able to define the limits of Entente military and naval capabilities.

The Guarantee to Poland Cramped Defense Planning

The peaceful settlement of the Czechoslovakian crisis at Munich liberated Paris and London to pursue in concert a ruthless policy of appeasement toward Germany. In the aftermath of Munich, the options in Paris were whether to pursue a long-term détente with Germany or merely to withdraw quietly from eastern Europe and allow events there to run their course. Either option amounted to appeasement. But Daladier rejected both options, caving in to Gamelin, who insisted on forming an "eastern bloc" against Germany and maintaining a neutral posture toward Italy. So Daladier, Gamelin, and Chamberlain moved in the direction of confronting Hitler and of appeasing Mussolini.

Out of step with that strategy was Admiral Jean François Darlan, whose attraction to appeasing Berlin matched his concern to shift French defense priorities toward the Mediterranean. He understood the fundamental point that withdrawing quietly from eastern Europe without making any commitments to Berlin promised to defer the dreaded Franco-German war into the future. This option was consistent with Entente military weakness in eastern Europe and Anglo-French naval strength in the Mediterranean. It meant appeasement in France's relations with Germany and power in her relations with Italy. It amounted to applying the policy of appeasement selectively and ruthlessly in the interest of turning the Reich toward the Soviets and buying time to pre-pare for any future war with Germany. This pragmatic version of appeasement remained an option when Hitler occupied the rump Czech state on March 15, for neither London nor Paris had announced any guarantee to Poland.

But Chamberlain abruptly abandoned the policy of appeasing Berlin at the critical moment, when a quiet withdrawal from the Polish imbroglio promised to defer the German war into the future. He opted instead for untimely com-mitments to Poland, which amounted to confronting Hitler with an ultima-tum in a region beyond the limits of Entente military or naval power. After he had relieved France in 1938 of the burdensome Czech alliance, Chamberlain failed in 1939 to exploit the advantage implicit at Munich of persisting with the policy of appeasing Germany. The guarantee to Poland liberated Moscow to partition rather than to defend Poland. It also set the stage for Berlin to defer the Soviet war into the future and simultaneously deny the Entente the advan-tage of imposing a two-front war on the Reich.

The announcement of the guarantee imposed heavy burdens on the Anglo-French military and naval staff consultations, which had opened just the day prior on March 30. The guarantee shifted control of the calendar to Berlin and cramped any dialogue between Entente soldiers and statesmen, as the diplo-mats had forfeited the option of remaining neutral in the event of a crisis in eastern Europe. Anglo-French staff consultations were therefore condemned to a narrow agenda that assumed a continental war whose outbreak and perim-eters would be defined in Berlin. Would it have been prudent to withhold the guarantee in the interest of buying time to bring defense and diplomatic plan-ning into harmony with each other?

It would seem so. Anglo-French defense planning, which proceeded on its own track, quickly confirmed that British military weakness condemned the Entente to a defensive posture on the continent. But with France con-sidering in December whether to withdraw from all commitments in eastern Europe, the stage had been set for London and Paris together to revisit that option in March to the end of planning for a more timely entry into the war. In the absence of a Soviet ally in eastern Europe, any military offensive on the French front hinged upon mobilizing over many months the full manpower and material resources of the two modern industrialized states and their colo-nial empires, which meant exploiting the Entente advantage in naval power to strengthen the military front in France prior to the Entente-German war. The guarantee to Poland aborted that strategy, however, as it would allow Berlin to provoke war prior to the reinforcement of the military front in France.

Appeasing Mussolini

The formation of the Entente in the spring of 1939 shifted the naval balance in the Mediterranean overwhelmingly against Italy. Yet at the moment when Chamberlain abandoned appeasement in eastern Europe, well beyond the limits of Entente military capabilities, he persisted with appeasement in the Mediterranean, where combined Anglo-French naval might had become more than sufficient to smash the Regia Marina. When Mussolini invaded Albania on April 7, a week after the guarantee to Poland, Chamberlain had already backed away from a guarantee to Albania, announcing on April 2 that "Great Britain has no specific interest in Albania."[1]

At the moment of the guarantee to Poland, Chamberlain effectively conceded Albania to Mussolini, and he continued to appease Rome after the German war broke out in September. He clung to appeasement in the one area where he enjoyed an overwhelming advantage in naval power, and he abandoned appeasement to challenge the Reich in a remote area of Europe where British military power was irrelevant. Why, then, did London continue to appease Italy after it had concluded a French alliance shifting the Mediterranean naval balance decisively to the Entente advantage?

The Admiralty Wished to Avoid a Mediterranean War

Chamberlain's policy of appeasing Mussolini meshed with the Admiralty's assumption that an Italian war, however winnable, was not worth the risk of disturbing naval communications between Gibraltar and Singapore. The British strategic focus, always broader than that of Paris, extended beyond the continent to include the Japanese threat in Asia. But the Royal Navy was stretched so thin in 1939 that it could not expect to fight Germany and simultaneously address the Japanese threat without the support of a strong naval ally. So while the French army focused its attention on the continent and the French navy on the Mediterranean, the Admiralty worried about the defense of Singapore and the British Empire in Asia.

In the view of the Admiralty, the main purpose of the alliance was to distribute Entente naval power to the end of neutralizing two of the three Axis powers. By forging a naval alliance with France, London brought into the British orbit 159 French warships built since 1920. These included the *Dunkerque* and *Strasbourg*, already in commission, and the *Richelieu* and *Jean Bart*, scheduled for completion in 1940 and 1941, to coincide with the completion of the first of five *King George V*–class battleships and the first of four aircraft carriers of the *Illustrious* and *Indomitable* classes. With the French fleet immediately available in 1939 to support the Royal Navy, British units would be liberated for assignment to Alexandria, to restrain Japanese ambitions in Asia. Although the combined fleets were still stretched thin in their Asian defense commitments, the alliance enabled the Admiralty to arrange an efficient distribution of assets so that units of the two fleets might be combined in the Atlantic to wage war against the Reich and distributed in the Mediterranean to wage peace against Italy and Japan. That strategy made good sense, as long as the military command managed to avoid losing the German war on the continent.

The Operational Value of the Alliance

As it turned out, the French navy proved to be a loyal and productive wartime ally, which British records confirm. In a 1941 report prepared at the Admiralty, British officers reviewed the whole question of Anglo-French planning and operational relations, citing both strengths and weaknesses. They heaped praise on naval relations at Maintenon, where Captain Cedric Holland presided over the British mission. They reported fewer problems with wartime operations than with wartime planning, burdened in many ways by organizational differences between the two naval commands. These problems, predictable results of different naval cultures, were sometimes irksome but never serious enough to threaten the stability of the alliance. The report cited differences in strategic objectives that led the French command sometimes to advance unrealistic proposals. But "if due allowance is made to differences of outlook and temperament," the report continued, "the cooperation given by the French at sea was excellent."[2]

It was indeed at sea that the two navies cooperated most productively. The report underscores Darlan's cordial relations with Admiral Sir Dudley Pound, citing specifically Darlan's prompt attention to Pound's request for a French squadron to operate out of Alexandria in cooperation with Admiral Sir Andrew Cunningham. It is on the whole complimentary of French assistance with convoy escorts, describing the excellent manner in which the *Dunkerque* cooperated with the *Hood* to escort French Canadian military units across the Atlantic, "a gesture of cooperation which had a heartening effect on the troops on board."[3]

The report reserved its most glowing praise to the sharing of naval bases, clearly a key French contribution to the alliance. It praised French naval cooperation in the South Atlantic, where the two fleets shared the big naval base at Dakar, where French ships "contributed materially" to operations against German surface raiders, and where the *Hermes* and the *Strasbourg* worked together under the orders of a French admiral. The French effort there "was sustained and valuable," and, as the report insisted, "They cooperated with us to the utmost of their ability and employed forces ranging from a battlecruiser and 8-inch cruisers, to sloops and submarines."[4]

British and American historians are tempted to dismiss the violent breakdown of the Entente at Mers el-Kébir as the aggravation of growing misunderstandings as the war wound down or as an accumulation of tensions dating back to the beginning of the war. To be sure, there were tensions and misunderstandings, many of which are catalogued in this study. But the report lends no support to any connection between Mers el-Kébir and tensions in the alliance. It reflects instead a reasonably high level of trust, particularly in the Atlantic, where close tactical cooperation between the two navies enabled the Entente to wage war successfully against the Kriegsmarine. It seems clear that Mers el-Kébir was a product of the armistice settlement ending the military campaigns in France, rather than one of accumulated wartime tensions between the two navies.

Did the Alliance Fulfill Its Strategic Expectations?

Given that the Entente was successful enough in addressing operational problems in the naval war against Germany, the question remains as to whether it accomplished its broader strategic objectives. How successful were the Admiralty and the Rue Royale in combining and distributing their assets to the end of addressing the challenge of three widely separated Axis powers, one of which was weak and within easy striking range?

In the view of the Admiralty, the alliance rested from the beginning on the assumption that combined Anglo-French naval power could be distributed in a pattern to isolate the three Axis navies in the interest of neutralizing two of them. It exploited the center of Axis naval weakness to the end of addressing the peripheries, where Axis naval power was stronger and harder to reach. The strategy therefore focused on the Mediterranean, where combined Anglo-French naval power outmatched that of Italy, whose navy was already isolated by geography from her two Axis allies.

But in London's view, the alliance was not intended to wage war against Italy. It was intended instead to keep Italy neutral. With overwhelming Entente naval power poised to strike against Italy and her African empire, London could see that Rome would be tempted to remain neutral at the outbreak of an Entente-German war. From London's perspective, Italian neutrality was the key to the success of the alliance, for waging peace in the Mediterranean kept open communications between Gibraltar and Singapore.

With Entente assets spread thin in terms of the global naval balance, the weakest link in the alliance was the force at Alexandria, with its dual role of restraining both Italy and Japan. But its role in restraining Japan hinged importantly upon keeping Mussolini neutral, for any war against Italy would isolate the Alexandria squadron until the Regia Marina could be defeated. The Alexandria squadron, even with its French reinforcements, remained too weak to wage war simultaneously against both Italy and Japan.

The alliance failed to head off what would later become a more hostile naval balance in the Mediterranean. Despite massive Anglo-French naval power poised to strike, London tolerated Italian neutrality in 1939 when crippling the Regia Marina and isolating Libya were within Entente capabilities. In tolerating Italian neutrality, London forfeited an opportunity to solve the Mediterranean problem early in the conflict.

Irrelevance of the Alexandria Squadron

The Italian entry into the war and the exit of the French ally in June 1940 isolated the Alexandria squadron, liberating Tokyo to unleash its naval and military power against Singapore and Hong Kong. Or so it seemed. The new strategic picture did indeed render the Alexandria squadron irrelevant, as Tokyo could easily see that the fall of France had isolated the Royal Navy to confront alone two European enemies. The Italian entry had also cut communications between Gibraltar and Alexandria so that the Alexandria squadron posed little threat to Japan. In the wake of the Mers el-Kébir attack, the Japanese naval attaché in France remarked optimistically to his American counterpart that the recent Anglo-French hostilities "gave Japan an absolutely free hand in the Far East."[5]

But he was mistaken. Instead of unleashing Japanese naval and military power in Asia, Tokyo moved cautiously in measured steps to pressure London into closing the Burma Road. Tokyo's restrained response to the collapse of the Entente seems surprising, as Great Britain was now isolated to wage war against two European enemies. So why did Tokyo not go ahead and seize Singapore, Hong Kong, and other British territories in Asia?

The answer is clear enough. What in fact had restrained Japan all along was not the Alexandria squadron; it was instead American naval power. Had it not been for the threat of the Pacific Fleet, based at Hawaii since the spring of 1940, Tokyo would have had no reason to withhold its naval power upon the collapse of the Entente. Significantly, Japan did not attack Singapore or any British possession in Asia until after it had crippled the American fleet at Pearl Harbor, more than a year later.

The View from the Rue Royale

In the view of the Rue Royale, the alliance failed to fulfill the urgent regional objective implicit in it, which was to exploit the overwhelming advantage that combined Anglo-French naval power enjoyed over the Regia Marina. The French naval staff, had it not been overruled by London, would have unleashed Entente naval power to wreck the Italian navy at the outset of the war, to isolate Libya, and to seize control of waters between Gibraltar and Suez—in sum, to solve the Mediterranean problem at the beginning of the war. The French wanted to combine and coordinate Entente naval power in the Mediterranean rather than distribute it. This is exactly what Darlan and Cunningham had proposed in 1939. French naval interests focused sharply on the Mediterranean, for the Rue Royale assigned less importance to defending Indochina than the Admiralty did to defending Singapore.

Although Darlan understood the importance of the Atlantic war, he viewed the alliance first of all as an instrument to wage war against Italy rather than to keep her neutral. He understood that destroying the weakest of the Axis powers at the outset was the key to quickly solving the strategic problem at the top of the British agenda, which was to protect communications with Singapore. The Italian naval command, well aware of its own weakness, expected the Entente to unleash its naval power in exactly the way Darlan had preferred. In the view of the Rue Royale, London's refusal to unleash combined Entente naval power forfeited an opportunity for the Entente to solve the Italian problem at the beginning of the war, when the two fleets together were capable of wrecking the Regia Marina, isolating Libya, and seizing control of the Mediterranean.

Mers el-Kébir or Taranto?

The seizure of French ships in British home ports during the predawn hours of July 3, 1940, is hardly controversial, but the decision to attack the French warships at Mers el-Kébir raises the question as to why Churchill risked provoking a third naval war when the Royal Navy was already burdened with two wars it could not win. French historians have asked why Churchill chose to attack the French fleet rather than the Italian, for crippling the Regia Marina in the summer of 1940 would have addressed directly the threatening naval imbalance and simultaneously underscore without any toxic reflux the British resolve to continue in the war.[6] That question deserves our consideration.

In 1940 the Royal Navy struck twice at widely separated targets in Mediterranean and Atlantic waters. The first of these was the largely unsuccessful attack on French targets at Mers el-Kébir and Dakar in early July, and the other was the clear victory over the Italian fleet anchored at Taranto on November 11–12, nearly six months later. The French targets at Mers el-Kébir and Dakar posed serious tactical problems, as the British naval staff report of June 24 had clearly warned. The targets were widely separated, and the ships at Mers el-Kébir were not positioned in a pattern friendly to aerial torpedo attack. These ships therefore had to be attacked initially by gunships with a poor view of the harbor. Naval aviation played mainly a supporting role until it was unleashed again on July 6, against the damaged *Dunkerque,* and on July 8, against the *Richelieu,* already isolated at Dakar. The failed operation at Mers el-Kébir alienated the entire French naval and colonial establishment at the expense of the future war effort. It also provoked undeclared naval hostilities with France, whose submarine fleet and the *Strasbourg* squadron at Toulon now emerged as a greater threat to British interests than had the French battleships prior to the attack.

In contrast, the November air raid at Taranto posed fewer tactical problems as numerous heavy ships of the Regia Marina were concentrated in one spacious harbor and positioned in a pattern suitable for aerial torpedo attack. The British attack on these ships was staged by naval aviation with gunships playing a supporting role, much the opposite of the attack at Oran and considerably more effective. In addition, the raid at Taranto carried with it no toxic political or strategic baggage, imposing no burden on the future conduct of the war.

The attack at Taranto, though more daring, was clearly within British naval capabilities, as evidenced by the obvious success of the operation. Admiral Pound had understood this capability even before the war when he took care to assign an aircraft carrier to Alexandria and to train air crews to attack specifically the ships anchored at Taranto. In 1940 aerial torpedo attacks on warships remained problematic and experimental, but Pound appears to have appreciated the technical advantage in naval aviation that the Royal Navy enjoyed over the Regia Marina. The outcome of the operation underscores that advantage. Whereas the conventional gunship attack at Mers el-Kébir failed to destroy either of the two modern French battleships in the harbor, the aviation attack at Taranto put three Italian battleships—including the modern *Littorio*—out of action.

Is it possible that Churchill selected the less attractive target because he had become obsessed to strike France? He clearly was more angered at the French exit from the war than the Italian entry into it, as he viewed the French withdrawal as a betrayal of the British ally. The Prime Minister's anger at the former ally shines through more than once in the minutes of the War Cabinet in late June and early July. He justified the attack on the grounds of heading off an unfavorable balance of naval power. That was indeed a legitimate concern given the completion of two new Italian battleships in 1940 and the German invasion threat from across the North Sea.

Churchill, however, ignored plans already in place to attack Taranto. As former First Lord, he surely would have known of these plans and of the prior training of British aircrews at Alexandria to carry out the operation. But the minutes of the War Cabinet in late June bear no evidence of any debate on whether to attack the Italian fleet rather than the French. It appears that Churchill was motivated to strike uniquely at the French fleet, that he gave no thought to attacking the Italian fleet, and that to attack the Regia Marina rather than the Marine Nationale was not an issue at that moment.

That a Taranto attack was not an issue fits neatly with Admiralty plans to appease Mussolini until a carefully planned attack on the Italian fleet could be staged later in the war. On the other hand, the rush to attack the French squadron at Mers el-Kébir denied London an occasion to consider whether the time had come to suspend the policy of appeasing Mussolini in favor of one appeasing French Africa and Darlan, who remained eager to preserve the cordial relations he enjoyed with the former ally.

In any event, Taranto was the easier target. Numerous units of the Regia Marina had taken refuge in the harbor upon the Italian entry into the war, and they were poorly protected against aerial attack. Although technical considerations may not have permitted an attack at Taranto as early as July 3, when Force H attacked Mers el-Kébir, Taranto was fast becoming a more attractive target. But Churchill, impatient to strike swiftly at four French battleships, forfeited the opportunity to consider whether to attack instead at Taranto, an easier and less toxic target.

Postscript

Although Mers el-Kébir is largely forgotten among Americans, it persists as a disturbing current in the French wartime memory. Early in the twenty-first century, as British and French defense staffs prepared again to combine their resources, the French assembled annually at various cities to honor the memory of the 1,297 French mariners who gave their lives at Mers el-Kébir. The ceremonies at Brest, held on Saturday, July 3, 2010, by the French Association of Mers el-Kébir Veterans, aimed importantly at reconciliation, as British officials participated in ceremonies marking the seventieth anniversary of the attack. The services began early that morning with a memorial mass at the Church of St. Louis and continued at nearby Kerfautras Cemetery, where lay the remains of an unknown victim of the attack at Mers el-Kébir.

Afterward official ceremonies were held at a nearby monument honoring French mariners who died in naval service.[7] Among the participants were the British ambassador, an admiral of the Royal Navy, and, significantly, a delegation representing the HMS *Hood* Association, all to honor the memory of French victims of the British attack. It would be a mistake to think that these occasions have erased entirely the current of bitterness still lingering among the French. Nevertheless, these ceremonies are entirely in step with the emerging new era in Anglo-French naval and military relations. As French and British staff officers assemble in the twenty-first century to consider anew the value of closer defense cooperation, the history of their prior relations remains relevant to the challenge before them. Cultural and geographical differences still linger. And although the political and strategic environments have changed dramatically since 1940, it seems reasonable to think that further study of the old alliance might be helpful as the two democratic states close ranks again in a new century.

NOTES

Abbreviations used in Notes

ADM   Admiralty records, British Public Records Office, London

AFSC   Anglo-French Staff Conversations, category of ADM

BB   Category of "B" [alphabetical] records, French Naval Archives, Vincennes

CAB   Cabinet records, British Public Records Office, London

DBFP   *Documents on British Foreign Policy, 1929–1939*, 2nd ser. 21 vols. London: Her Majesty's Stationery Office, 1946–85.

DGFP   U.S. Department of State, *Documents on German Foreign Policy, 1918–1945*, ser. D. 13 vols. Washington, D.C.: U.S. Government Printing Office, 1949–64.

EMG/SE   État Major Général/Section d'Études

FRUS   U.S. Department of State, *Papers Relating to the Foreign Relations of the United States, 1919: The Paris Peace Conference*. 13 vols. Washington, D.C.: U.S. Government Printing Office, 1919. Available at the University of Wisconsin Digital Collections, http://digital.library.wisc.edu/1711.dl/FRUS.

NARA   National Archives and Records Administration, Washington, D.C.

ONI   Office of Naval Intelligence

PRO   Public Records Office, London

RG   Record Group

SHM   Service Historique de la Marine, Vincennes, France

Chapter 1. Toward a Global Imbalance

1. Stephen Roskill, *Naval Policy between the Wars*, vol. 1 (New York: Walker and Company, 1968), 73–74. For a French perspective covering roughly the same time period, see Louis de la Monneraye [Espagnac Du Ravay, pseud.], *Vingt ans de politique navale, 1919–1939* (Grenoble: Arthaud, 1941). This book, published during the German occupation of France, was authored by the paymaster of the French navy and a friend of Admiral Jean François Darlan. In a 1982 interview, Monneraye indicated that Darlan had helped to write the book.

2. FRUS, vol. 3, art. 181, 184, 185, and com., pp. 337–47.

3. Ibid., art. 190, p. 348.

4. See Monneraye, *Vingt ans de politique navale, 1919–1939*, 62, 260.

5. Roskill, *Naval Policy between the Wars*, 1:71.

6. See ibid.

7. Monneraye, *Vingt ans de politique navale*, 51.

8. See Roskill, *Naval Policy between the Wars*, 1:310–11.

9. Monneraye, *Vingt ans de politique navale*, 53.

10. Ibid., 53–54.

11. Ibid., 54–55.

12. The figures are from Roskill, *Naval Policy between the Wars*, 1:71.

13. For an excellent study of the Treaty Cruisers, see John Jordan, *Warships after Washington: The Development of the Five Major Fleets, 1922–1930* (Annapolis, Md.: Naval Institute Press, 2012), chap. 6.

14. See Monneraye, *Vingt ans de politique navale*, 175.

15. Ibid., 57.

16. See Correlli Barnett, *The Collapse of British Power* (Gloucestershire: Sutton, 1997), 251–55.

17. Roskill, *Naval Policy between the Wars*, 1:71.

18. Ibid., 1:215.

19. See ibid., app. C, 1:580.

20. See M. J. Whitley, *Destroyers of World War II* (Annapolis, Md.: Naval Institute Press, 1988), 157–62.

21. Leygues had political and family connections with the future admiral Jean François Darlan, whose father, Jean-Baptiste Darlan, served in the Chamber of Deputies with Leygues.

22. See Whitley, *Destroyers of World War II*, 35–37; and Jordan, *Warships after Washington*, chap. 8.

23. Roskill, *Naval Policy between the Wars*, app. C, 1:580–82.

24. See Jordan, *Warships after Washington*, 109.

25. See David Miller, *Warships from 1860 to the Present Day* (St. Paul, Minn.: MBI Publishing, 2001), 10–12, 34–39, 58–59; and Jordan, *Warships after Washington*, chap. 7.

26. See Roskill, *Naval Policy between the Wars*, 1:234–68.

27. Bernard Ireland and Eric Grove, *Jane's War at Sea, 1987–1997* (New York: Collins Reference, 1997), 128–32.

28. See Roskill, *Naval Policy between the Wars*, app. C, 1:580–85.

29. Monneraye, *Vingt ans de politique navale*, 59–60.

30. Roskill, *Naval Policy between the Wars*, 1:498–99.

31. NARA, RG 38, ONI, C-9-b, Reg. 18625, "Address of the Honorable Hugh S. Gibson," August 1927.

32. Ibid.; and Roskill, *Naval Policy between the Wars*, 1:506.

33. NARA, RG 38, ONI C-9-b, Reg. 18625, "Address of the Honorable Hugh S. Gibson," August 1927.

34. See Richard W. Fanning, *Peace and Disarmament: Naval Rivalry and Arms Control, 1922–1933* (Lexington: University Press of Kentucky, 1995).

35. NARA, RG 38, ONI, 6-10-e, Reg. 20228-C, "United States Cruisers under Construction," December 16, 1929.

36. See NARA, RG 38, ONI, Reg. 15139, Naval Attaché Report, "Proposed Franco-British Naval Treaty," August 11, 1928; Monneraye, *Vingt ans de politique navale*, 64–65; Fanning, *Peace and Disarmament*, 87–89; and David Carlton, "The Anglo-French Compromise on Arms Limitations, 1928," *Journal of British Studies* 8, no. 2 (1969): 141–62, doi:10.1086/385574.

37. American naval attachés in European and other capital cities reported the response of the press. See NARA, RG 30, ONI, C-9-e.

38. See, for example, the October 26, 1928, edition of the Paris daily *Le Temps*. Editorials defending the agreement are contained in NARA, RG 38, ONI, C-9-e, Reg. 19447A, Naval Attaché Report, October 30, 1928.

39. NARA, RG 38, ONI, C-9-e, Reg. 19447-B, November 5, 1928.

40. NARA, RG 38, ONI, C-9-e, Reg. 19447-A, October 30, 1928.

41. NARA, RG 38, ONI, C-9-e, Reg. 19447-A, November 23, 1928.

42. Roskill, *Naval Policy between the Wars*, 1:549.

43. NARA, RG 38, ONI, 6-10-e, Reg. 20228-C, December 16, 1929.

44. Ibid.

45. Ibid.; Roskill, *Naval Policy between the Wars*, app. C, 1:580–82; and Stephen Howarth, *To Shining Sea: A History of the United States Navy, 1775–1991* (New York: Random House, 1991), 348.

46. Roskill, *Naval Policy between the Wars*, 1:564–65; and NARA, RG 38, ONI, 6-10-e, Reg. 20228C.

47. For technical details, see M. J. Whitley, *German Capital Ships of World War Two* (London: Arms and Armour Press, 1989), 20–23, 214.

48. Fanning, *Peace and Disarmament*, 127; and Ireland and Grove, *Jane's War at Sea*, 139.

49. James K. Sadkovich, *The Italian Navy in World War II* (Westport, Conn.: Greenwood, 1994), 6–7.

50. Correlli Barnett, *Engage the Enemy More Closely: The Royal Navy in the Second World War* (New York: Norton, 1991), 24, 28.

51. Roskill, *Naval Policy between the Wars*, app. C, 1:583–84.

52. For details, see ibid., 2:89–94.

53. Ireland and Grove, *Jane's War at Sea*, 140; and Barnett, *Engage the Enemy More Closely*, 30–31.

54. SHM, 1BB2, EMG/SE, Carton 208, Dossiers Amiral Darlan, "Note pour le Ministre," June 9, 1936.

55. This summary of the Geneva negotiations is based on SHM, 1BB2, EMG/SE, Carton 193, "Négotiations navales de Genève"; Carton 193, "NÉGO-CIATIONS NAVALES, 1 Mars—1 Avril 1931"; and SHM, 1BB2, EMG/SE, Carton 196, "HISTORIQUE SUCCINCT DES NÉGOCIATIONS DU 10 NOVEMBRE 1929 AU 20 AVRIL 1931."

56. See John Jordan and Robert Dumas, *French Battleships, 1922–1956* (Annapolis, Md.: Naval Institute Press, 2009).

57. See Monneraye, *Vingt ans de politique navale*, annexe 5.

Chapter 2. Fascist Aggression in the Mediterranean

1. See Richard Lamb, *Mussolini and the British* (London: John Murray, 1997), 108–11.

2. See Richard Davis, *Anglo-French Relations before the Second World War* (London: Palgrave, 2001), 79–93.

3. Eden was also head of the British delegation to the League of Nations.

4. SHM, 1BB2, EMG/SE, Carton 208, Dossiers Amiral Darlan, "Note pour le Ministre," June 9, 1936.

5. NARA, RG 38, ONI, C-9-e, Reg. 15812, "Confidential Letter No. 80," October 25, 1935.

6. Lamb, *Mussolini and the British*, 130.

7. Ibid., 132; and Anthony Eden, *Facing the Dictators: The Memoirs of Anthony Eden, Earl of Avon* (Boston: Houghton Mifflin, 1962), 317.

8. NARA, RG 38, ONI, C-9-e, Reg. 15812, "Confidential Letter No. 82," November 6, 1935.

9. NARA, RG 38, ONI, C-9-e, Reg. 15812, "Confidential Letter No. 83," December 2, 1935.

10. PRO, ADM 116/3398, untitled memorandum, January 3, 1936.

11. Arthur J. Marder, *From the Dardanelles to Oran* (London: Oxford University Press, 1974), 93.

12. PRO, ADM 116/3398, "Record of Meeting Held in C.N.S.'s Room on Wednesday, 15th January, 1936, to Discuss Questions of Co-operation with the French in the Event of Hostilities."

13. See PRO, ADM 116/3398, "Questions To Be Put to the English Admiralty, Arising Out of the Staff Agreements of April, 1936," April 23, 1936; and "Answer to French Questionnaire Dated 23.4.36."

14. Darlan had anticipated this scenario. See SHM, 1BB2, EMG/SE, Carton 208, Dossiers Amiral Darlan, "Politique navale," January 17, 1934.

15. See SHM, 1BB2, EMG/SE, Carton 208, Dossiers Amiral Darlan, ministère de la marine, état-major génèral, section d'étude des Armaments Navals, "La situation navale en juin 1936 envisagée du point de vue français," June 9, 1936, p. 19.

16. SHM, 1BB2, EMG/SE, Carton 203, "Entretiens franco-britanniques du 5 août 1936 a l'amiraute britannique," August 5, 1936.

17. Hugh Thomas, *The Spanish Civil War* (New York: Harper and Row, 1963), 257, 279.

18. SHM, 1BB2, EMG/SE, Carton 203, "Note pour le Ministre," November 4, 1936.

19. SHM, 1BB2, EMG/SE, 1BB2, Carton 208, Dossiers Amiral Darlan, "Politique navale"; and "Note sur une question posée par le gouvernement du reich," January 22, 1934.

20. Lamb, *Mussolini and the British*, 174–75.

21. Eden, *Facing the Dictators*, 483–84.

22. Ibid., 486.

23. Ibid., 487.

24. Ibid.

25. Lamb, *Mussolini and the British*, 177–78.

26. Thomas, *Spanish Civil War*, 395.

27. Lamb, *Mussolini and the British*, 178–79.

28. Ibid., 181–83.

Chapter 3. Tensions in Spanish Waters

1. SHM, 1BB2, EMG/SE, Carton 202, "Incidents No. 1," 1937–38; and several miscellaneous folders.

2. SHM, 1BB2, EMG/SE, Carton 203, Ministre de la Marine, État-Major Générale, No. 101 E.M.G. 3, January 27, 1937.

3. *New York Times*, January 18, 1937, 6.

4. SHM, 1BB2, EMG/SE, Carton 203, "Bulletin d'Information," December 17, 1937; see also Stephen Roskill, *Naval Policy between the Wars* (London: Collins, 1976), 2:382.

5. Hugh Thomas, *The Spanish Civil War* (New York: Harper and Row, 1963), 439–40; SHM, 1BB1, EMG/SE, Carton 202, "Incidents No. 1," 1937–38.

6. SHM, 1BB2, EMG/SE, Carton 202, "Incidents No. 1," 1937–38.

7. Ibid.

8. Ibid., and various reports contained in the folder.

9. SHM, 1BB2, EMG/SE, Carton 202, "Le Ministre des Affaires Étrangeres à Monsieur le Ministre de la Marine," June 9, 1937.

10. SHM, 1BB2, EMG/SE, Carton 202, "Incidents No. 1," 1937–38; and press reports contained in the folder.

11. SHM, 1BB2, EMG/SE, Carton 202, Note no. 86 to Paris from French naval attaché in Berlin, June 3, 1937; and no. 967 to Paris from French ambassador André François-Poncet in Berlin, June 9, 1937.

12. Thomas, *Spanish Civil War*, 456.

13. SHM, 1BB2, EMG/SE, Carton 202, "Incidents No. 1," Note no. 86 from the French naval attaché in Berlin to Paris, June 7, 1937.

14. SHM, 1BB2, EMG/SE, Carton 203, "Situation des Forces Navales," August 20, 1937.

15. SHM, 1BB2, EMG/SE, Carton 202, "Incidents No. 1," 1937–38, press reports contained in the folder.

16. Thomas, *Spanish Civil War*, 457; Anthony Eden, *Facing the Dictators: The Memoirs of Anthony Eden, Earl of Avon* (Boston: Houghton-Mifflin, 1962), 503; and NARA, College Park, Md., RG 38, ONI, C-9-e, Reg. 21555-E, Naval Attaché Report from Paris, July 6, 1937.

17. SHM, 1BB2, EMG/SE, Carton 203, "Bulletin d'Informations," no. 42, August 20, 1937.

18. Robert Mallett, *The Italian Navy and Fascist Expansionism, 1935–1940* (London: Frank Cass, 1998), 94, 97.

19. SHM, 1BB2 EMG/SE, Carton 203, "Bulletin d'Informations," no. 43, August 27, 1937.

20. SHM, 1BB2, EMG/SE, Carton 203, "Bulletin d'Informations," no. 42, August 20, 1937; Mallette, *Italian Navy and Fascist Expansionism*, 97; Galeazzo Ciano, *Ciano's Hidden Diary, 1937–1938*, introduction by Malcolm Muggeridge (New York: E. P. Dutton, 1953), 6; and DGFP, vol. 3, *Germany and the Spanish Civil War, 1936–1939*, nos. 407, 408, 409.

21. SHM, 1BB2, EMG/SE, Carton 203, "Bulletin d'Informations," no. 41, August 13, 1937; DBFP, vol. 19, *European Affairs, July 1937–August 1938*, 180n5; and PRO, ADM 116, 3522, Eden conversation with A.C.N.S. (AIR), August 25, 1937.

22. Malcolm Muggeridge, ed., *Ciano's Diplomatic Papers* (London: Odhams Press, 1948), 134–35; and DBFP, 19:186–88.

23. SHM, 1BB2, EMG/SE, Carton 203, "Bulletin d'Informations," no. 41, August 13, 1937, and no. 42, August 20, 1937.

24. SHM, 1BB2, EMG/SE, Carton 203, "Bulletin d'Informations," no. 41, August 13, 1937, and no. 42, August 20, 1937; and PRO, ADM 116, 3522, "Attacks on Ships in Which Italian Activity Has Been Suggested."

25. SHM, 1BB2, EMG/SE, Carton 203, "Bulletin d'Informations," no. 42, August 20; and SHM, 1BB2, EMG/SE, Carton 203, "Bulletin d'Informations," no. 42, August 20, 1937. See also Peter Gratton, "The Nyon Conference: The Naval Aspect," *English Historical Review* 90, no. 354 (January 1975): 104–5, doi:10.1093/ehr/XC.CCCLIV.103.

26. SHM, 1BB2, EMG/SE, Carton 203, "Bulletin d'Informations," no. 42, August 20.

27. Ibid.; and DBFP, 19:212–13.

28. DBFP, no. 90.

29. Ibid., no. 91.

30. Ibid.

31. Ibid., no. 94, 181.

32. Ibid., no. 94.

33. Ibid., no. 96.

34. NARA, RG 38, ONI, C-9-e, Reg. 21555-E, Naval Attaché Report, from Paris, August 24, 1937.

35. DBFP, no. 103, 191n2.

36. "Italy's Naval Aid for Franco," *Manchester Guardian*, August 20, 1937, p. 191.

37. DBFP, nos. 99, 100, 102, 104; and Muggeridge, *Ciano's Diplomatic Papers*, 134–36.

38. PRO, ADM 116, 3522, "Note of Conversation between Foreign Secretary and A.C.N.S. (AIR) on 25th August 1937."

39. Ibid.; see also "Attacks on Shipping in the Mediterranean," *Manchester Guardian*, August 27, 1937, p. 164.

40. See Thomas, *Spanish Civil War*, 471; and "Mussolini's Speech" *Manchester Guardian*, August 27, 1937, pp. 162, 170

41. "French Criticism of the Speech," *Manchester Guardian*, August 27, 1937, pp. 162–63, 170.

42. SHM, 1BB2, EMG/SE, Carton 203, "Bulletin d'Informations," no. 44, September 3, 1937; PRO, ADM 116, 3552.

43. SHM, 1BB2, EMG/SE, Carton 203, "Bulletin d'Informations," no. 44, September 3, 1937; and NARA, RG 39, ONI, C-10-k, Reg. 22407, "Mediterranean Piracy and the Nyon Conference."

44. "Piracy in the Mediterranean," *Manchester Guardian*, September 3, 1937, pp. 184–85.

45. SHM, 1BB2, EMG/SE, Carton 203, "Bulletin d'Informations," no. 44, September 3, 1937; and PRO, ADM 116, 3522.

46. John E. Dreifort, *Yvon Delbos at the Quai d'Orsay* (Lawrence: University Press of Kansas, 1973), 60–62.

47. DBFP, no. 103.

48. Ibid., no. 108.

49. Ibid., nos. 108, 110, 146.

Chapter 4. The Road to Nyon

1. PRO, ADM 116/3522, "Mediterranean Situation," August 31, 1937.

2. Ibid.

3. DBFP, vol. 19, *European Affairs, July 1937–August 1938*, nos. 111, 114

4. Ibid., no. 114.

5. Ibid.

6. NARA, RG 38, ONI, C-10-k, Reg. 22407, "Mediterranean 'Piracy' and the Nyon Conference," September 14, 1937.

7. DBFP, vol. 19, no. 116, and n4.

8. Ibid., no. 119.

9. PRO, ADM 116/3522, no. 472, telegram, Ingram to Eden, September 3, 1937.

10. DBFP, vol. 11, *Far Eastern Affairs, November 1936–July 1938*, no. 120; and Anthony Eden, *Facing the Dictators: The Memoirs of Anthony Eden, Earl of Avon* (Boston: Houghton Mifflin, 1962), 520–21.

11. See DBFP, vol. 19, no. 146.

12. Ibid., and John E. Dreifort, *Yvon Delbos at the Quai d'Orsay* (Lawrence: University Press of Kansas, 1973), 64.

13. Count Galeazzo Ciano, *Ciano's Hidden Diary, 1937–1938*, introduction by Malcolm Muggeridge (New York: E. P. Dutton, 1953), 8.

14. Ibid., 9.

15. DBFP, vol. 19, no. 122.

16. Ibid., 124.

17. Ibid., 126.

18. PRO, ADM 116/3522, report of Lord Chilston in Moscow to the Foreign Office, September 4, 1937.

19. Ibid., September 7, 1937.

20. Ciano, *Ciano's Hidden Diary*, 10.

21. DBFP, vol. 19, no. 126.

22. Ibid., no. 129.

23. Ciano, *Ciano's Hidden Diary*, 10.

24. DBFP, vol. 19, no. 128.

25. Ibid., no. 133.

26. Ibid., no. 130.

27. Ibid., no. 136.

28. Ibid., no. 140.

29. See ibid., no. 138.

30. PRO, ADM 116/3522, "Message to C-in-C Mediterranean," September 9, 1937.

31. DGFP, vol. 3, *Germany and the Spanish Civil War, 1936–1939*, no. 417.

32. Ibid., no. 418.

33. DBFP, vol. 19, nos. 232 and 233.

34. SHM, 1BB2, EMG/SE, Carton 203, "Note pour le Ministre," September 7, 1937.

35. Ibid.

36. Ibid., "Note," September 7, 1937.

37. Ibid.

38. Ibid.

39. PRO, ADM 116/3522, minute sheet, unnumbered, September 9, 1937.

40. DBFP, vol. 19, no. 134.

41. Ibid.

42. "Pirates," *Daily Herald*, September 6, 1937, p. 10.

43. "No Delay," *Daily Herald*, September, 7, 1937, p. 10; and "There Is Work to Do," *Daily Herald*, September 8, 1937, p. 8.

44. "A Clear Policy," *Manchester Guardian*, September 10, 1937, p. 202.

45. "Eden's Discussions in Paris," London *Times*, September 10, 1937, p. 10.

46. See "French Policy for Nyon," *Manchester Guardian*, September 10, 1937, p. 204.

47. "Prevention of Piracy," London *Times*, September 10, 1937, p. 12.

48. "Four British Destroyers Sail," *Manchester Guardian*, September 10, 1937, p. 204.

49. "Carry It Through," *Daily Herald*, September 10, 1937, p. 2; and "Prevention of Piracy," London *Times*, September 10, 1937, p. 12.

Chapter 5. Solving a Mediterranean Problem

1. "A Clear Policy," *Manchester Guardian*, September 10, 1937, p. 202.

2. "Carry It Through," *Daily Herald*, September 10, 1937, p. 8.

3. PRO, ADM 116, 3522, "Technical Considerations Underlying the Anglo-French Proposal"; and 3523, "Telegram to Foreign Office," September 10, 1937.

4. SHM, 1BB2, EMG/SE, Carton 204, folder no. 1, "CONFERENCE MEDITERRANEENNE, COMITE PERMANENT, Procès-verbal provisiore de la première séance (privée) tenue à Nyon le vendredi 10 septembre 1937 à 17 heures 40."

5. SHM, 1BB2, EMG/SE, Carton 204, folder no. 1, "CONFERENCE MEDITERRANEENNE, Compte rendu sténographique de première séance plénière," September 10, 1937.

6. The protocol required submarines to rise to the surface and ensure the safety of crews and passengers before sinking merchant ships. It was adopted by the London Naval Conference in 1936.

7. SHM, 1BB2, EMG/SE, Carton 204, folder no. 1, "CONFERENCE MEDITERRANEENNE, Compte rendu sténographique de première séance plénière," September 10, 1937.

8. Ibid. See also the "Piracy Talk," *Daily Herald*, September 11, 1937, p. 2.

9. SHM, 1BB2, EMG/SE, Carton 204, folder no. 1, "CONFERENCE MEDITERRANEENNE, Compte rendu sténographique de première séance plénière," September 10, 1937

10. SHM, 1BB2, EMG/SE, Carton 204, folder no. 1, CONFERENCE MEDITERRANEENNE, COMITE PERMANENT, "Procès-verbal de la

première séance (privée) tenue à Nyon, le vendredi 10 septembre 1937, a 17 heures 40."

11. Ibid.

12. Ibid.

13. Ibid.

14. Ibid.

15. Ibid.

16. Ibid.

17. Ibid.

18. Ibid.

19. See "Italy Asked to Help Track Pirates," *Daily Herald*, September 11, 1937, p. 1.

20. Anthony Eden, *Facing the Dictators: The Memoirs of Anthony Eden, Earl of Avon* (Boston: Houghton Mifflin, 1962), 526.

21. PRO, ADM 116/3523, no. 27 (R), September 10, 1937.

22. Eden, *Facing the Dictators*, 526–27.

23. Ibid.

24. SHM, 1BB2, EMG/SE, Carton 204, folder no. 1, "CONFERENCE MEDITERRANEENNE, Proces-verbal provisiore de la deuxieme séance (privée) tenue à NYON, le samedi, 11 Septembre 1937, à 16 heures 30."

25. SHM, 1BB2, EMG/SE, Carton 204, "ARRANGEMENT DE NYON."

26. Ibid.

27. Ibid.

28. Ibid.

29. DBFP, vol. 19, *European Affairs, July 1937–August 1938*, 294–98.

30. PRO, ADM 116/3523, September 14, 1937.

31. Ibid., September 21, 1937.

32. "Bad for Pirates," *Daily Herald*, September 13, 1937.

33. "Partners for Peace," *Daily Herald*, September 16, 1937, p. 10.

34. Count Galeazzo Ciano, *Ciano's Hidden Diary, 1937–1938*, introduction by Malcolm Muggeridge (New York: E. P. Dutton, 1953), 12.

35. PRO, ADM 116/3523, telegram, Ingram to Foreign Office, no. 28, September 13, 1937.

36. PRO, ADM, 116/3522, no. 508, September 13, 1937.

37. Ciano, *Ciano's Hidden Diary*, 12.

38. DBFP, vol. 19, no. 165.

39. Ciano, *Ciano's Hidden Diary*, 13.

40. PRO, ADM 116/3528, September 17, 1937.

41. DBFP, vol. 19, no. 173, and n2.

42. Ibid.

43. Ibid., nos. 176, 177.

44. Ibid., no. 179.

45. Ibid., no. 180.

46. Ciano, *Ciano's Hidden Diary*, 15.

Chapter 6. An Informal Naval Entente

1. SHM, 1BB2, EMG/SE, Carton 204, "Agreement Supplementary to the Nyon Arrangement," September 17, 1937.

2. SHM, 1BB2, EMG/SE, Carton 204, "Accord entre les États-Majors Navals britannique et français, 13 Septembre 1937."

3. Ibid.

4. Ibid.

5. Anthony Eden, *Facing the Dictators: The Memoirs of Anthony Eden, Earl of Avon* (Boston: Houghton Mifflin, 1962), 528.

6. PRO, ADM 116/3522, "Notes of Meeting between Lord Chatfield and Admiral Godfroy," September 15, 1937.

7. "French Preparations for Patrol," London *Times*, September 14, 1937, p. 12.

8. SHM, 1BB2, EMG/SE, Carton 203, "Situation des Forces Navales," September 24, 1937.

9. PRO, ADM 116/3523, no. 28, Geneva to Foreign Office, September 11, 1937.

10. DGFP, vol. 3, *Germany and the Spanish Civil War, 1936–1939*, 422.

11. PRO, ADM 116/3524, no. 1933/17, C-in-C Mediterranean to Admiralty, September 18, 1937.

12. SHM, 1BB2, EMG/SE, Carton 204, "Instruction No. 1," September 18, 1937.

13. SHM, 1BB2, EMG/SE, Carton 203, Dossier no. 8, "Guerre de Espagne, EMG-2, 1936–1939"; and PRO, ADM 116/3522, First Sea Lord to C-in-C Mediterranean, no. 2045/13, September 13, 1937.

14. PRO, ADM 116/3524, C-in-C Mediterranean to Admiralty, no. 0028/19, September 19, 1937.

15. SHM, 1BB2, EMG/SE, Carton 204, "Instruction No. 1," September 18, 1937.

16. "Italy and Nyon," London *Times*, September 22, 1937, p. 12.

17. NARA, RG 38, ONI, C-9-e, Reg. 21555-E, Naval Attaché Report, September 28, 1937.

18. PRO, ADM 116/3527, Roger M. Bellairs from Geneva to the Admiralty, September 20, 1937.

19. PRO, ADM 116/3523, from Switzerland, no. 62, September 20, 1937.

20. PRO, ADM 116/3528, no. 45, September 22, 1937.

21. PRO, ADM 116/3528, no. 1705114/37, Naval Attaché Paris, September 22, 1937.

22. PRO, ADM 116/3528, no. 1705114/37, minute sheet, September 22, 1937.

23. PRO, ADM 116/2523, James to Admiralty, September 27, 1937.

24. Ibid.

25. PRO, ADM 116/3523, D.C.N.S. Paris to First Sea Lord, September 28, 1937.

26. PRO, ADM 116/3528, no. 180, telephone, Phipps to Foreign Office, September 28, 1937.

27. See "Führer and Duce," London *Times*, September 30, 1937, p. 12.

28. See DBFP, vol. 19, *European Affairs, July 1937–August 1938*, no. 214, pp. 356–58.

29. PRO, ADM 116/3528, no. 183, Phipps to Foreign Office, September 29, 1937.

30. See PRO, ADM 116/3523, minutes from Paris no. 184, September 29, 1937; and Robert Mallet, *The Italian Navy and Fascist Expansionism, 1935–1940* (London: Frank Cass, 1998), 99–100.

31. PRO, ADM 116/3523, no. 183, Phipps to Foreign Office, September 29, 1937.

32. PRO, ADM 116/3523, Admiralty to C-in-C Mediterranean, nos. 234, 235, October 1, 1937. See also SHM, 1BB2, EMG/SE, Carton 948, October 20, 1937.

33. PRO, ADM 116/3524, nos. 1828/2 and 1833/2, C-in-C Mediterranean to Admiralty, October 2, 1937.

34. PRO, ADM 116/3524, no. 2033, C-in-C Mediterranean to Admiralty, October 30, 1937; and French Naval Archives, SHM, 1BB2, EMG/SE, Carton 203, "Bulletin d'Information," November 5, 1937.

35. PRO, ADM, 116/3524, no. 1621/28, Admiralty to C-in-C Mediterranean, October 28, 1937.

36. See Mallett, *Italian Navy and Fascist Expansionism*, 101; and Count Galeazzo Ciano, *Ciano's Hidden Diary, 1937–1938*, introduction by Malcolm Muggeridge (New York: E. P. Dutton, 1953), 13, September 15, 1937.

37. PRO, ADM 116/3529, no. 1784/6, C-in-C Mediterranean to Admiralty, October 6, 1937; PRO, ADM 116/3529, no. 1438/8, October 8, 1937; and PRO, ADM 116/3529, October 23, 1937.

38. PRO, ADM, 116/3529, telegram no. 276, Admiralty to C-in-C Mediterranean, October 11, 1937.

39. PRO, ADM, 116/3525, no. 1145/15, Naval Delegation Geneva to C-in-C Mediterranean, September 15, 1937.

40. PRO, ADM, 116/3527, no. 540, Thomas in Paris to London, September 18, 1937.

41. French Naval Archives, SHM, 1BB2, EMG/SE, Carton 204, "Rapport de Mission," December 24, 1937.

42. PRO, ADM 116/3530, Air to James, November 15, 1937.

43. PRO, ADM 116/3530, Phillips minute sheet no. 3, November 16–17, 1937.

44. PRO, ADM 116/3530, Phillips minute sheet no. 3, November 22, 1937.

45. PRO, ADM 116/3530, no. 1447, Paris Embassy, December 17, 1937.

46. PRO, ADM, 116/3525, no. 2008/2, C-in-C Mediterranean to Rome, January 2, 1938.

47. NARA, RG 38, ONI, C-9-e, Reg. 22407-H, Naval Attaché Report, February 10, 1938.

48. Ibid., Reg. 21555-H, Naval Attaché Report no. 76, February 8, 1938; SHM, 1BB2, EMG/SE, Carton 203, "Supplement au Bulletin d'Information no. 67."

49. PRO, ADM 116/3529, no. 1950/5, Admiralty to C-in-C Mediterranean, February 5, 1938; and NARA, RG 38, ONI, C-9-e, Reg. 21555-H, Naval Attaché Report no. 76, February 8, 1938.

50. PRO, ADM 116/3580, no. 1156/1, Admiralty to C-in-C Mediterranean, March 1, 1938; and PRO, ADM 116/3580, no. M02959/38, Military Branch to Mounsey, Foreign Office, May 21, 1938.

51. PRO, ADM, 116/3530, no. 2008/31, Admiralty to C-in-C Mediterranean, May 31, 1938; PRO, ADM, 116/3530, no. 1857/24, June 24, 1938; and two Admiralty memoranda dated June 24 and 25, 1938.

52. PRO, ADM, 116/3530, no. 11307/38, Board of Trade to Jarrett, August 2, 1938.

53. PRO, ADM, 116/3531, no. 82, April 6, 1939; NARA, RG 38, ONI, C-10-k, Reg. 22407-H, Naval Attaché Report, April 17, 1939.

Chapter 7. From Nyon to Munich

1. Winston S. Churchill, *The Second World War*, vol. 1, *The Gathering Storm* (Boston: Houghton Mifflin, 1948), 247.

2. NARA, RG 38, ONI, M975, Reel 1, Translation of Report Submitted by Finance Commission of French Chamber in Submitting Naval Budget for Year 1937, January 27, 1937.

3. SHM, 1BB2, EMG/SE, Carton 208, "Des conditions de la guerre dans la situation internationale présent," November 12, 1937.

4. NARA, RG 38, ONI, C-9-e, Reg. 19447-C, from an article in *CHOC*.

5. SHM, 1BB2, EMG/SE, Carton 208, "Politique navale," undated, housed among early 1938 papers.

6. Anthony Eden, *Facing the Dictators: The Memoirs of Anthony Eden, Earl of Avon* (Boston: Houghton Mifflin, 1962), 540–41, 577.

7. Ibid., 576–85.

8. Ibid., 566–67.

9. PRO, CAB 29/159, Anglo-French Staff Conversations, 1939, United Kingdom delegation, serial no. 3, "Summarized History," 3–6.

10. Keith Feiling, *The Life of Neville Chamberlain* (London: Macmillan, 1946), 331.

11. DBFP, vol. 19, *European Affairs, July 1937–August 1938*, no. 453, January 21, 1938.

12. See Richard Lamb, *Mussolini and the British* (London: John Murray, 1997), 210–11.

13. SHM, 1BB2, EMG/SE, Carton 207, "Directives pour les Plans d'Opérations," June 5, 1937.

14. Ibid.

15. Ibid.

16. Ibid.

17. SHM, 1BB2, EMG/SE, Carton 208, "Des conditions de la guerre dans la situation internationale présent," November 12, 1937.

18. M. J. Whitley, *German Capital Ships of World War Two* (London: Arms and Armour Press, 1989), app. 2.

19. Larry H. Addington, *The Patterns of War since the Eighteenth Century* (Bloomington: University of Indiana Press, 1984), 169.

20. Stephen Roskill, *Naval Policy between the Wars* (London: Collins, 1976), 2:216–18, 418.

21. Winston S. Churchill, *The Second World War*, vol. 2, *Their Finest Hour* (Boston: Houghton-Mifflin, 1949), 464. See also NARA, RG 38, ONI, C-9-e, Reg. 21555-F, Naval Attaché Report from Paris, November 15, 1937.

22. See Roskill, *Naval Policy between the Wars*, 2:422; Churchill, *Second World War*, 1:464; and Correlli Barnett, *Engage the Enemy More Closely* (London: Norton, 1991), 13.

23. M. J. Whitley, *Destroyers of World War II* (Annapolis, Md.: Naval Institute Press, 1988), 114–15.

24. See NARA, RG 38, ONI, C-9-d, Reg. 3536, Bingham to Secretary of State, October 28, 1936.

25. Churchill, *Second World War*, 1:465.

26. NARA, RG 38, ONI, M975, Reel 1.

27. Barnett, *Engage the Enemy More Closely*, 13.

28. PRO, CAB 29/159, AFC, serial no. 3, "Summarized History," 1–4, annex 2 and app., pp. 19–32.

29. Ibid., 4–11.

30. Ibid., 12–13, and annex V.

31. SHM, 1BB2, EMG/SE, Carton 208, "Note sur la nouvelle organisation du commandement et de la répartition des forces navales françaises," September 28, 1938.

32. Ibid.

33. Ibid.

34. PRO, CAB 29/159, AFC, serial no. 3, "Summarized History," 13.

Chapter 8. An Anglo-French Naval Alliance

1. See Reynolds M. Salerno, *Vital Crossroads: The Mediterranean Origins of the Second World War, 1935–1940* (Ithaca, N.Y.: Cornell University Press, 2002), 54–59.

2. SHM, 1BB2, EMG/SE, Carton 208, "L'Angleterre et la France pouvent-elles soutenir un conflit, contre l'Allemagne et l'Italie?" January 24, 1939.

3. See Reynolds M. Salerno, "The French Navy and the Appeasement of Italy, 1937–9, *English Historical Review* 112, no. 445 (February 1997): 66–104.

4. See Martin S. Alexander and William J. Philpott, eds., *Anglo-French Defense Relations between the Wars* (London: Palgrave Macmillan, 2002), 92–93, 142–45. In chapter 5 Talbot Imlay suggests that the reports of a German attack on the Netherlands were also a ruse that the French military command never took seriously.

5. PRO, CAB 29/159, Anglo-French Staff Conversations, 1939, "Summarized History," 15–16.

6. PRO, CAB 29/159, Anglo-French Staff Conversations, 1939, British strategical memorandum, part 1, p. 9.

7. Ibid.

8. Ibid.

9. Ibid., 13.

10. Ibid., 8–9, 14.

11. Ibid., 14.

12. Ibid., part 3, p. 40.

13. Ibid., part 2, p. 16.

14. Ibid., 23.

15. Ibid., 17.

16. Ibid., part 3, p. 40.

17. PRO, ADM 116/5458, P.D. 07596, minutes of the meeting of March 30, 1939; PRO, CAB 29/161, AFSC, 1939, minutes of the naval staff meeting held at the Admiralty on March 30–31, 1939.

18. PRO, ADM116/5458, Dispositions, April 1, 1939.

19. PRO, CAB 29/161, AFSC, 2nd minutes, March 31, 1939.

20. Ibid.

21. PRO, ADM 116/5458, D. of P. minute, April 14, 1939, 14. 4. 39.

22. PRO, ADM 116/5458, "Notes on Franco-British Conversations Held on 17th April, 1939."

23. Ibid.; and PRO, CAB 29/160, "Allied Naval Cooperation," May 8, 1939.

24. PRO, ADM 116/5458, "Notes on Franco-British Conversations Held on 17th April, 1939"; and PRO, CAB 29/160, "Allied Naval Cooperation," May 8, 1939.

25. PRO, ADM 116/5458, minute sheet no. 1, May 2, 1939; PRO, ADM 116/5458, "Report of a Meeting Held at the Admiralty on 3rd May 1939"; and CAB 29/160, "Allied Naval Cooperation," May 8, 1939.

26. PRO, ADM 116/5458, minute sheet no. 1, May 2, 1939; PRO, ADM 116/5458, "Report of a Meeting Held at the Admiralty on 3rd May 1939"; and CAB 29/160, "Allied Naval Cooperation," May 8, 1939.

27. PRO, ADM 116/5458, minute sheet no. 1, May 2, 1939; PRO, ADM 116/5458, "Report of a Meeting Held at the Admiralty on 3rd May 1939"; and CAB 29/160, "Allied Naval Cooperation," May 8, 1939.

28. PRO, CAB 29/159, AFSC, part 2, 33.

29. PRO, ADM 116/5458, Report of conference between the Commander-in-Chief Mediterranean and the Vice-Admiral Commandant, French Mediterranean Fleet.

30. Ibid.

31. Ibid.

32. Ibid.

33. Ibid.

34. *The Cunningham Papers*, vol. 1, *The Mediterranean Fleet, 1939–1942*, ed. Michael Simpson (London: Ashgate for the Naval Records Society, 1999), 22–24, letter of July 24, 1939, Pound to Cunningham.

35. Ibid., July 26, 1939, Cunningham to Pound.

36. SHM, 1BB2, EMG/SE, Carton 208, "Directives de l'Amiral de la Flotte, Chef d'État-Major Général; comment se déroulera la guerre maritime?" August 3, 1939.

37. Ibid.

38. PRO, ADM 116/5458, Anglo-French Naval Liaison, March–December 1939, "Exchange of Information, 1939–1940."

39. SHM, 1BB2, EMG/SE, Carton 182, "Résumé de la conférence tenue le 8 août 1939 à bord *l'Enchantress* entre l'Amiral de la Flotte Darlan et l'Admiral of the Fleet Sir Dudley Pound," August 8, 1939; and SHM, 1BB2, EMG/SE, Carton 182, "Mémento," August 8, 1939.

40. *Cunningham Papers*, 31, letter of August 18, 1939.

41. Robert Mallett, *The Italian Navy and Fascist Expansionism, 1935–1940* (London: Frank Cass, 1998), 146–47, 153–57.

42. Corelli Barnett, *Engage the Enemy More Closely: The Royal Navy in the Second World War* (New York: Norton, 1991), 55.

43. DGFP, vol. 7, *The Last Days of Peace, August 9–September 3, 1939*, 286.

44. Ibid., 7:326.

45. Ibid., 7:431.

46. Henri Ballande, *De l'Amirauté à Bikini* (Paris: Presses de la Cité, 1972), 37; and SHM, 1BB2, EMG/SE, Carton 208, Dossiers Amiral Darlan, August 1939.

47. NARA, RG 38, ONI, C-9-e, Reg. 21555q, Naval Attaché Report from Rome, August 25, 1939.

48. Count Galeazzo Ciano, *Ciano's Hidden Diary, 1937–1938*, introduction by Malcolm Muggeridge (New York: E. P. Dutton, 1953), 136.

49. Ibid., 128.

50. Ibid., 141.

51. See Mallett, *Italian Navy and Fascist Expansionism*, 158; and Richard Lamb, *Mussolini and the British* (London: Murray, 1997), 262.

52. PRO, CAB 65/1, Conclusions of the meeting of September 11, 1939.

53. Ciano, *Ciano's Hidden Diary*, 146.

Chapter 9. War on the Periphery

1. Winston S. Churchill, *The Second World War*, vol. 1, *The Gathering Storm* (Boston: Houghton Mifflin, 1948), 415.

2. PRO, ADM 205/2, Report of the First Lord of the Admiralty to the War Cabinet, no. 1, September 18, 1939. See also Churchill, *Second World War*, 1:436.

3. NARA, RG 38, U.S. Naval Attaché Reports on microfilm, M975, Roll 1, "Summary of Estimate of Potential Military Strength," report of Naval Attaché Berlin, E-1–28, August 18, 1939.

4. PRO, ADM 205/4, Darlan to Pound, September 17, 1939.

5. PRO, ADM 205/4, Pound to Darlan, September 19, 1939.

6. PRO, ADM 205/4, Holland to Pound, October 25, 1939.

7. PRO, ADM 205/4, Holland to Pound, November 11, 1939.

8. PRO, ADM 205/4, Pound to Holland, November 11, 1939.

9. See Churchill, *Second World War*, 1:499–500.

10. See PRO, ADM 205/12, file no. 10, B, General Naval Policy and War Strategy, September 5, 1939; Arthur J. Marder, *From the Dardanelles to Oran* (London: Oxford University Press, 1974), 120–21; Corelli Barnett, *Engage the Enemy More Closely: The Royal Navy in the Second World War* (New York: Norton, 1991), 68–69; and Churchill, *Second World War*, 1:435.

11. See Churchill, *Second World War*, 1:462–64 and app. B; Barnettt, *Engage the Enemy More Closely*, 92–96; and Marder, *From the Dardanelles to Oran*, 140–47.

12. SHM, 1BB2, EMG/SE, Carton 208, Darlan Diary, September 8, 1939.

13. SHM, 1BB2, EMG/SE, Carton 208, Darlan Diary, September 20, 1939. For a thorough account of Entente relations with Italy in 1939 and 1940, see Reynolds M. Salerno, *Vital Crossroads; Mediterranean Origins of the Second World War, 1935–1940* (Ithaca, N.Y.: Cornell University Press, 2002), 147–54.

14. SHM, 1BB2, EMG/SE, Carton 208, Darlan Diary, September 22, 1939.

15. See Salerno, *Vital Crossroads*, 168–72.

16. SHM, 1BB2, EMG/SE, Carton 208, Darlan Diary, December 11, 1939; and Andrew Browne Cunningham, *A Sailor's Odyssey*, 2 vols. (London: Arrow Books, 1961), 1:161–62.

17. PRO, ADM 116/5458, aide-memoir no. 67, October 26, 1939.

18. PRO, ADM 116/5458, L/155/39, October 26, 1939.

19. PRO, ADM 116/5458, notes of meeting held at Marceau on November 3, 1939.

20. See SHM, 1BB2, EMG/SE, Carton 208, Darlan Diary, September 30–October 10, 1939.

21. PRO, ADM 116/5458, notes of meeting held at Marceau on November 3, 1939.

22. Ted Briggs, "Remembering the *Hood*," HMS *Hood* Association, http://hmshood.com/crew.

23. See Churchill, *Second World War*, 1:514–15.

24. PRO, ADM 116/5458, notes of meeting with the French naval staff in London on December 20, 1939.

25. PRO, ADM 205/2, file no. 10, report of the First Lord of the Admiralty to the War Cabinet, September 18, 1939.

26. PRO, ADM 205/5, War Cabinet, Naval Program, 1940–41, February 1940.

27. SHM, 1BB2, EMG/SE, Carton 208, Darlan Diary, December 14, 1939.

28. SHM, 1BB2, EMG/SE, Carton 207, untitled report, December 22, 1939.

29. SHM, 1BB2, EMG/SE, Carton 207, "Note sur les moyens d'arrêter les pétroles du Caucase," January 26, 1940.

30. SHM, 1BB2, EMG/SE, Carton 207, untitled report, December 22, 1939.

31. SHM, 1BB2, EMG/SE, Carton 207, "Operations sous la Finlande du Nord," n.d.

32. SHM, 1BB2, EMG/SE, "Note sur l'étude du 23 Janvier 1940 et les décisions de la première expédition B.K.," January 15, 1940.

33. SHM, 1BB2, EMG/SE, Carton 207, "Première Tentative d'Expédition Scandinave," March 10, 1940; and Churchill, *Second World War*, 1:560–61.

34. SHM, 1BB2, EMG/SE, Carton 207, "Avril 1940, Résumé succinct (of governmental decisions and correspondence with General Gamelin)"; and SHM, 1BB2, EMG/SE, Carton 207, "Histoire de l'expédition B.K. bis," April 11, 1949.

35. SHM, 1BB2, EMG/SE, Carton 207, "Résumé succinct"; and SHM, 1BB2, EMG/SE, Carton 208, Darlan Diary, April 9, 1940.

36. Churchill, *Second World War*, 1:593.

37. SHM, 1BB2, EMG/SE, Carton 207, "L'Amiral de la Flotte Darlan . . . à Monsieur le Ministre de la Défense Nationale," April 12, 1940.

38. Larry H. Addington, *The Patterns of War since the Eighteenth Century* (Bloomington: Indiana University Press, 1984), 186.

39. See Barnett, *Engage the Enemy More Closely*, chaps. 4 and 5.

40. See ibid., 136–38.

41. SHM, 1BB2, EMG/SE, Carton 207, "La situation maritime," May 8, 1940; and SHM, 1BB2, EMG/SE Carton 207, no. 926 F.M.F.3, April 13, 1940, Darlan to the minister of national defense.

42. SHM, 1BB2, EMG/SE, Carton 207, "La situation maritime," May 8, 1940; and SHM, 1BB2, EMG/SE, Carton 207, "Avril 1940, Résumé succinct, Avril 1940.

43. SHM, 1BB2, EMG/SE, Carton 208, Darlan Diary, April 27 and May 3, 1940.

44. PRO, CAB 65/7, War Cabinet Conclusions, 109, May 1, 1940.

45. PRO, CAB 65/7, War Cabinet Conclusions, 122, May 14; 123, May 15; and 124, May 16, 1940.

46. PRO, CAB 65/7, War Cabinet Conclusions, 122, May 14, 1940.

47. *The Cunningham Papers*, vol. 1, *The Mediterranean Fleet, 1939–1942*, ed. Michael Simpson (London: Ashgate for the Naval Records Society, 1999), 47.

48. PRO, CAB 65/7, War Cabinet Conclusions, 124, May 16, 1940.

49. PRO, CAB 65/7, War Cabinet Conclusions, 122, 124, May 14 and 16, 1940.

50. *Cunningham Papers*, 45.

51. Author interview with Captain Henri Ballande, Parc Isthmia, Toulon, May 26, 1982.

52. Henri Ballande, *De l'Amirauté à Bikini* (Paris: Presses de la Cité, 1972), 73.

Chapter 10. Twilight of the Anglo-French Naval Alliance

1. SHM, 1BB2, EMG/SE, Carton 208, Darlan Diary, May 28, 1940.

2. See Winston S. Churchill, *The Second World War*, vol. 2, *Their Finest Hour* (Boston: Houghton Mifflin, 1949), 58–59, 83–84.

3. SHM, 1BB2, EMG/SE, Carton 208, Darlan Diary, May 31, 1940.

4. Alain Darlan, *L'Amiral Darlan parle* (Paris: Amiot-Dumont, 1952), 56.

5. Paul Baudouin, *The Private Diaries of Paul Baudouin*, trans. Charles Petrie (London: Eyre and Spotteswood, 1948), 75.

6. Letter of Darlan to Ollive, July 7, 1940, compliments of Claude Huan.

7. Baudouin, *Private Diaries*, 94.

8. PRO, ADM 205/5, First Sea Lord Papers, Demolition of Cross-Channel Ports, May–June 1940.

9. Author's interview with Captain Henri Ballande, Parc Isthmia, Toulon, May 26, 1982.

10. Henri Ballande, *De L'Amirauté à Bikini* (Paris: Presses de la Cite, 1972), 314.

11. Ibid., 315.

12. SHM, 1BB2, EMG/SE, Carton 208, "Note pour l'Amiral le Luc," May 28, 1940.

13. Hervé Coutau-Bégarie and Claude Huan, *Darlan* (Paris: Fayard, 1989), 235.

14. Darlan's accepting the promotion, instead of bolting with his fleet to the side of the English, marks the origin of his reputation as an opportunist motivated by political ambitions. See Churchill, *Second World War*, 2:229–231.

15. See Coutau-Bégarie and Huan, *Darlan*, 239.

16. Amiral Jules Docteur, *La grande énigme de la guerre: Darlan, Amiral de la Flotte* (Paris: Editions de la Caronne, 1949), 81–82.

17. SHM, 1BB2, EMG/SE, Carton 208, Darlan Diary, June 20, 1940.

18. DGFP, vol. 9, *The War Years, March 18–June 22, 1940*, 673.

19. See Baudouin, *Private Diaries*, 130–35; Yves Bouthillier, *Le Drame de Vichy*, 2 vols. (Paris: Plon, 1950), 1:103–7; DGFP, 9:665; and Maxime Weygand, *Recalled to Service: Memoirs* (London: William Heinemann, 1952), 195–99.

20. DGFP, 9:666.

21. Hervé Coutau-Bégarie and Claude Huan, *Lettres et notes de l'Amiral Darlan* (Paris: Economica, 1992), 211–12.

22. Jacques Raphaël-Leygues and François Flohic, *Darlan* (Paris: Plon, 1986), 112–13.

23. Docteur, *Darlan*, 82. See also Coutau-Bégarie and Huan, *Lettres et notes de l'Amiral Darlan*, 212–13.

Chapter 11. Toward a Violent Solution

1. Winston S. Churchill, *The Second World War*, vol. 2, *Their Finest Hour* (Boston: Houghton Mifflin, 1949), 87–89.

2. SHM, 1BB2, EMG/SE, Carton 208, Darlan Diary, June 11, 1940.

3. NARA, RG 38, U.S. Naval Attaché Reports on microfilm, "Summary of Estimate of Potential Military Strength, " Naval Attaché Paris, M975, Roll 1, B, p. 12.

4. PRO, ADM 205/4, First Sea Lord's Personal War Records, "Minutes of a Meeting Held in the First Sea Lord's Room at the Admiralty at 1830 on Friday, 7th June 1940."

5. Ibid.

6. Ibid.

7. PRO, CAB 65/13, W.M. (40) 167th Conclusions, minute 6, confidential annex, June 15, 1940, 10:00 a.m.

8. PRO, CAB 65/13, 168th Conclusions, minute 1, confidential annex, June 16, 1940, 10:15 a.m.

9. Ibid.

10. SHM, 1BB2, EMG/SE, Carton 208, Darlan Diary, June 18, 1940.

11. PRO, ADM 205/4, First Sea Lord's Personal Records, "Record of Conversation Held at Bordeaux on 18th June, 1940, between First Sea Lord & Admiral Darlan."

12. Ibid.

13. SHM, 1BB2, EMG/SE, Carton 208, Darlan Diary, June 20, 1940.

14. PRO, CAB 65/13, 176th Conclusions, June 22, 1940, 9:30 p.m.

15. Ibid.

16. Ibid.

17. Ibid.

18. PRO, ADM 205/4, Pound to Darlan, June 23, 1940.

19. Hervé Coutau-Bégarie and Claude Huan, *Mers el-Kébir (1940): la rupture franco-britannique* (Paris: Economica, 1994), 66.

20. SHM, 1BB2, EMG/SE, Carton 208, Darlan Diary, June 23 and 24, 1940.

21. Great Britain, *Parliamentary Debates,* 5th series, CCLXII, 1940, 304; and Churchill, *Second World War,* 2:231.

22. PRO, CAB 65/13, 179th and 180th Conclusions, June 24, 1940.

23. PRO, ADM 205/4, letter of Admiral Jean Odend'hal to Admiral Pound, June 27, 1940.

24. Albert Kammerer, *La passion de la flotte française, de Mers el-Kébir à Toulon* (Paris: Fayard, 1951), 132.

25. PRO, CAB 65/13, 180th Conclusions, June 24, 1940, 10:30 a.m.

26. Ibid.

27. Ibid.

28. PRO, CAB 65/13, 178th Conclusions, June 24, 1940, 12:00 noon.

29. Ibid.

30. Although these minutes do not identify the speaker, the style of the composition easily betray them as Churchill's comments. See also PRO, CAB 65/13, 179th Conclusions, June 24, 1940, 6:00 p.m.

31. Ibid.

32. PRO, CAB 65/13, 182nd and 183rd Conclusions, June 25 and 26, 1940.

33. PRO, CAB 65/13, 183rd Conclusions, June 26, 1940, 11:30 a.m.

34. PRO, CAB 65/13, 184th Conclusions, June 27, 1940, 12:00 noon.

35. PRO, CAB 65/13, 185th Conclusions, June 28, 1940.

36. PRO, CAB 65/14, 190th Conclusions, July 1, 1940.

37. *La délégation française auprès de la commission allemande d'armistice; recueil de documents publié par le gouvernement français*, (Paris: Impremerie Nationale, 1947–59), 1:10–13, 20, 27.

38. See Paul Auphan and Jacques Mordal, *The French Navy in World War II*, trans. A. C. J. Sabalot (Annapolis, Md.: Naval Institute Press, 1959), 120.

39. Quoted in David Brown, *The Road to Oran: Anglo-French Naval Relations, September 1939–July 1940* (London: Frank Cass, 2004), 167.

40. Ibid.

41. See Coutau-Bégerie and Huan, *Mers el-Kébir*, 68–69.

Chapter 12. Blunder at Mers el-Kébir

1. PRO, CAB 65/13, 184th Conclusions, June 27, 1940.

2. See PRO, CAB 65/13, 188th Conclusions, June 30, 1940; and PRO, CAB 65/13, 190th Conclusions, July 1, 1940.

3. PRO, CAB 65/13, 184th Conclusions, June 27, 1940.

4. PRO, CAB 65/13, 190th Conclusions, July 1, 1940.

5. *The Somerville Papers: Selections from the Private and Official Correspondence of Admiral of the Fleet Sir James Somerville, G.C.B., G.B.E., D.S.O,* ed. Michael Simpson (London: Scholar Press for the Navy Records Society, 1995), 88.

6. Ibid., 88–89.

7. Ibid., 89.

8. Ibid.

9. See ibid., 89; and David Brown, *The Road to Oran: Anglo-French Naval Relations September 1939–July 1940* (London: Frank Cass, 2004).

10. See Brown, *Road to Oran*, 165–66.

11. PRO, CAB 65/14, 190th Conclusions, July 1, 1940.

12. *Somerville Papers*, 93–95.

13. Hervé Coutau-Bégarie and Claude Huan, *Mers el-Kébir, 1940: la rupture franco-britannique* (Paris: Economica, 1994), 118.

14. PRO, CAB 65/14, 190th Conclusions, July 1, 1940.

15. Coutau-Bégarie and Huan, *Mers el-Kébir*, 120.

16. Ibid., 122.

17. *The Cunningham Papers*, vol. 1, *The Mediterranean Fleet, 1939–1942*, ed. Michael Simpson (London: Ashgate for the Naval Records Society, 1999), 80.

18. Ibid., 87.

19. Ibid., 88.

20. Ibid., 89.

21. Ibid., 94–96.

22. Ibid., 97.

23. *Somerville Papers*, 90–91.

24. See Brown, *Road to Oran*, 183–84.

25. PRO, ADM 205/6, Mers el-Kébir narrative by Captain Holland; Brown, *Road to Oran*, 182–86; and Coutau-Bégarie and Huan, *Mers el-Kébir*, 132–37.

26. Coutau-Bégarie and Huan, *Mers el-Kébir*, 136.

27. Ibid., 137.

28. PRO, ADM 1/10321, Force H, Diary of Events, Wednesday, July 3, 1940, 1.

29. See *Somerville Papers*, 99.

30. PRO, CAB 65/14, 192nd Conclusions, minute 5, confidential annex, July 3, 1940, 11:30 a.m.

31. See PRO, ADM 1/10321, Force H, Diary of Events, Wednesday, July 3, 1940, 1; and Brown, *Road to Oran*, 187–188.

32. *Somerville Papers*, 99.

33. Coutau-Bégarie and Huan, *Mers el-Kébir*, 135.

34. Ibid., 136.

35. Ibid., 137–38.

36. Ibid., 138. Also see Brown *Road to Oran*, 188–89.

37. Brown, *Road to Oran*, 189.

38. Ibid., 191; and PRO, ADM 205/6, Captain Holland's Mers el-Kébir narrative, "Interview with Admiral Gensoul."

39. PRO, ADM 205/6, Captain Holland's Mers el-Kébir narrative, "Interview with Admiral Gensoul."

40. Ibid.

41. *Somerville Papers*, 101.

42. NARA, RG 38, Report of Naval Attaché Paris, September 13, 1940, from information provided by the French Ministry of Marine in Vichy.

43. *Somerville Papers*, 102.

44. Ibid.

45. Coutau-Bégarie and Huan, *Mers el-Kébir*, annex 3, "Premier rapport de l'amiral Gensoul," 209.

46. *Somerville Papers*, 102–3.

47. Ibid., 103.

48. Ibid., 103–4.
49. Coutau-Bégarie and Huan, *Mers el-Kébir*, annex 7, "Gensoul's Second Report," 235.

Chapter 13. The Cover-Up and After

1. Henri Ballande, *De l'Amirauté à Bikini* (Paris: Presses de la Cité, 1972), 107; Paul Baudouin, *The Private Diaries of Paul Baudouin* (London: Eyre and Spotteswoode, 1948), 147.
2. *The Somerville Papers: Selections from the Private and Official Correspondence of Admiral of the Fleet Sir James Somerville, G.C.B., G.B.E., D.S.O.*, ed. Michael Simpson (London: Scholar Press for the Navy Records Society, 1995) 108–11.
3. Ibid.
4. Ibid.
5. Alexander Cadogan, *The Diaries of Sir Alexander Cadogan, 1938–1945* (New York: Putnam, 1972), 310.
6. See "Text of the Address of Prime Minister Churchill to the House of Commons," *New York Times*, July 5, 1940, p. 4.
7. This is a summary of the speech that Churchill made over the BBC the day before, on July 14. *New York Times*, July 15, 1940.
8. Winston S. Churchill, *The Second World War*, vol. 2, *Their Finest Hour* (Boston: Houghton-Mifflin, 1949), 237–38.
9. One historian who made that point was Michael Simpson, editor of the Somerville Papers. See *Somerville Papers*, introduction, 40.
10. PRO, CAB 65/13, 176th Conclusions, June 22, 1940, 9:30 p.m.
11. PRO, CAB 65/13, 178th Conclusions, June 24, 1940, 12:00 noon.
12. PRO, CAB 65/13, 187th Conclusions, July 6, 1940, 10:00 a.m.
13. Ibid.
14. See PRO, CAB 65/13, 188th Conclusions, June 30, 1940, 7:00 p.m.
15. PRO, CAB 65/13, 192nd Conclusions, July 3, 1940, 11:00 a.m.
16. Richard Bond, dir., *Churchill's Deadly Decision*, PBS, May 11, 2010, http://www.pbs.org/wnet/secrets/churchills-deadly-decision-watch-the-full-episode/620/.
17. PRO, ADM 205/6, Churchill to Pound, July 7, 1940.
18. This account of Operation Menace is based on PRO, ADM 205/6, The Dakar Operation, 1940. For the French side and for a summary of the diplomatic settlement following the operation, see Hervé Coutau-Bégerie and Claude Huan, *Darlan* (Paris: Fayard, 1984), 322–33.

Conclusions

1. Count Galeazzo Ciano, *Ciano's Diary, 1939–1943*, ed. Malcolm Muggeridge (London: Heinemann, 1947), 62.

2. PRO, ADM 1/11328, Fulfillment of Our Promises to France; Naval Co Operation, February 22, 1941.

3. Ibid.

4. Ibid.

5. NARA, RG 38, ONI, Reel M975, Selected Naval Attaché Reports Related to the World Crisis, vol. 2, Naval Attaché Paris, August 6, 1940.

6. See Hervé Coutau-Bégarie and Claude Huan, *Mers el-Kébir (1940): la rupture franco-britannique* (Paris: Economica, 1994), 186.

7. The information about the ceremonies at Brest were provided to the author by Madame Francine Hezez, niece of Admiral Darlan.

BIBLIOGRAPHY

Special Collections

The Cunningham Papers: Selections from the Private and Official Correspondence of Admiral of the Fleet Viscount Cunningham of Hyndhope, O.M., K.T., G.C.B., D.S.O. and Two Bars. Vol. 1, *The Mediterranean Fleet, 1939–1942.* Edited by Michael Simpson. London: Ashgate for the Naval Records Society, 1999.

The Somerville Papers: Selections from the Private and Official Correspondence of Admiral of the Fleet Sir James Somerville, G.C.B., G.B.E., D.S.O. Edited by Michael Simpson. London: Ashgate for the Navy Records Society, 1995.

Published Works

Addington, Larry H. *The Patterns of War since the Eighteenth Century.* Bloomington: University of Indiana Press, 1984.

Alexander, Martin S., and William J. Philpott, eds. *Anglo-French Defense Relations between the Wars.* London: Palgrave Macmillan, 2003.

Auphan, Paul, and Jacques Mordal. *The French Navy in World War II,* trans. A. C. J. Sabalot. Annapolis, Md.: Naval Institute Press, 1959.

Ballande, Henri. *De l'Amirauté à Bikini.* Paris: Presses de la Cité, 1972.

Barnett, Corelli. *Engage the Enemy More Closely: The Royal Navy in the Second World War.* New York: Norton, 1991.

———. *The Collapse of British Power.* Gloucestershire: Sutton, 1997.

Baudouin, Paul. *The Private Diaries of Paul Baudouin,* trans. Charles Petrie. London: Eyre and Spotteswood, 1948.

Bond, Richard, dir. *Churchill's Deadly Decision.* PBS, May 11, 2010, http://www.pbs.org/wnet/secrets/churchills-deadly-decision-watch-the-full-episode/620/.

Bouthillier, Yves. *Le Drame de Vichy.* 2 volumes. Paris: Plon, 1950.

Brown, David. *The Road to Oran: Anglo-French Naval Relations, September 1939–July 1940.* London: Frank Cass, 2004.

Cadogan, Alexander. *The Diaries of Sir Alexander Cadogan, 1938–1945.* New York: Putnam, 1972.

Carlton, David. "The Anglo-French Compromise on Arms Limitations, 1928." *Journal of British Studies* 8, no. 2 (1969): 141–62. Doi:10.1086/385574.

Churchill, Winston S. *The Second World War.* Vol. 1, *The Gathering Storm.* Boston: Houghton-Mifflin, 1948.

———. *The Second World War.* Vol. 2, *Their Finest Hour.* Boston: Houghton-Mifflin, 1949.

Ciano, Count Galeazzo. *Ciano's Hidden Diary, 1937–1938.* Introduction by Malcolm Muggeridge. New York: Dutton, 1953.

Coutau-Bégarie, Hervé, and Claude Huan, eds. *Darlan.* Paris: Fayard, 1989.

———. *Lettres et notes de l'Amiral Darlan.* Paris: Economica, 1992.

———. *Mers el-Kébir, 1940: La rupture franco-britannique.* Paris: Economica, 1994.

Cunningham, Andrew Browne, Viscount of Hyndhope. *A Sailor's Odyssey*, 2 vols. London: Arrow Books, 1961.

Darlan, Alain. *L'Amiral Darlan parle.* Paris: Amiot-Dumont, 1952.

Davis, Richard. *Anglo-French Relations before the Second World War.* London: Palgrave, 2001.

Docteur, Amiral Jules. *La grande énigma de la guerre: Darlan, Amiral de la Flotte.* Paris: Editions de la Caronne, 1949.

Dreifort, John E. *Yvon Delbos at the Quai d'Orsay.* Lawrence: University of Kansas Press, 1973.

Eden, Anthony. *Facing the Dictators: The Memoirs of Anthony Eden, Earl of Avon.* Boston: Houghton-Mifflin, 1962.

Fanning, Richard W. *Peace and Disarmament: Naval Rivalry and Arms Control, 1922–1933.* Lexington: University Press of Kentucky, 1995.

Feiling, Keith. *The Life of Neville Chamberlain.* London: Macmillan, 1946.

France. *La délégation française auprès de la commission allemands d'armistice: recueil de documents publié par le gouvernement français.* 5 vols. Paris: Imprimerie Nationale, 1947–59.

Gratton, Peter. "The Nyon Conference: The Naval Aspect," *English Historical Review* 90, no. 354 (January 1975): 103–12. Doi:10.1093/ehr/XC.CCCLIV.103.

Great Britain. *Documents on British Foreign Policy, 1919–1939.* 2nd ser., *1929–1938.* Vol. 11, *Far Eastern Affairs, October 1932–June 1933*, edited by W. N. Medlicott, et al. London: Her Majesty's Stationery Office, 1970.

———. *Documents on British Foreign Policy, 1919–1939.* Second series, *1929–1938.* Vol. 19, *European Affairs, July 1937–August 1938*, edited E. L. Woodward, R. Butler, J. P. T. Bury, W. N. Medlicott, D. Dakin, and M. E. Lambert. London: Her Majesty's Stationery Office, 1982.

———. *Parliamentary Debates*, 5th series, 263, 304. London: Her Majesty's Stationery Office.

Howarth, Stephen. *To Shining Sea: A History of the United States Navy, 1775–1991.* New York: Random House, 1991.

Ireland, Bernard, and Eric Grove, *Jane's War at Sea, 1987–1997.* New York: Collins Reference, 1997.

Jordan, John. *Warships after Washington: The Development of the Five Major Fleets, 1922–1930.* Annapolis, Md.: Naval Institute Press, 2012.

Jordan, John, and Robert Dumas. *French Battleships, 1922–1956.* Annapolis, Md.: Naval Institute Press, 2009.

Kammerer, Albert. *La passion de la flotte française, de Mers el-Kébir à Toulon.* Paris: Fayard, 1951.

Lamb, Richard. *Mussolini and the British.* London: John Murray, 1997.

Mallett, Robert. *The Italian Navy and Fascist Expansionism, 1935–1940*. London: Frank Cass, 1998.

Marder, Arthur J. *From the Dardanelles to Oran*. London: Oxford University Press, 1974.

Miller, David. *Warships from 1860 until the Present Day*. St. Paul, Minn.: MBI Publishing, 2001.

Monneraye, Louis de la [Espagnac Du Ravay, pseud.]. *Vingt ans de politique navale, 1919–1939*. Grenoble: Arthaud, 1941.

Muggeridge, Malcolm, ed. *Ciano's Diplomatic Papers*. London: Odhams Press, 1948.

Raphaël-Leygues, Jacques, and François Flohic. *Darlan*. Paris: Plon, 1986.

Roskill, Stephen. *Naval Policies between the Wars*. 2 vols. New York: Walker and Company, 1968, 1981.

Sadkovich, James K. *The Italian Navy in World War II*. Westport, Conn.: Greenwood, 1994.

Salerno, Reynolds M. "The French Navy and the Appeasement of Italy, 1937–9." *English Historical Review* 112, no. 445 (February 1997): 66–104.

———. *Vital Crossroads: The Mediterranean Origins of the Second World War, 1935–1940*. Ithaca, N.Y.: Cornell University Press, 2002.

Thomas, Hugh. *The Spanish Civil War*. New York: Harper and Row, 1963.

U.S. Department of State. *Documents on German Foreign Policy: 1918–1945*, ser. D. Vol. 3, *Germany and the Spanish Civil War, 1936–1939*. Washington, D.C.: U.S. Government Printing Office, 1949.

———. *Documents on German Foreign Policy: 1918–1945*, ser. D. Vol. 7, *The Last Days of Peace, August 9–September 3, 1939*. Washington, D.C.: U.S. Government Printing Office, 1949.

———. *Documents on German Foreign Policy: 1918–1945*, ser. D. Vol. 9, *The War Years, March 18–June 22, 1940*. Washington, D.C.: U.S. Government Printing Office, 1949.

———. *Papers Relating to the Foreign Relations of the United States, 1919: The Paris Peace Conference*. 13 vols. Washington, D.C.: U.S. Government Printing Office, 1919. Available at the University of Wisconsin Digital Collections, http://digital.library.wisc.edu/1711.dl/FRUS.

Weygand, Maxime. *Recalled to Service: Memoirs*. London: William Heinemann, 1952.

Whitley, M. J. *Destroyers of World War II*. Annapolis, Md.: Naval Institute Press, 1988.

———. *German Capital Ships of World War II*. London: Arms and Armour Press, 1989.

INDEX

ABOUT THE AUTHOR

George Melton grew up in a working-class suburb of Charlotte, NC, during the Great Depression and World War II. His childhood memories of the war years sparked in him an enduring interest in World War II and in naval affairs. He was fortunate to win a scholarship to Davidson College, where he split his time between academics and athletics. In graduate school at the University of North Carolina, Chapel Hill, he explored connections between naval power and diplomacy as he earned a PhD in modern European history with an emphasis on French naval and diplomatic history during World War II. A member of the faculty of St. Andrews University in Laurinburg, North Carolina, since 1968, he has traveled frequently to explore naval and diplomatic archival collections in Washington, London, and Paris. He also served at St. Andrews as chair of the History Department and as interim vice president and dean of the college (1984–86). His biography of French admiral Jean François Darlan was published by Praeger in 1998. A French-language edition of it was published by Pygmalion in Paris in 2002.